I0605704

For Côme, Clément and Mademoiselle delOdA.

LUCAS TUBIANA

BARTENDER & PEDAGOGUE

THE

CLASSIC COCKTAIL RECIPES TO MASTER THE ART OF MIXOLOGY

PHOTOGRAPHS BY PIERRE JAVELLE

ILLUSTRATIONS BY YANNIS VAROUTSIKOS

ADDITIONAL SCIENTIFIC INFORMATION BY ANNE CAZOR

STYLING BY ORATHAY SOUKSISAVANH

MITCHELL BEAZLEY

CONTENTS

FOREWORD BY THE AUTHOR

Having started out as a self-taught bartender, before progressing to become a professional alongside expert bartenders, I soon became aware of the rather vague nature of the cocktail world, which evolved with no real rules, or ones that simply came too late. It is a discipline whose methods, recipes and uses vary tremendously from one country to another.

Unlike cooking, where culinary pioneers such as Auguste Escoffier laid the foundations for the cuisines of the entire western hemisphere, the bar world has never had a similar work of reference. Thus, technical terms are duplicated, with the result that a slight variation in spelling can lead to radically different results. The laws that govern the production of alcohol are also numerous, complex and littered with exceptions.

The aim of this book is to provide clear answers to questions posed by curious readers and to demonstrate precise step-by-step methods for making a successful cocktail. I hope you enjoy reading the book and tasting the results!

NOTE

We have used capital letters for the names of alcoholic drinks and spirits, whether the brand is registered or not.

HOW TO USE THIS BOOK

1. THE BASICS

Discover the key principles involved in making a cocktail, find out about the basic spirits and other ingredients used in the recipes, learn about the different skills required for making them, as well as adding ice and decorations. In addition, there are detailed illustrations and diagrams plus explanations of the features specific to each one.

2. COCKTAIL RECIPES

Put into practice the basic skills for making cocktails. Each recipe has references to the basic knowledge you will need, detailed graphics to show the cocktail's ingredients and a photograph to show you how it should look.

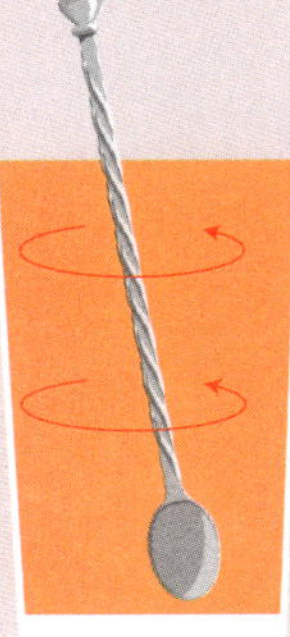

3. ILLUSTRATED GLOSSARY

Become familiar with the bar's equipment and glassware; broaden your knowledge by going deeper into the technical aspects of cocktail making and getting to know the recipes through tasting them.

CHAPTER 1

THE BASICS

CATEGORIES

The Lowdown

WHAT DOES THIS MEAN?

Finding out the best way to serve a particular cocktail. It is very difficult to classify cocktails in a definitive way and, to date, there is no classification that is recognized throughout the entire profession. For this reason, the cocktails featured in this book are divided into two categories – short and long drinks – as this classification is most commonly used.

WHY CLASSIFY?

- To know which techniques to use and learn how to master them through repetition.
- To be able to anticipate the end result and create it consistently each time.
- To know what the desired balance should be for the chosen cocktail family and how to adapt it if necessary.
- To identify a cocktail's origins and be familiar with its derivatives.
- To understand the structure of a cocktail family and draw inspiration from it.

A DEEPER DIVE

Logic would suggest that the difference between a short drink and a long drink is simply down to the size of the cocktail, but the reality is more nuanced. When served in a tumbler over ice, some short drinks will practically fill the whole glass, just like a long drink.

LONG DRINK

Generally speaking, this is long, diluted and served in a tall glass. Anything served in a highball or similar-shaped glass (tumbler, sling), such as Snappers, Bucks, Fizzes, Mules, Highballs or Collins.

SHORT DRINK

Generally speaking, this is short, concentrated, powerful and served in a small glass. Anything served in a coupette (coupe) or similar-shaped glass (such as a Martini or Nick & Nora, among others), as well as Ancestral cocktails, Duos, Trios, Daisies, Spirit Forwards, Reinforced Sours, Juleps, non-elongated Smashes and Flips.

THE MAIN COCKTAIL FAMILIES

The Lowdown

WHAT DOES THIS MEAN?

It is a way of classifying cocktails that have a similar structure in order to understand their character and to know what to expect in terms of balance. The following list of families is not exhaustive, but it covers the 22 families whose composition can be summarized systematically.

ANCESTRAL

BUCK

+ Ginger ale
Bitters and/or sweetener (optional)

CHAMPAGNE COCKTAIL

+ Sparkling wine. With the optional addition of an acidic ingredient and/or sweetener

COLLINS

+ Sparkling water
Traditionally made in the glass

DAISY

+ Egg white (optional)
Liqueur often triple sec

DUO

FIZZ

+ Soda + egg white (optional)
Always shaken

FLIP

+ Whole egg. The spirit can be replaced with fortified wine

HIGHBALL

+ Soda

JULEP

+ Egg white (optional)
Traditionally served over crushed ice

LADDER

+ Alcoholic or non-alcoholic additive (vermouth, liqueur, cream, syrups, and others) + bitters (liqueur)

MULE

+ Ginger beer
Bitters and/or sweetener (optional)

NOG

+ Cream + milk + whole egg
Brown spirit

RICKEY

+ Sparkling water + fresh lime juice
Traditionally made in a cocktail shaker

SLING

+ Fruit juice

SMASH

SNAPPER

+ Aromatic mix + tomato juice.
Liqueur generally triple sec

SOUR

+ Egg white (optional)

REINFORCED SOUR

+ Alcoholic or non-alcoholic additive (vermouth, liqueur, cream, syrups, and others) + bitters (liqueur)

SPIRIT FORWARD

Wine-based aperitifs
+ fortified wines + bitters (liqueur)

TIKI

+ Alcoholic or non-alcoholic additive (vermouth, liqueur, cream, syrups, among others + fruit juice)

TRIO

+ vermouth/cream

Spirit — Liqueur — Bitters (concentrated aromatic) — Acidifier — Sweetener — Fresh herbs

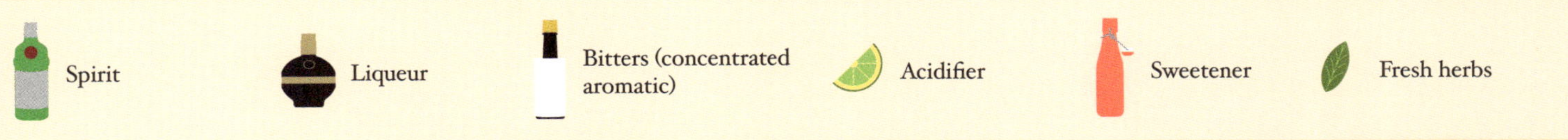

FLAVOURS & BALANCE

The Lowdown

WHAT DOES THIS MEAN?

The balance of a cocktail is very relative, its aim being to please the drinker. There are four main components to play around with: sweetness, acidity, bitterness and the perception of alcohol, which in combination should all enhance the spirit.

FASHION

As with cooking, cocktails follow trends, and the craze for a new flavour or previously rare ingredient that suddenly becomes available can propel a recipe centre stage.

CULTURE

For a taste that is considered well-balanced, it is very important to take into account where in the world or in which country the cocktail is served. Depending on the culture, local palates will be more accustomed to bitter flavours (as found in bitters and some Italian liqueurs), while others are fonder of sweeter flavours.

PUBLIC HEALTH

Many of the recipes in this book date from the 19th century, or even earlier, and have had to be adapted so they can be drunk today and will suit modern tastes, while at the same time retaining their original flavour profile. The quantities of alcohol in the original recipes were much higher than those allowed in current legislation, meaning that many of those cocktails could not be served today.

UNITS AND LOCAL LAWS

Units of measure vary from one country to another, which means it is not always possible to simply convert a recipe word for word. Bartenders, therefore, have to work out how to adapt a recipe, while at the same time retain the balance of flavours.

BALANCE

Certain cocktails are perfectly balanced. They are not excessively sweet, the acidity does not make your palate cringe, the level of alcohol is acceptable, and they leave no bitter aftertaste (for example, Horse's Neck with a Kick, see page 197; Paloma, see page 194; Breakfast Martini, see page 130).

UNBALANCED

Certain cocktails are intentionally unbalanced and focus more on a specific flavour, such as bitterness (for example, Negroni, see page 86; Boulevardier, see page 146, among others), acidity (Tom Collins, see page 170) or even sugar (for example, Brandy Alexander, see page 88).

BENCHMARKS

The Lowdown

WHAT DOES THIS MEAN?

The proportions shown here work for most cocktails, depending on the family to which they belong.

COMPOSITION

Increasing the number of ingredients can result in the flavour becoming blurred but, when mastered, the result can be a truly elegant and complex cocktail (for example, Singapore Sling, see page 92; Ramos Gin Fizz, see page 167).

DUO

2 measures of spirit for
1 measure of liqueur

TRIO

For a bitters cocktail
1 measure of vermouth
1 measure of bitters
1 measure of spirit

MULE, BUCK AND RICKEY

2 measures of spirit for
1 measure of an acidifier

SOUR, DAISY, FIZZ, SMASH

2 measures of spirit for
1 measure of sugar and
1 measure of an acidifier

WINE-BASED

APERITIFS

The Lowdown

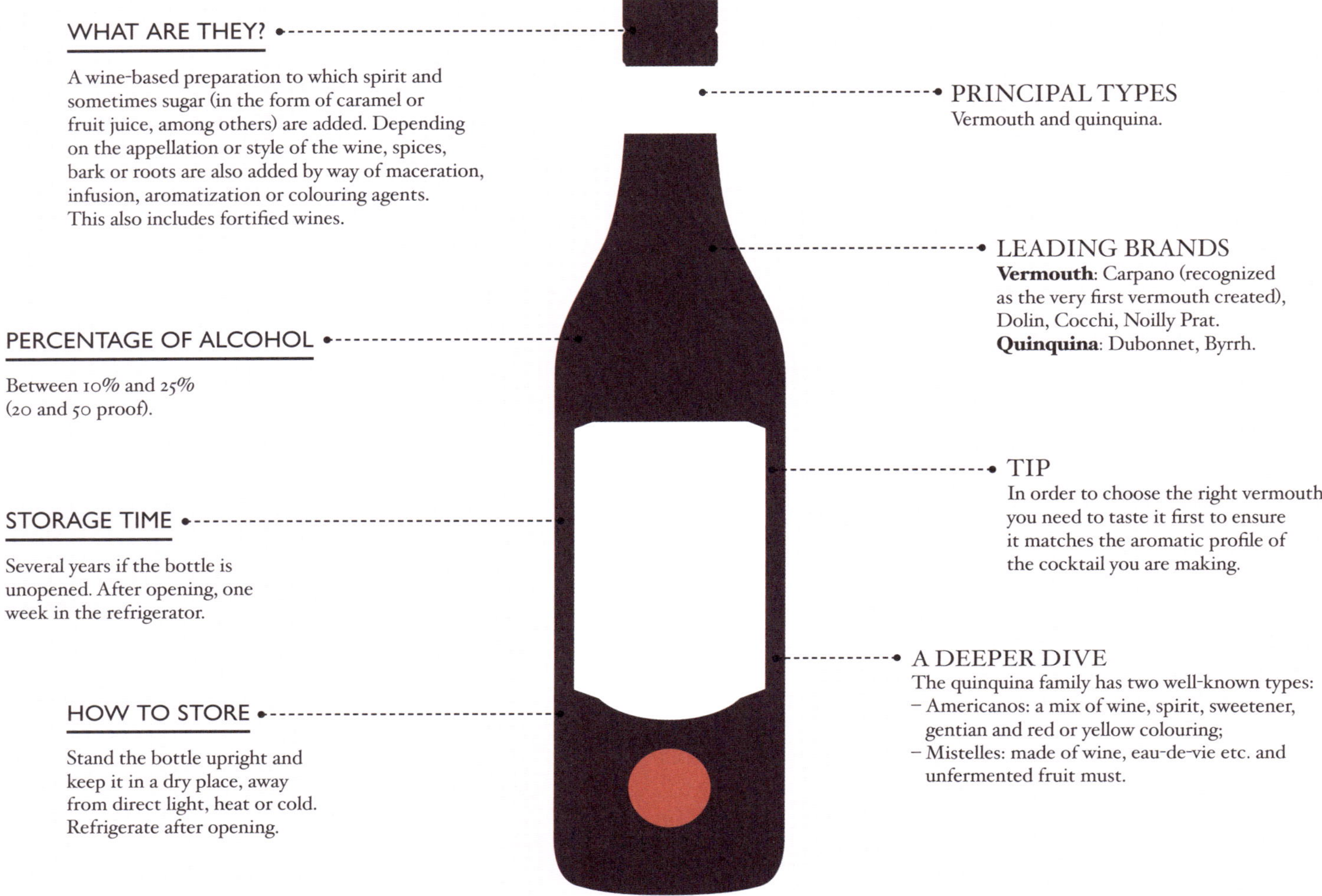

WHAT ARE THEY?

A wine-based preparation to which spirit and sometimes sugar (in the form of caramel or fruit juice, among others) are added. Depending on the appellation or style of the wine, spices, bark or roots are also added by way of maceration, infusion, aromatization or colouring agents. This also includes fortified wines.

PRINCIPAL TYPES

Vermouth and quinquina.

LEADING BRANDS

Vermouth: Carpano (recognized as the very first vermouth created), Dolin, Cocchi, Noilly Prat.
Quinquina: Dubonnet, Byrrh.

PERCENTAGE OF ALCOHOL

Between 10% and 25% (20 and 50 proof).

TIP

In order to choose the right vermouth, you need to taste it first to ensure it matches the aromatic profile of the cocktail you are making.

STORAGE TIME

Several years if the bottle is unopened. After opening, one week in the refrigerator.

A DEEPER DIVE

The quinquina family has two well-known types:

- Americanos: a mix of wine, spirit, sweetener, gentian and red or yellow colouring;
- Mistelles: made of wine, eau-de-vie etc. and unfermented fruit must.

HOW TO STORE

Stand the bottle upright and keep it in a dry place, away from direct light, heat or cold. Refrigerate after opening.

VERMOUTH

WHAT IS IT?
Wine that has been aromatized with herbs (chamomile, mint, artemisia [mugwort], fennel, among others).
To bear the appellation, the degree of alcohol must be between 14.5% and 22%.

INGREDIENTS
Wine + spirit + sweetener + artemisia (mugwort).

TYPES
Sweet vermouth, red (known as Italian): slightly sweet, with a mildly bitter flavour.
Dry or extra dry vermouth (known as French): dry and quite floral.
White: sweet and floral.

AROMATIC PROFILE
Each vermouth is made to its own recipe. Its aromatic profile and sugar level are therefore specific to it.

QUINQUINA

WHAT IS IT?
An aperitif wine traditionally aromatized with bark from the quinquina tree, which contains quinine.

INGREDIENTS
Wine + spirit + sweetener + quinine.

AROMATIC PROFILE
Due to the quinine, its aromatic profile is bitter. This family of wine-based aperitifs is being used less and less in cocktails.

FORTIFIED WINES

The Lowdown

WHAT ARE THEY?

A drink based on 'fortified' or 'mutated' wine, i.e. one to which neutral alcohol has been added to halt fermentation. The wines contain no other additives, such as sugar or flavourings, and most of them hold PDO (Protected Designation of Origin) status.

HOW TO STORE

Stand the bottle upright and keep it in a dry place, away from direct light, heat or cold. Refrigerate after opening.

PERCENTAGE OF ALCOHOL

Between 10% and 20% (20 and 40 proof).

STORAGE TIME

Several years if the bottle is unopened. After opening, one month in the refrigerator.

PRINCIPAL TYPES

Port, Madeira and sherry.

PORT

WHAT IS IT?
A fortified wine produced in a defined geographical region of Portugal, according to a strictly controlled production process.

TYPES
Different types of port are available: red, white, rosé, old or younger styles.

AROMATIC PROFILE
A characteristic aromatic profile that is always very rounded and sweet.

MADEIRA

WHAT IS IT?
A fortified wine produced on the island of Madeira in the Portuguese archipelago, according to a strictly controlled production process.

TYPES
Available as red or white, and in old or younger styles.

AROMATIC PROFILE
Madeira is characterized by more acidity and sometimes more complexity. Be careful not to confuse this fortified wine with the table wine produced by the Château de Madère in Bordeaux.

SHERRY

WHAT IS IT?
A fortified white wine produced in a defined geographical region of Spain, according to a strictly controlled production process.

TYPES
There are many types and the most well-known are Pedro Ximénez, Palo Cortado, Oloroso, Fino, Amontillado, Manzanilla and Moscatel.

AROMATIC PROFILE
A sweet wine, the aromatic profile of which can vary according to its type.

SPIRIT

VODKA

The Lowdown

WHAT IS IT?

A spirit produced by distilling fermented agricultural mash, such as cereals (wheat, barley, rye, maize, buckwheat, among others), grapes, potatoes or beetroot molasses. Often only one of these ingredients is used, the most common these days being wheat.

PRINCIPAL TYPES

Neutral vodkas, complex vodkas, flavoured vodkas.

PERCENTAGE OF ALCOHOL

Minimum 37.5% (75 proof).

LEADING BRANDS

Neutral vodkas: Ketel One, Absolut, Smirnoff, Grey Goose.
Complex vodkas: Polugar, Sauvelle, Chopin.
Flavoured vodkas: Grey Goose la Poire, Chase Marmalade Orange.

STORAGE TIME

Several years if the bottle is unopened.

TIP

Neutral vodkas are generally used to add alcohol to cocktails where the spirit is not the star (Moscow Mule, see page 180, for example) but without introducing an aromatic note which would interfere with the balance of the cocktail. Character vodkas are more often used in Spirit Forward cocktails (such as Martinis, for example).

HOW TO STORE

Stand the bottle upright and keep it in a dry place, away from direct light, heat or cold.

NEUTRAL VODKAS

WHAT ARE THEY?
They are often distilled several times and highly filtered, which results in a very neutral end product with a simple ethanol taste, the sweetness of which varies depending on the quality chosen.

COMPLEX VODKAS

WHAT ARE THEY?
Generally produced through ageing in cask with less distillation and filtration than neutral vodkas to preserve the more fragrant notes of the basic ingredient. Their aromatic profile is more pronounced.

FLAVOURED VODKAS

WHAT ARE THEY?
Flavoured vodkas (strawberry, cinnamon, cherry, pear, chocolate, among others) are produced either by maceration directly in the distillate of fruits or spices, or by adding chemical or natural extracts. Unfortunately, these days they are often of poor quality.

SPIRIT

GIN

The Lowdown

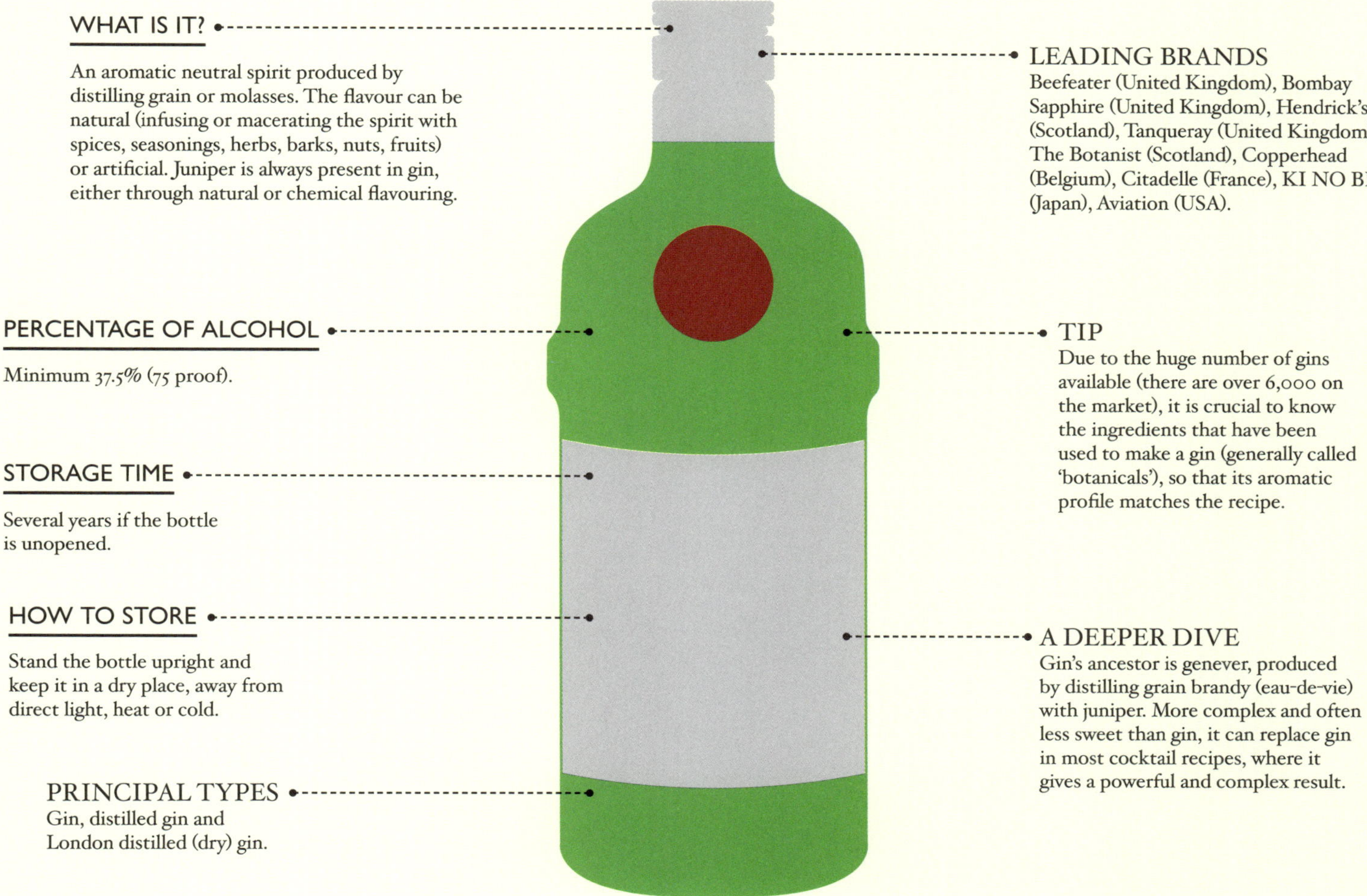

WHAT IS IT?

An aromatic neutral spirit produced by distilling grain or molasses. The flavour can be natural (infusing or macerating the spirit with spices, seasonings, herbs, barks, nuts, fruits) or artificial. Juniper is always present in gin, either through natural or chemical flavouring.

LEADING BRANDS

Beefeater (United Kingdom), Bombay Sapphire (United Kingdom), Hendrick's (Scotland), Tanqueray (United Kingdom), The Botanist (Scotland), Copperhead (Belgium), Citadelle (France), KI NO BI (Japan), Aviation (USA).

PERCENTAGE OF ALCOHOL

Minimum 37.5% (75 proof).

TIP

Due to the huge number of gins available (there are over 6,000 on the market), it is crucial to know the ingredients that have been used to make a gin (generally called 'botanicals'), so that its aromatic profile matches the recipe.

STORAGE TIME

Several years if the bottle is unopened.

HOW TO STORE

Stand the bottle upright and keep it in a dry place, away from direct light, heat or cold.

A DEEPER DIVE

Gin's ancestor is genever, produced by distilling grain brandy (eau-de-vie) with juniper. More complex and often less sweet than gin, it can replace gin in most cocktail recipes, where it gives a powerful and complex result.

PRINCIPAL TYPES

Gin, distilled gin and London distilled (dry) gin.

GIN

WHAT IS IT?
A neutral eau-de-vie base flavoured when cold with natural or chemical extracts. Most often, the lowest quality gin.

INGREDIENTS
Eau-de-vie + flavourings + sugar + authorized colourings.

DISTILLED GIN

WHAT IS IT?
A neutral eau-de-vie that has to be re-distilled with the main ingredients (juniper, bark, fruit, among others). The name is widely used and is no guarantee that it is a higher-quality spirit than simple gin.

INGREDIENTS
Eau-de-vie + flavourings. Can be artificially coloured and other natural or chemically produced flavours can be added when cold.

LONDON DRY GIN

WHAT IS IT?
An eau-de-vie base that must be re-distilled with all the ingredients used to produce it. Contrary to what its name might suggest, this type of gin is not subject to any control as to where, geographically, it can be produced.

INGREDIENTS
Eau-de-vie + flavouring ingredients. No cold or post-distillation aromatization is allowed.

SPIRIT

WHISKY, WHISKEY

The Lowdown

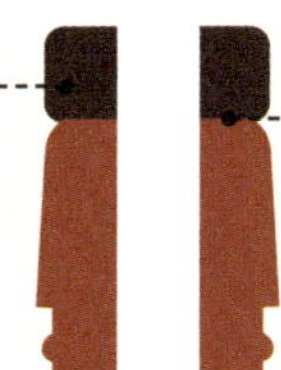

WHAT IS IT?

Eau-de-vie obtained by distilling a beer produced from the fermentation of cereals and then aged in casks. The only permitted ingredients that can be used are water, yeast, cereals and maybe caramel, which gives a darker colour.

LEADING BRANDS

Whisky

- Scotch single malt: Craigellachie, Glenlivet, Glenmorangie, Dalmore, Glenfiddich.
- Peated: Ardbeg, Lagavulin, Laphroaig, Aberfeldy.
- Blended Scotch whisky: Johnnie Walker (black, double black, green), Monkey Shoulder, Dewar's.
- Japanese single malt: Nikka, Yamazaki, Hakushu.
- Indian: Amrut, Paul John.
- France: Alfred Giraud, Armorik, Michel Couvreur.

Whiskey

- USA Bourbon: Bulleit, Jim Beam, Blanton's, Four Roses, Maker's Mark, FEW, Woodford Reserve.
- USA Rye: Bulleit, Jim Beam, Wild Turkey, Rittenhouse, WhistlePig, FEW, Lot 40.

PERCENTAGE OF ALCOHOL

Minimum 40% (80 proof).

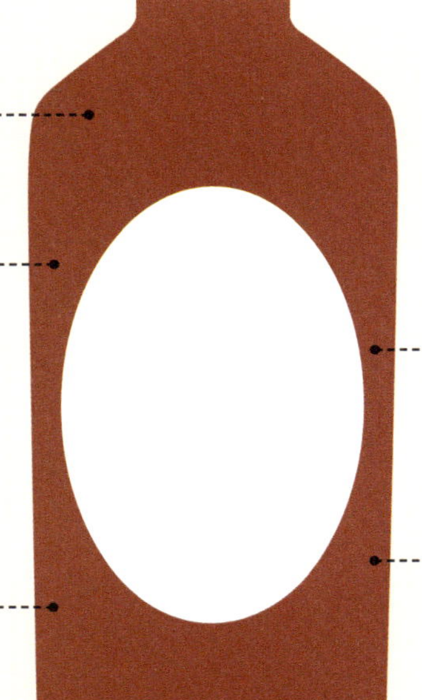

STORAGE TIME

Several years.

HOW TO STORE

Stand the bottle upright and keep it in a dry place, away from direct light, heat or cold. After opening, to ensure safer conservation of quality whiskies or whiskeys, re-seal the bottle with plumber's-grade Teflon sealing tape (also known as PTFE tape – they are one and the same) to prevent oxidation causing the spirit to deteriorate.

TIP

Despite the similarity in their names, these are very different spirits, so take careful note of how they are made.

PRINCIPAL TYPES

Whisky: single malt, grain, blended, blended malt, single grain.
Whiskey: bourbon, rye whiskey.

A DEEPER DIVE

The colour of whiskies and whiskeys depends on the casks that are used. In all cases, the age on the bottle always denotes that of the youngest eau-de-vie in the bottle.

WHISKY

WHAT IS IT?

The style of whisky made in Scotland, which is distilled in alembic stills and aged in casks. Legislation differs from country to country but, in general, the eau-de-vie has to be aged for a minimum of three years for it to be called 'whisky'.

TYPES

Single malt: produced from the distillation of beer from a 100% malted barley fermentation and made in a single distillery.
Grain: produced from the distillation of beer from a fermentation of cereals with a small amount of malted barley.
Blended: produced from the distillation of beer from a blend of single malt and grain, which may come from several distilleries.
Blended malt: produced from the distillation of beer from a blend of single malts from several distilleries.
Irish whiskeys: although spelt with an 'e', they are 'whiskies' in the sense of the way they are manufactured.

WHISKEY

WHAT IS IT?

An eau-de-vie produced from the distillation of beer from a mixture of cereals. Column still distillation, rather than by alembic still, with the spirit then aged in new oak casks. Mainly American whiskeys.

TYPES

Bourbon: a blend of cereals (minimum 51% corn), aged for at least two years in new American oak casks. Bourbon tends towards roundness with notes of vanilla.
Rye whiskey: a blend of cereals (including a minimum of 51% rye), aged for at least two years in new American oaks casks. Rye displays very pronounced spicy notes and is quite dry.

SPIRIT

RUM

The Lowdown

WHAT IS IT?

A spirit produced by distilling fermented sugar cane as a juice, syrup or molasses. It may or may not be aged (if it is labelled white, silver or light, it will not have been). It has different names in different languages: for example, *rhum* (French), rum (English) or *ron* (Spanish). Two criteria determine the right to use the name: it must comply with the minimum alcohol content, and the rum must be produced from sugar cane grown in its country of origin.

LEADING BRANDS

Hispanic or Cuban rum: Flor de Cana, Havana Club, Ron Santiago de Cuba.
Rhum agricole: La Mauny, HSE, Saint James, Trois Rivières.
Jamaican rum: Appleton Estate, Hampden Estate, Wray & Nephew Overproof (> 50%)

PERCENTAGE OF ALCOHOL (ABV)

Minimum 37.5% (75 proof) in the European Union and the UK, 40% (80 proof) in the USA.

STORAGE TIME

Several years.

HOW TO STORE

Stand the bottle upright and keep it in a dry place, away from direct light, excess heat or cold. After opening, to ensure good quality rums are stored safely, re-seal the bottle with plumber's-grade Teflon sealing tape to prevent oxidation, which would cause the spirit to deteriorate.

A DEEPER DIVE

Depending on the laws in individual countries, and unlike whiskies or cognac, the age indicated on a bottle of rum can refer to the oldest spirit it contains, even if that only amounts to 1% of the final blend. Also, since colouring is permitted (except for white/silver/light rums), a very dark hue does not necessarily indicate long ageing. Cachaça is a type of rum made in Brazil from sugarcane juice and its production is subject to strict rules.

MAIN TYPES

Hispanic or Cuban colony rum, Rhum agricole, Jamaican rum.

HISPANIC OR CUBAN RUM

WHAT IS IT?

Rum that is produced in Spanish-speaking countries from sugarcane molasses.

AROMATIC PROFILE

Its subtle herbaceous notes and sugarcane aromas mean it is frequently used in cocktails.

RHUM AGRICOLE

WHAT IS IT?

Produced in French overseas territories and islands that grow sugarcane, it is made from sugarcane juice and not molasses. In the main production areas, the rum can be white (three months' minimum ageing), amber (eighteen months' minimum ageing), aged (three years' minimum ageing) or out of age (aged for more than six years).

AROMATIC PROFILE

More herbaceous than its Hispanic cousins, it is also much fruitier. Its pronounced herbaceous notes make it difficult to use in a cocktail.

JAMAICAN RUM

WHAT IS IT?

Produced in Jamaica, it is made from molasses. If labelled 'estate rum', this indicates that it was produced entirely in the area where the sugarcane was grown. It is always aged at different stages of maturation.

AROMATIC PROFILE

Rich and often quite dark. It has fruity and herbaceous notes but also aromas of leather, hay and even a hint of petrol. In a cocktail, it adds complexity and density to the flavour (in a Daiquiri, for example). This rum, and older rums in general, come into their own in spirit-forward cocktails.

SPIRIT

TEQUILA, MEZCAL

The Lowdown

WHAT ARE THEY?

Spirits made by distilling fermented agave nectar (obtained by cooking agave plants, which are then pressed to extract their sap). The spirits are aged in barrels or vats and are only produced in certain Mexican states.

MAIN TYPES

- Mezcal *joven/blanco* (young), mezcal *reposado* (rested) or mezcal *añejo* (aged).
- Tequila silver/*blanco*, tequila *reposado*, tequila *añejo*.

PERCENTAGE OF ALCOHOL (ABV)

Minimum 37.5% (75 proof).

LEADING BRANDS

Tequila: Patrón, Milagro, Don Julio.
Mezcal: Del Maguey, Bruxo, Los Siete Misterios.

STORAGE TIME

Several years.

TIP

Mezcal has a tendency to overpower many flavours, so use it sparingly. Pick a young mezcal for a cocktail that contains juices and sweeteners to retain its freshness, while an aged, more complex, mezcal can enhance a spirit-forward cocktail. The same applies to tequila, where it is best to choose a 100% agave blue tequila, usually an indication of superior quality.

HOW TO STORE

Stand the bottle upright and keep it in a dry place, away from direct light, excess heat or cold. After opening, to ensure better quality agave spirits are stored safely, re-seal the bottle tightly with plumber's-grade Teflon sealing tape to prevent oxidation causing the spirit to deteriorate.

MEZCAL

WHAT IS IT?
Mezcal must be made with at least one type of thirty possible agaves (wild or not) and can be produced in ten Mexican states.

TYPES
***Joven/blanco*:** not aged or aged for a maximum of two months.
***Reposado*:** aged for at least two months in oak casks.
***Añejo*:** aged for a minimum of a year in oak casks.

AROMATIC PROFILE
It is smoky and can reach levels of complexity that match those of whisky or cognac.

TEQUILA

WHAT IS IT?
Tequila is made with a minimum of 51% blue agave, and it can be produced in five Mexican states.

TYPES
Silver/*blanco*: aged in casks for less than two months. No colouring is allowed to be added.
***Reposado*:** aged in casks for at least two months. Colouring and the addition of sugar are allowed.
***Añejo*:** aged in cask for a minimum of one year and sealed by the government. Colouring and the addition of sugar are allowed.

AROMATIC PROFILE
Sweeter than mezcal and, primarily, little or no smokiness, but often less complex.

SPIRIT

BRANDY

The Lowdown

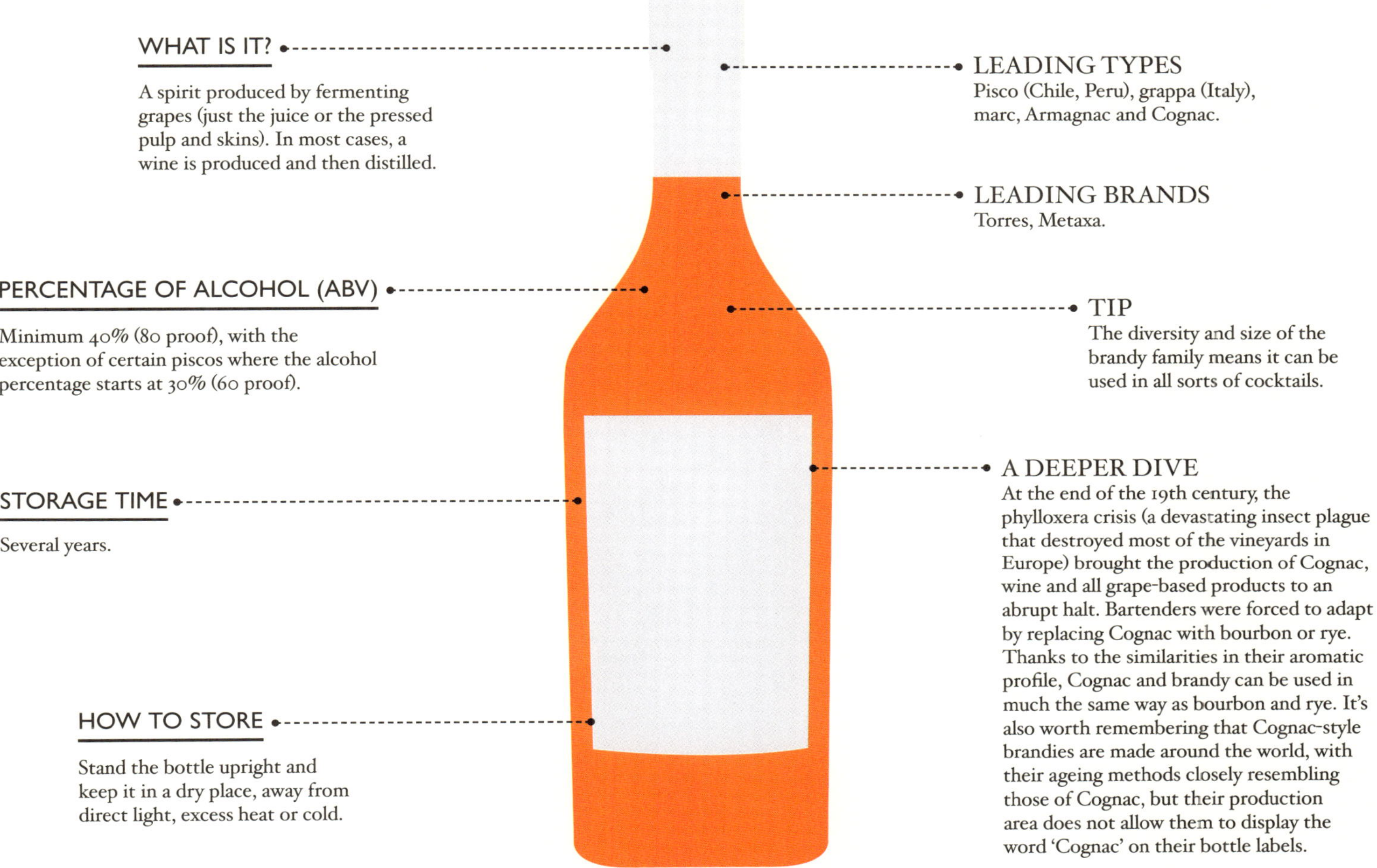

WHAT IS IT?

A spirit produced by fermenting grapes (just the juice or the pressed pulp and skins). In most cases, a wine is produced and then distilled.

LEADING TYPES

Pisco (Chile, Peru), grappa (Italy), marc, Armagnac and Cognac.

LEADING BRANDS

Torres, Metaxa.

PERCENTAGE OF ALCOHOL (ABV)

Minimum 40% (80 proof), with the exception of certain piscos where the alcohol percentage starts at 30% (60 proof).

TIP

The diversity and size of the brandy family means it can be used in all sorts of cocktails.

STORAGE TIME

Several years.

A DEEPER DIVE

At the end of the 19th century, the phylloxera crisis (a devastating insect plague that destroyed most of the vineyards in Europe) brought the production of Cognac, wine and all grape-based products to an abrupt halt. Bartenders were forced to adapt by replacing Cognac with bourbon or rye. Thanks to the similarities in their aromatic profile, Cognac and brandy can be used in much the same way as bourbon and rye. It's also worth remembering that Cognac-style brandies are made around the world, with their ageing methods closely resembling those of Cognac, but their production area does not allow them to display the word 'Cognac' on their bottle labels.

HOW TO STORE

Stand the bottle upright and keep it in a dry place, away from direct light, excess heat or cold.

PISCO

WHAT IS IT?
A brandy produced in Peru or Chile which, with a few exceptions, is unusual in that it is not aged. There is a list of the specific grape varieties that can be used to produce it.

INGREDIENTS
The entire bunch of grapes is used to make pisco: juice, pulp and skins.

AROMATIC PROFILE
These days, muscat and *quebranta* are to the fore, but the list is pretty long. Pisco often has quite dry and floral notes.

ARMAGNAC

WHAT IS IT?
Brandy produced from certain grape varieties that is always aged in casks (with the exception of 'white Armagnac').

AROMATIC PROFILE
When young, there are usually floral, fruity and even vegetal notes. As it ages, Armagnac develops aromas of candied fruits, wood and spices.

COGNAC

WHAT IS IT?
Brandy produced in the Cognac region from certain grape varieties (98% *ugni blanc*), following regulated manufacturing and ageing methods. It holds AOC (*appellation d'origine contrôlée;* French protected designation of origin) classification.

NOTE
The terms VS, VSOP, XO indicate the age of the youngest eau-de-vie in the bottle.
VS: Very Special, aged for two years minimum.
VSOP: Very Superior Old Pale, aged for a minimum of four years.
XO: Extra Old. Before 2018, it had to be aged for at least six years. Since 2018, this has risen to a minimum of ten years.

SPIRIT

BITTERS

The Lowdown

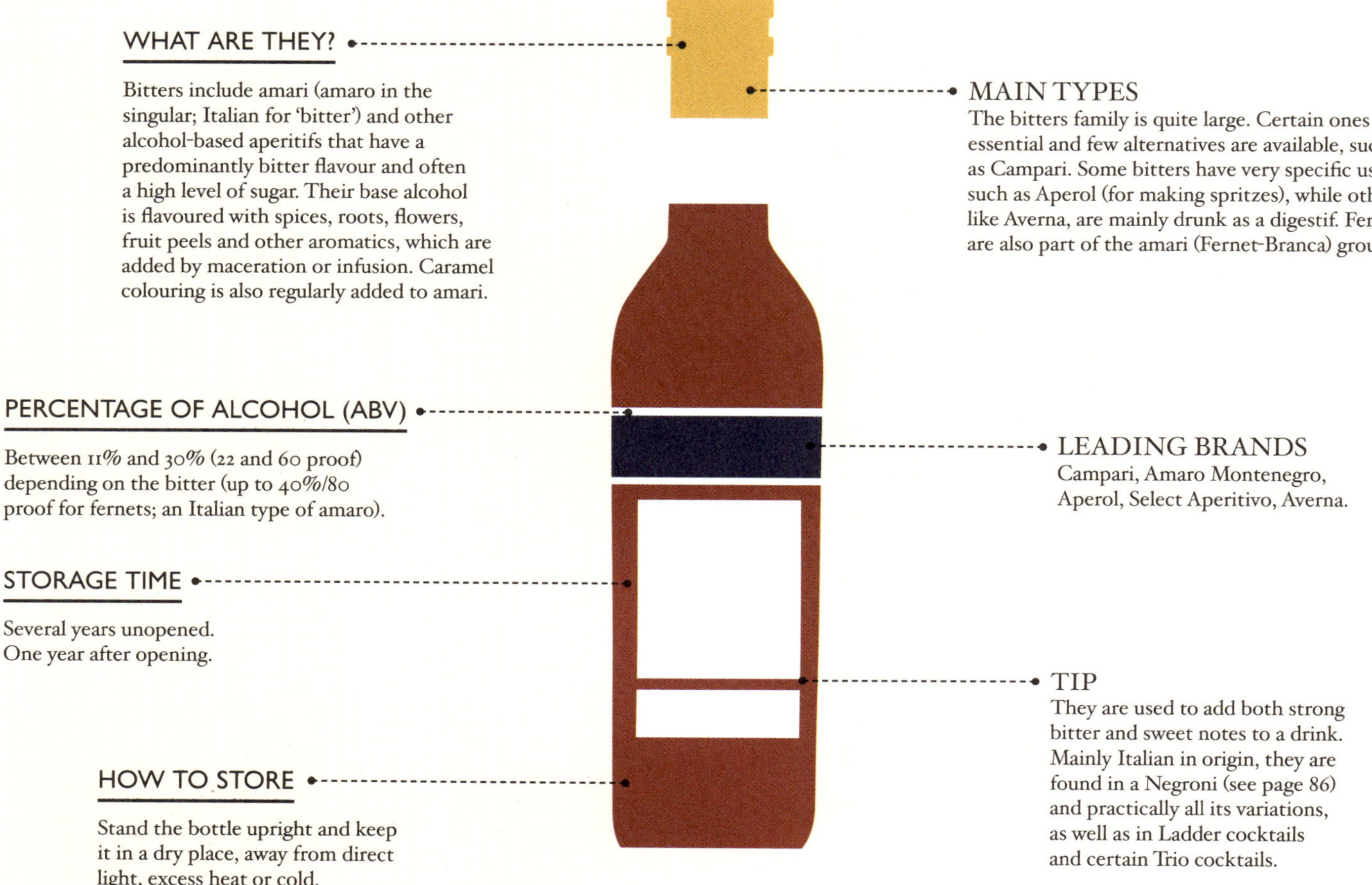

WHAT ARE THEY?

Bitters include amari (amaro in the singular; Italian for 'bitter') and other alcohol-based aperitifs that have a predominantly bitter flavour and often a high level of sugar. Their base alcohol is flavoured with spices, roots, flowers, fruit peels and other aromatics, which are added by maceration or infusion. Caramel colouring is also regularly added to amari.

MAIN TYPES

The bitters family is quite large. Certain ones are essential and few alternatives are available, such as Campari. Some bitters have very specific uses, such as Aperol (for making spritzes), while others, like Averna, are mainly drunk as a digestif. Fernets are also part of the amari (Fernet-Branca) group.

PERCENTAGE OF ALCOHOL (ABV)

Between 11% and 30% (22 and 60 proof) depending on the bitter (up to 40%/80 proof for fernets; an Italian type of amaro).

LEADING BRANDS

Campari, Amaro Montenegro, Aperol, Select Aperitivo, Averna.

STORAGE TIME

Several years unopened.
One year after opening.

TIP

They are used to add both strong bitter and sweet notes to a drink. Mainly Italian in origin, they are found in a Negroni (see page 86) and practically all its variations, as well as in Ladder cocktails and certain Trio cocktails.

HOW TO STORE

Stand the bottle upright and keep it in a dry place, away from direct light, excess heat or cold.

A DEEPER DIVE

They were originally made mainly for medicinal purposes but, as time went on, their popularity increased and they became drinks to be enjoyed on their own or in a cocktail.

CONCENTRATED AROMATIC

BITTERS

The Lowdown

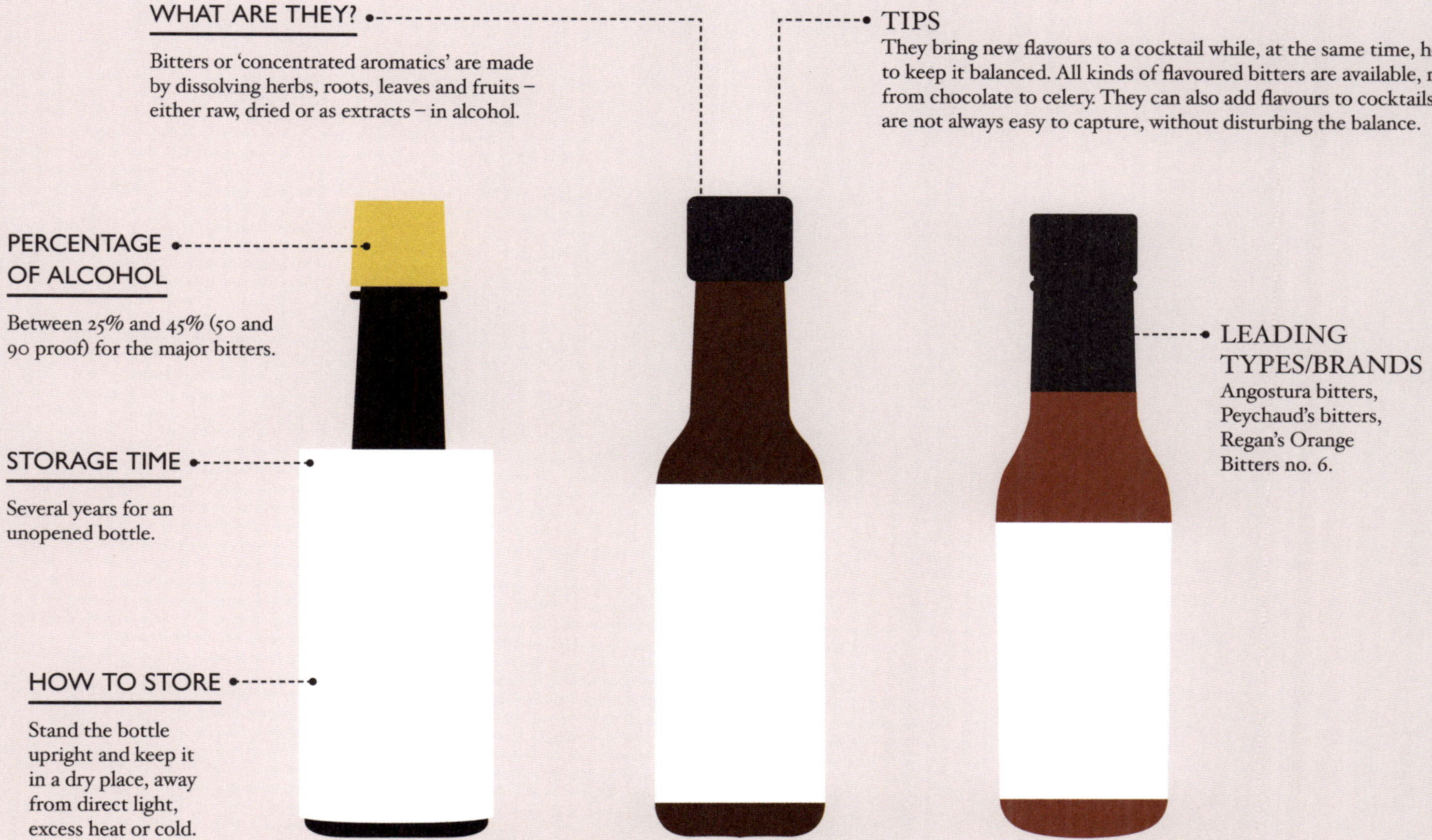

ANGOSTURA

WHAT IS IT?
A bitters with a rum base (44.7%) made with more than 44 plants. Right up to the present day, the recipe remains secret.

AROMATIC PROFILE
Bitter, with strong spicy notes and a hint of cinnamon, cloves and star anise. It's added to many classic cocktails, as Angostura has been unique since the 19th century and as yet has no alternative.

PEYCHAUD'S BITTERS

WHAT IS IT?
A bitters named after its creator with a neutral alcohol (35%) base. Flavoured with gentian and many other unknown ingredients; its recipe also remains secret.

AROMATIC PROFILE
Bitter with acidic notes and a powerful hint of bubble gum. It, too, is used in many classic cocktail recipes, as it has been around since the 19th century. Peychaud's bitters is also unique with no alternative available to date.

ORANGE BITTERS

WHAT IS IT?
A bitters that contains orange. Many different recipes for it are on the market (25% minimum ABV/minimum 50 proof).

AROMATIC PROFILE
A marked orange fragrance, often made more complex with the addition of spices, seeds and roots, such as caraway, star anise, cardamom and gentian. Its aroma resembles that of bitter oranges.

LIQUEUR

TRIPLE SEC

The Lowdown

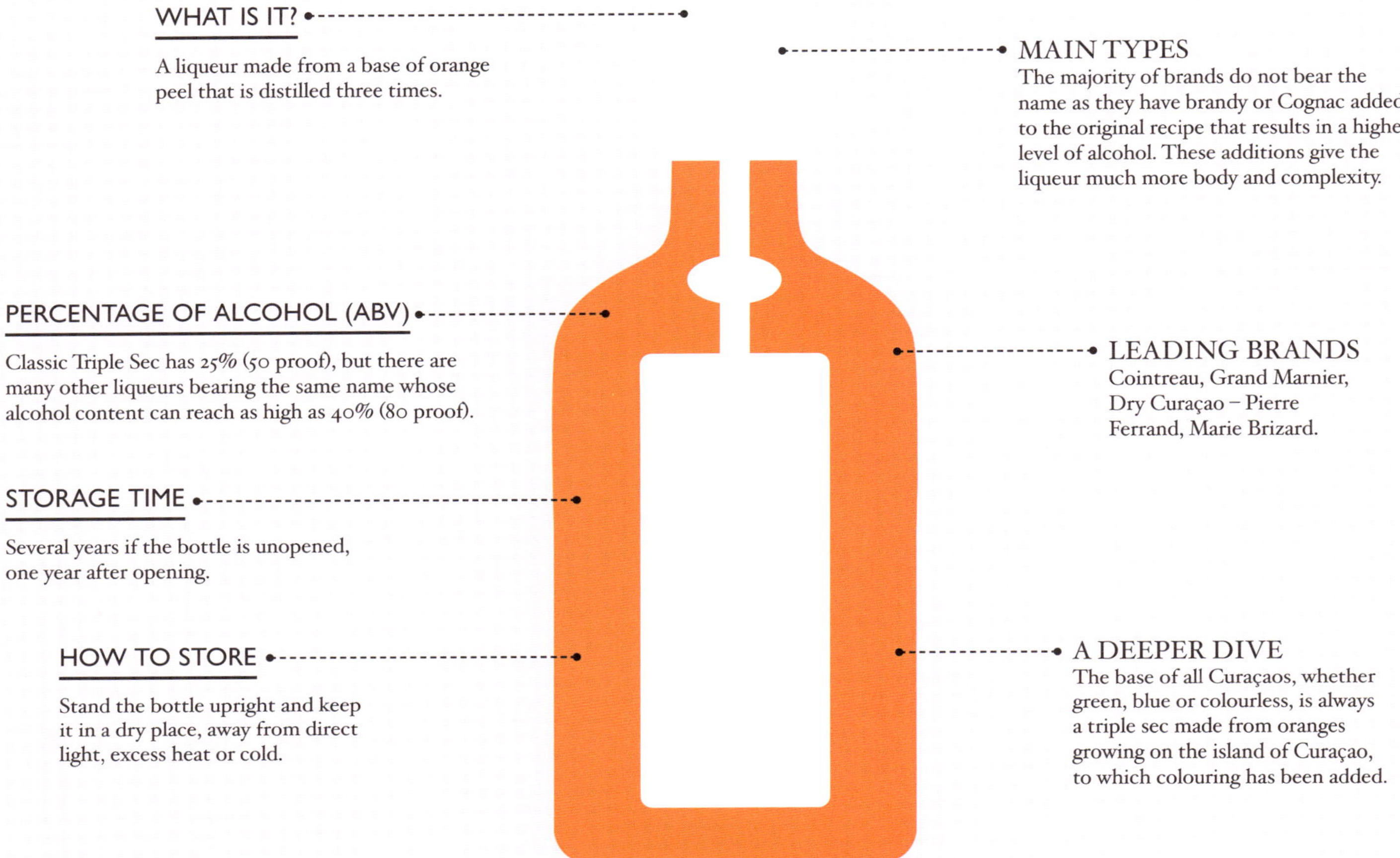

COINTREAU

Made with both sweet and bitter oranges. It's one of the most balanced triple secs and suitable for most cocktails that require it.

GRAND MARNIER

A base of bitter orange with Cognac added. It has a more bitter flavour, meaning it suits fewer cocktails, but it can enhance some classic ones (such as El Presidente, see page 143).

DRY CURAÇAO – PIERRE FERRAND

Curaçao-based with the addition of wine spirit and Cognac. Very well balanced and complex, it is similar to Cointreau but contains 25% less sugar.

CREAMS &

LIQUEURS

The Lowdown

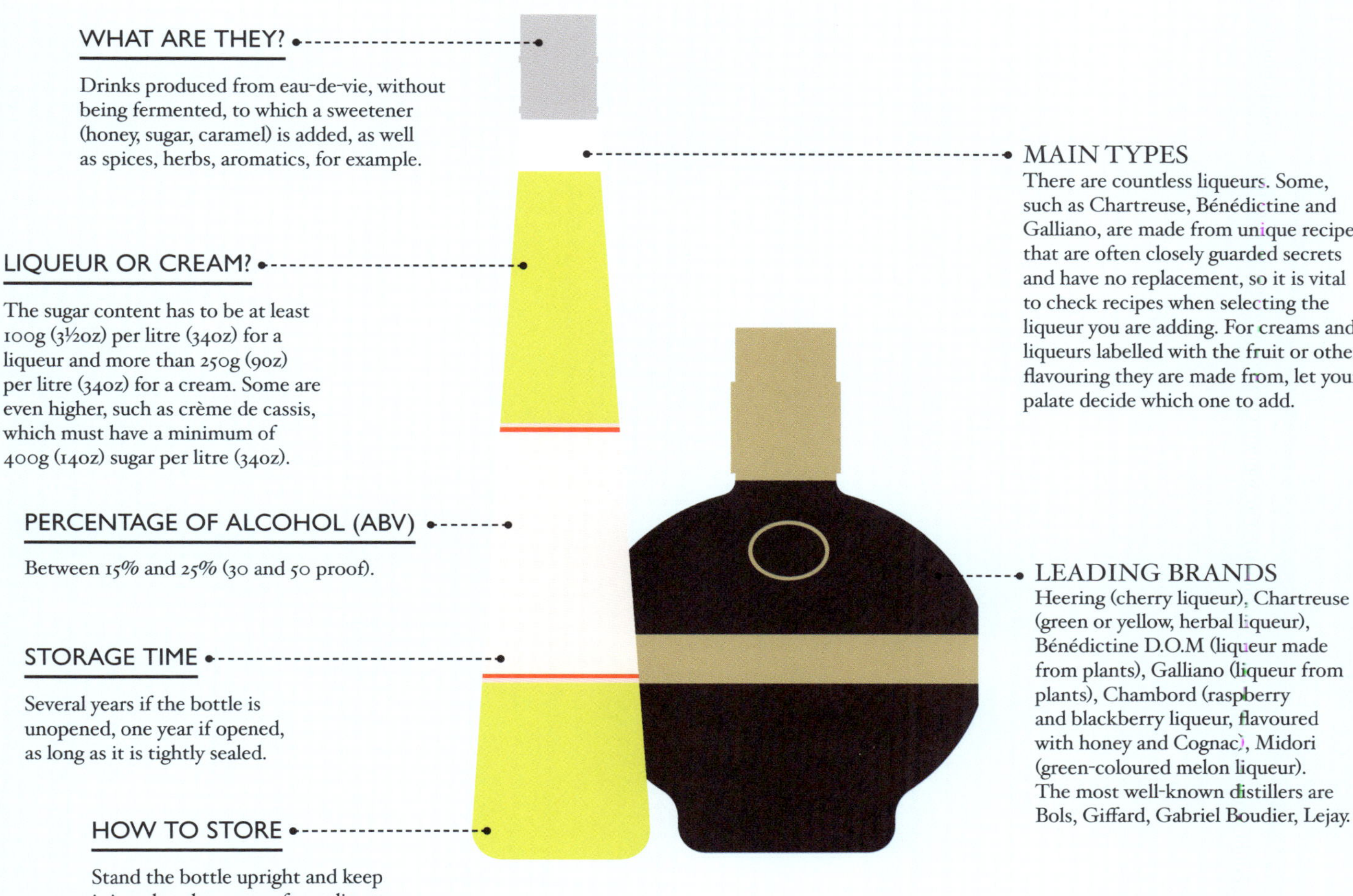

WHAT ARE THEY?

Drinks produced from eau-de-vie, without being fermented, to which a sweetener (honey, sugar, caramel) is added, as well as spices, herbs, aromatics, for example.

LIQUEUR OR CREAM?

The sugar content has to be at least 100g (3½oz) per litre (34oz) for a liqueur and more than 250g (9oz) per litre (34oz) for a cream. Some are even higher, such as crème de cassis, which must have a minimum of 400g (14oz) sugar per litre (34oz).

PERCENTAGE OF ALCOHOL (ABV)

Between 15% and 25% (30 and 50 proof).

STORAGE TIME

Several years if the bottle is unopened, one year if opened, as long as it is tightly sealed.

HOW TO STORE

Stand the bottle upright and keep it in a dry place, away from direct light, excess heat or cold.

MAIN TYPES

There are countless liqueurs. Some, such as Chartreuse, Bénédictine and Galliano, are made from unique recipes that are often closely guarded secrets and have no replacement, so it is vital to check recipes when selecting the liqueur you are adding. For creams and liqueurs labelled with the fruit or other flavouring they are made from, let your palate decide which one to add.

LEADING BRANDS

Heering (cherry liqueur), Chartreuse (green or yellow, herbal liqueur), Bénédictine D.O.M (liqueur made from plants), Galliano (liqueur from plants), Chambord (raspberry and blackberry liqueur, flavoured with honey and Cognac), Midori (green-coloured melon liqueur). The most well-known distillers are Bols, Giffard, Gabriel Boudier, Lejay.

A DEEPER DIVE

Liqueurs and creams play an important part in cocktail making, not just by upping the alcohol level a bit, but, more importantly, by adding sweetness and often a strong, deep flavour that lingers in the mouth. The quality of a liqueur or cream will always influence the final quality of a cocktail.

SPIRIT

EAU-DE-VIE

The Lowdown

WHAT IS IT?

A spirit made by macerating fruits, nuts or berries that is partially fermented or unfermented. It can be strengthened with agriculturally produced neutral alcohol or a distillate of the fruit, nut or berry used to make it. No colouring (except caramel for spirits matured in oak casks) or flavouring of any kind is added, but sweeteners might be, up to a maximum of 18g (¾oz) per litre (34oz). This very restricted amount guarantees the chosen ingredient has a very pure taste.

LEADING BRANDS

Lehmann, Massenez, Morand, Miclo.

TIP

The fact that eaux-de-vie are low in sugar and have no additives is a double-edged sword, as their flavours can easily be overwhelmed by other ingredients in a cocktail and their sole contribution is a not-very-pleasant alcoholic edge. For this reason, they are rarely used, despite being around for several centuries.

PERCENTAGE OF ALCOHOL (ABV)

Minimum 37.5% (75 proof).

STORAGE TIME

Several years.

HOW TO STORE

Stand the bottle upright and keep it in a dry place, away from direct light, heat or cold.

A DEEPER DIVE

Before legislation put a stop to permits for home distillers being renewed, stills could be found in every village growing fruits, berries or nuts and proved that home distilling was an ancient craft that had evolved over time. In France, the term 'eau de vie' is also used to cover all spirits. In Europe, an eau-de-vie can only contain one ingredient, in addition to alcohol and water. The list is limited to 35 elements.

ABSINTHE

WHAT IS IT?

An absinthe-based spirit made by distillation, where plant extracts are dissolved in neutral alcohol or the plants macerated in alcohol. Those most commonly used are grand wormwood, little wormwood (also known as Roman wormwood), lemon balm, hyssop and fennel.

PERCENTAGE OF ALCOHOL (ABV)

Between 60% and 75% (120 and 150 proof).

DIFFERENT TYPES

Absinthes with an alcohol content below 60% (120 proof) are almost all of very poor quality as, broadly speaking, the content of quality absinthes is between 66% and 75% (132 and 150 proof). White absinthes are often destined for tastings rather than making cocktails as they have pronounced characteristics.

A FINAL WORD

Banned in France in 1915 for close to 100 years, absinthe is now seeing a resurgence in popularity. Its production and consumption is unrestricted in the UK but, in the US, it must not contain thujone (the chemical compound in absinthe spirit that can allegedly cause hallucinations and madness).

EGGS

The Lowdown

WHY INCLUDE EGGS IN A COCKTAIL BOOK?

When making cocktails, raw hen's eggs can be added; the white, the yolk, or the whole egg.

TIPS

Never use eggs that have flecks of blood in their white or yolk. Do not crack an egg on the rim of a cocktail shaker. This reduces the risk of salmonella contamination and avoids tiny amounts of shell or egg yolk mixing with the white.

HOW ARE THEY USED?

White: this acts as an emulsifier, adding texture and producing a beautiful, silky foam.
Yolk: this adds texture and taste, making a cocktail smooth and giving it a rich, creamy flavour.
Whole egg: this also adds texture and taste, plus a foamy mousse on top.

HOW TO USE

Remove eggs kept in the refrigerator ahead of time so they can come to room temperature. Break the egg and keep it separate from the other ingredients, either in a bowl or in the top part of an empty cocktail shaker. Use immediately; it is the last step before a dry shake (see page 58).

WHICH TYPE OF EGG IS BEST?

Preferably standard-size eggs and as fresh as possible. Avoid large ones or the cocktail can taste too 'eggy'. An average egg white is 30ml (1oz). Use organic eggs with care as they can give a sulphurous taste.

WHY DOES AN EMULSION WORK BETTER WITH AN EGG AT ROOM TEMPERATURE RATHER THAN ONE STRAIGHT FROM THE REFRIGERATOR?

The proteins in an egg will change depending on its temperature. When cold, these proteins will curl up on themselves, while at room temperature, they will unroll a little. By being more 'unrolled', the parts of the egg that have emulsifying properties will become more exposed, meaning emulsions will bind together more quickly.

SWEETENER

SYRUPS

The Lowdown

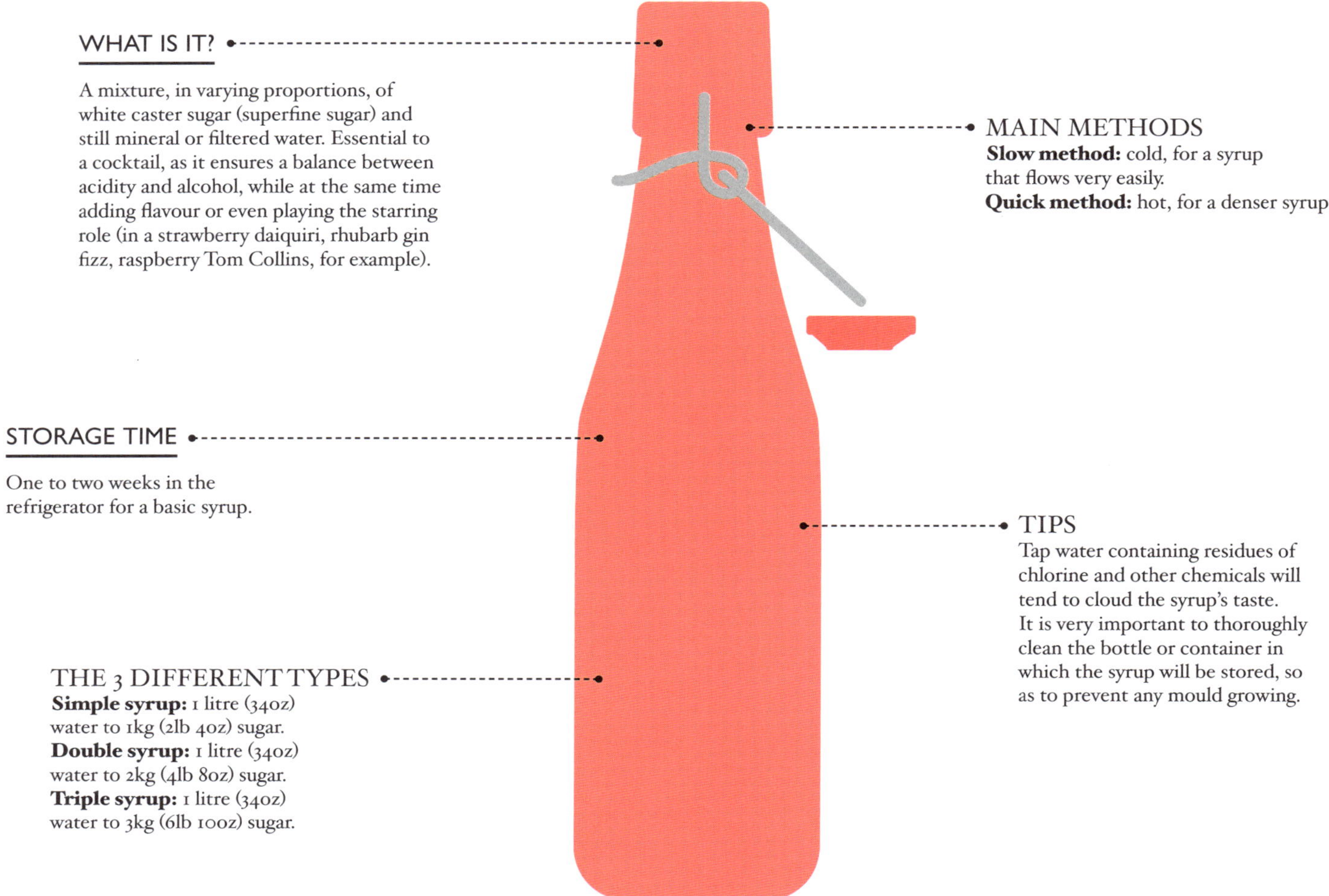

WHAT IS IT?

A mixture, in varying proportions, of white caster sugar (superfine sugar) and still mineral or filtered water. Essential to a cocktail, as it ensures a balance between acidity and alcohol, while at the same time adding flavour or even playing the starring role (in a strawberry daiquiri, rhubarb gin fizz, raspberry Tom Collins, for example).

MAIN METHODS

Slow method: cold, for a syrup that flows very easily.
Quick method: hot, for a denser syrup.

STORAGE TIME

One to two weeks in the refrigerator for a basic syrup.

TIPS

Tap water containing residues of chlorine and other chemicals will tend to cloud the syrup's taste.
It is very important to thoroughly clean the bottle or container in which the syrup will be stored, so as to prevent any mould growing.

THE 3 DIFFERENT TYPES

Simple syrup: 1 litre (34oz) water to 1kg (2lb 4oz) sugar.
Double syrup: 1 litre (34oz) water to 2kg (4lb 8oz) sugar.
Triple syrup: 1 litre (34oz) water to 3kg (6lb 10oz) sugar.

THE BASICS

Slow method (for simple syrup): combine the sugar and water in a bowl. Whisk thoroughly every 10 minutes, taking care to ensure the undissolved sugar does not settle at the bottom of the bowl. When the liquid is clear, the syrup is ready.
Quick version: pour the water into a saucepan. When steam rises from it, add the sugar and whisk, without letting the water boil. When the liquid becomes clear, the syrup is ready.
Storage: pour the syrup into a clean, sterilized bottle or other container and wait until the syrup is cold before sealing. Store for 1–2 weeks in the refrigerator.

TRIPLE HONEY SYRUP (A BLEND OF WHITE SUGAR, AGAVE NECTAR AND HONEY)

Heat a measured quantity of water in a saucepan. When steam rises from it, add three times the weight of the water in honey syrup and whisk in. Store in the refrigerator for one month.

GINGER SYRUP

This syrup is prepared cold. Pass fresh ginger through a centrifugal juice extractor and weigh the juice. Using a whisk, mix in the same weight of white sugar. Store for one week in the refrigerator.

SWEETENER

CORDIALS

The Lowdown

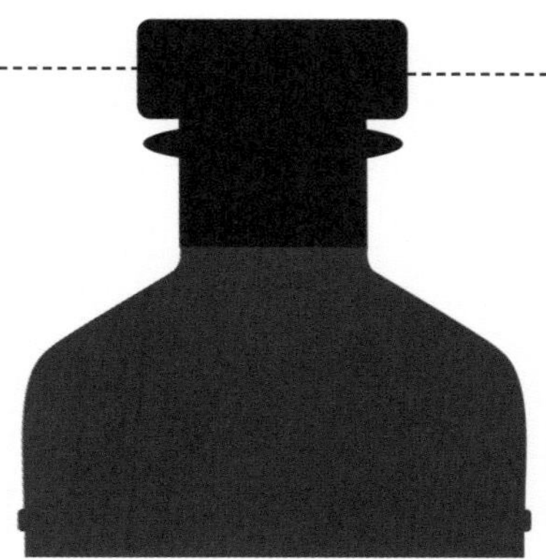

WHAT IS IT?

A non-alcoholic drink, usually not as sweet as a syrup, made from one or more fruits and sometimes essential citrus oils.

LEADING BRANDS

Rose's Lime Juice Cordial, Bottlegreen, Belvoir and Monin.

STORAGE TIME

One to seven days, according to type, in the refrigerator.

TIPS

With a fragrance that is often more balanced than that of a syrup, a cordial adds a slight bitterness and a tangy note. The most classic is lime cordial, which is added to a Gimlet (see page 132), which never goes out of fashion.

SHRUB

WHAT IS IT?

A purée of cooked fruits or vegetables, sometimes enhanced with spices, oil or another ingredient for extra flavour, then mellowed with vinegar and sometimes concentrated by reduction. Almost exclusively intended for a bar. Keeps for one week in the refrigerator.

NOTE

Not to be confused with Shrubb, which is a liqueur from the Antilles.

OLEO SACCHARUM

WHAT IS IT?

In Latin it means 'sugar oil' and it is a type of syrup made by kneading sugar and citrus peel together to extract the oils from the zest before diluting with water. A little citrus juice can also be added. Often used to make mixes more complex, from an aromatic point of view, than simply adding a syrup. It will keep for one or two days in the refrigerator.

ORGEAT

WHAT IS IT?

A syrup made from almond milk and orange flower water. However, the term can be used for any plant-based drink, such as orgeat of pistachio, hazelnut, walnut, rice, and others. Usually a simple syrup where the water is replaced with a plant-based drink before extracts, aromatics such as herbs, or spices are added to boost the flavour and add complexity. It will keep for 1–2 weeks in the refrigerator. Shake before using.

NECTAR, PURÉES &

FRUIT JUICES

The Lowdown

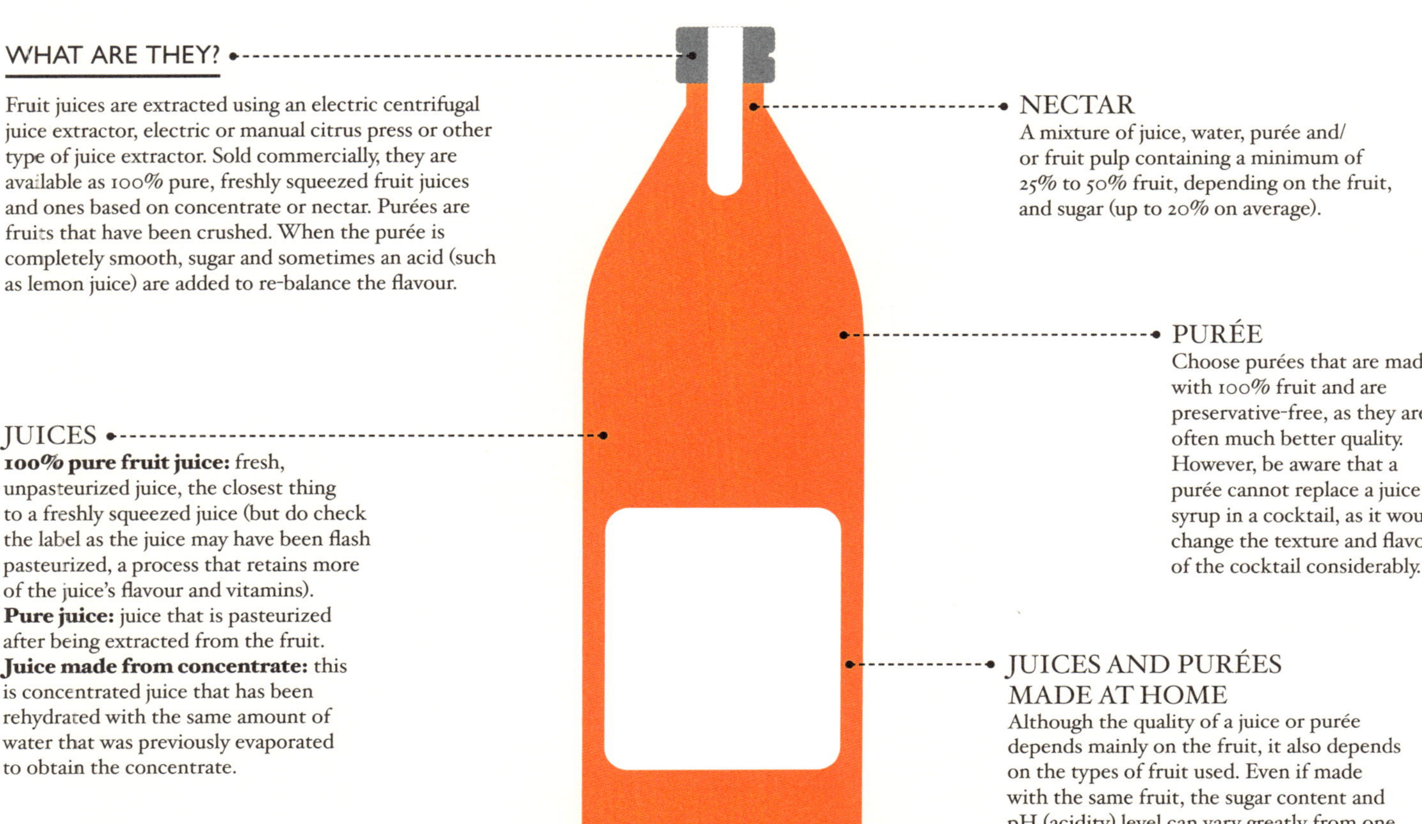

WHAT ARE THEY?

Fruit juices are extracted using an electric centrifugal juice extractor, electric or manual citrus press or other type of juice extractor. Sold commercially, they are available as 100% pure, freshly squeezed fruit juices and ones based on concentrate or nectar. Purées are fruits that have been crushed. When the purée is completely smooth, sugar and sometimes an acid (such as lemon juice) are added to re-balance the flavour.

NECTAR

A mixture of juice, water, purée and/or fruit pulp containing a minimum of 25% to 50% fruit, depending on the fruit, and sugar (up to 20% on average).

PURÉE

Choose purées that are made with 100% fruit and are preservative-free, as they are often much better quality. However, be aware that a purée cannot replace a juice or syrup in a cocktail, as it would change the texture and flavour of the cocktail considerably.

JUICES

100% pure fruit juice: fresh, unpasteurized juice, the closest thing to a freshly squeezed juice (but do check the label as the juice may have been flash pasteurized, a process that retains more of the juice's flavour and vitamins).
Pure juice: juice that is pasteurized after being extracted from the fruit.
Juice made from concentrate: this is concentrated juice that has been rehydrated with the same amount of water that was previously evaporated to obtain the concentrate.

JUICES AND PURÉES MADE AT HOME

Although the quality of a juice or purée depends mainly on the fruit, it also depends on the types of fruit used. Even if made with the same fruit, the sugar content and pH (acidity) level can vary greatly from one juice to another. Fresh juices can be made at home using a centrifuge or cold press juicer. For a fruit purée, use a blender or liquidizer, as the fruit pulp left behind in a centrifugal juicer will be too dry and will have lost too much of its flavour to be used as a purée.

LIME JUICE AND LEMON JUICE

These are predominantly added to cocktails for their acidity. They help to balance a cocktail, bringing not just freshness but also citrus notes that combine very well with other flavours.

SEASONALITY

Lemon trees produce fruit all year round but the best quality is the fruit harvested between mid-autumn and late spring. Lime trees have a shorter fruiting season, lasting from mid-autumn to early winter.

WHEN BUYING

Choose fruit that is untreated and unwaxed, from sustainable agriculture or organically grown.
Lemons: smell them (they must be strongly scented) and press them gently to make sure they are firm. Look for normal-sized or smaller lemons (as larger fruits can be dry with little juice).
Limes: smell them (they must have a strong, sweet aroma). Choose good-sized fruit and make sure they are firm.

PRESSING

Ideally, cut and squeeze them just before using to preserve their vitamins.

USING

Taste the juice before using it. If it seems more acidic than usual, reduce the quantity (by 5ml/1 tsp) or add a little sugar to restore the balance. Store lemons at room temperature to ensure the greatest amount of juice can be squeezed from them. Ideally, use a lemon hand press (also known as a Mexican elbow squeezer). Filter the juice through a double strainer to eliminate impurities.

ALTERNATIVES

Commercially produced lemon juices cannot really replace a freshly squeezed juice. They will often contain too much sugar, which makes them lose their acidic bite, or be far too acidic and have no aroma.

SODAS

The Lowdown

WHAT ARE THEY?

Alcohol-free drinks that contain CO_2 naturally or have been carbonated (the gas incorporated). Sodas can be flavoured (with, for example, different aromas and extracts) and sweetened.

LEADING BRANDS

Sparkling mineral water: Perrier, San Pellegrino.
Soda water: Thomas Henry, Fever-Tree, Schweppes Premium Mixer.
Ginger ale: Canada Dry, Schweppes, Fentimans.
Ginger beer: Belvoir, Bundaberg, Fentimans, Old Jamaica.
Tonic water: Fever-Tree, Thomas Henry, Fentimans, 1724, Schweppes, Archibald, The London Essence Co., Three Cents.

STORAGE TIME

Several months.

HOW TO STORE

Keep away from direct heat. After opening, drink on the same day.

MAIN TYPES

Sparkling mineral water, Seltz, soda water, ginger ale, ginger beer, tonic water. There are many other sodas on the market, all of which have their place in a cocktail. Choose ones with natural flavourings, plenty of fizz, a low sugar content and no added sweeteners.

TIP

When using a soda in a cocktail, always check it's not a soda 'light' or 'zero'. Sweeteners – in particular stevia – react poorly with acidifiers such as lemon, producing an unpleasant taste.

MINERAL WATER OR SELTZ

Water that is full of minerals and sometimes salt. Whether naturally carbonated or not, it very rarely has a neutral pH. Low carbonation can negatively affect a cocktail's balance, causing it to lack sparkle.

SODA WATER

Water that is filtered and sometimes demineralized, with a pH close to neutral and very strongly carbonated. This prevents it affecting the taste of a cocktail, and it does not alter its effervescence despite the addition of other liquids (even an egg white or aquafaba emulsion).

GINGER ALE

A fairly lightly carbonated mixture based on ginger bug (fermented ginger), lime juice and sugar. Nowadays, ginger flavourings or extracts are used instead, and true ginger ale is hard to find. It is preferable to look for a balanced product that has plenty of bubbles and is not too sweet.

GINGER BEER

Produced by fermenting ginger, but the fermentation is stopped just before it becomes alcoholic (and therefore very strong), completed with water and sugar. It can be naturally carbonated or have the gas incorporated. These days, many ginger beers are made using extracts or flavourings, meaning they lose much of the intensity of the ginger's characteristics in the original recipe. The presence of a deposit at the bottom of a bottle indicates that the ginger beer was produced from fermented ginger and is a guarantee of quality.

TONIC WATER

Soda that contains quinine and, usually, sugar. Sometimes other plant extracts, artificial or natural flavourings and essential oils are added to give the tonic a more complex flavour. A wide variety of different tonics are available.

GLASSWARE

The Lowdown

WHAT IS IT?

Containers made of glass or, in a few cases, stainless steel, of varying capacities and shapes, in which cocktails are served.

SHAPES

Chalice shaped, straight sided, fancy, and with or without a stem and foot.

MATERIAL

For preference: materials that conduct heat well and keep cocktails cool (glass, copper, stainless steel).
Type: 'tempered' glass as it lasts longer and is resistant to temperature changes.
Avoid: plastic or polycarbonate plastic, both of which do not wear well and conduct heat poorly, encouraging ice to melt and leading to unwanted dilution of a cocktail.

WHICH TO CHOOSE?

The choice of glass is governed by the cocktail recipe and whether or not ice is added when it is served. It's not set in stone that you must prefer one shape of glass over another. This can be down to the personal preference of the cocktail's creator, who could well set a new trend by doing so.

AESTHETIC

In some cases, the choice of glass can simply be down to how it looks. Choose one with a very minimalist design or unusual shape and your cocktail can become a real talking point.

CARE

Taking care of glassware is as essential for its longevity as for its appearance. Careful washing and wiping with a microfibre cloth will ensure a flawless shine and clarity.

ESSENTIAL GLASSES

1 OLD FASHIONED (OR ON THE ROCKS):

A low glass with a capacity of approximately 200ml (7oz).Used for cocktails served with or without ice.

2 DOUBLE OLD FASHIONED (OR DOUBLE ON THE ROCKS)

A low glass with a capacity of approximately 360ml (12oz plus 1 tsp). Used for cocktails served with or without ice.

3 MARTINI (OR COCKTAIL GLASS)

A stemmed glass with a capacity of around 150ml (5oz). Used for cocktails traditionally served without ice.

4 TUMBLER

A tall glass holding approximately 350ml (12oz). Used for cocktails served with ice.

ICE

The Lowdown

WHAT IS IT?

Water in solid, cut or shaped form. When added to a cocktail, ice brings it to the right drinking temperature and is the link between the ingredients and the correct amount of dilution.

SHOULD I BUY IT?

The sale of quality ice to individual customers is a growing business. Globally, when ice is bought commercially, it must be clear, without impurities.

WATER

Use filtered or mineral water.

TEMPERATURE

The outer surface must be around -10°C (14°F). To know when ice is at the correct temperature, wait until the opaque haze caused by the cold is no longer visible.

TIPS

Avoid stirring the water first so no air becomes trapped in the ice, which would make it less attractive and more fragile.

STORAGE

Transfer ice to an insulated container that will keep it at the ideal temperature for 1–2 hours before using.

WHY DOES ICE SHATTER DUE TO THERMAL SHOCK?

Like all crystals, ice is a jumble of three-dimensional meshes, and these icy meshes contract when the temperature increases. When an ice cube is plunged into a liquid, the meshes inside it become wider while, on the surface and warmed by the liquid around it, the meshes contract. The tension created causes the ice cube to break.

HOW DOES ICE LOWER THE ALCOHOL CONTENT OF A COCKTAIL?

By adding ice to a cocktail, you are adding water. It dilutes the cocktail and thus the alcohol content of it decreases.

WHY USE FILTERED WATER?

Filtering water removes any particles suspended in it that could make the ice cloudy. Use of this type of water means that the ice is clear, more attractive to look at and without any taste.

HOW DO THERMAL EXCHANGES WORK?

When an ice cube comes into contact with a cocktail, it will draw energy from the cocktail. The surface of the ice cube (and gradually all of it) will warm up to 0°C (32°F). At this temperature the ice cube gradually melts, and its transition from a solid to a liquid absorbs heat from its surroundings, which in turn cools the cocktail.

THE THREE KINDS OF ICE

1 BLOCK OF ICE

See page 40.

2 ICE CUBE

See page 38.

3 CRUSHED ICE

See page 39.

ICE CUBES

The Lowdown

WHAT ARE THEY?

Water in solid form, moulded into different shapes, most commonly cubes.

EQUIPMENT

Use silicone moulds (or others made of a flexible material) so that the ice cubes can be unmoulded easily and without damage.

DILUTION

Medium, ideal for shaken cocktails.

USES

Suitable for all cocktails served with ice cubes. Can be used for a cocktail made in a shaker or one prepared in a mixing glass. However, considerable skill is needed to achieve the right level of dilution, depending on the shaking or mixing time.

TEMPERATURE

The surface area of an ice cube must be around -10°C (14°F).

STORAGE

Transfer the unmoulded ice cubes to an insulated container that will keep them at an optimum temperature so they can be used for up to 1–2 hours.

SIZE

Ice cubes must be sufficiently large (between 3–5cm/1–2in) to avoid the cocktail being diluted too rapidly.

SHAPE

Cubes, spheres or with a conical base.

TIPS

Ice cubes should not contain any holes as, if they do, they may explode or melt too quickly. Do not use ice taken directly out of a conventional freezer (with a temperature below or equal to -18 °C/-0.4°F) as the thermal shock could cause it to shatter, creating unsightly shards of ice in your cocktail.

1. Pour filtered, boiled or mineral water into the ice cube moulds, filling each cavity right to the top.
2. Freeze at -18°C (-0.4°F) for 24 hours.
3. About 5–15 minutes before using (depending on the room temperature) unmould the ice cubes and store them in an insulated container.

DOES AN ICE CUBE MELT DIFFERENTLY DEPENDING ON THE TECHNIQUE USED TO MAKE A COCKTAIL?

With a shaken cocktail, the energy necessary to melt an ice cube is transferred more rapidly than one that is stirred, as the shaking action is stronger. It explains why, for an equivalent amount of ice cubes and cocktail mix, the ice melts faster when the cocktail is shaken than when stirred with a spoon.

CRUSHED ICE

The Lowdown

WHAT IS IT?
Water in solid form, broken or crushed into small shards.

EQUIPMENT
If possible, use a crushed ice maker (see page 211) to make regular-sized pieces. You can also break up ice cubes using a pestle or heavy blunt utensil (such as a hammer or rolling pin) but the shards will be of irregular shape, resulting in a different dilution rate each time.

DILUTION
Rapid, and even faster if you use only a small amount. Ideal if you want a very refreshing cocktail.

USE
Suitable for cocktails that taste strongly of alcohol (Caipirinha, see page 70). The low temperature from the crushed ice helps to showcase the flavour of the spirit by reducing the taste of alcohol. It is also used to deliver freshness (in a Bramble, see page 102 and Mojito, see page 178) or, less often, for aesthetic reasons, such as holding decorations in place (Mai Tai, see page 184).

TEMPERATURE
Use as soon as you take it out of the freezer, at -18°C (-0.4°F).

SIZE
The ideal size for the fragments of ice is about 5–7mm (¼in).

STORAGE
Crushed ice can be kept for a few hours by packing it into an insulated container.

SHAPE
Shards.

TIPS
Crushed ice is fragile and very heat sensitive. It is best to use it as soon as you take it out of the freezer.

1. Pour filtered, boiled or mineral water into ice cube moulds, filling each cavity right to the top.
2. Freeze at -18°C (-0.4°F) for 24 hours.
3. Unmould the ice cubes and pass immediately through a crushed ice maker. Keep in an insulated container.

WHY DOES CRUSHED ICE PRODUCE AN IMMEDIATE SENSE OF FRESHNESS?

The contact surface of the ice is much greater, meaning the cocktail becomes colder more quickly.

LARGE

ICE BLOCKS

The Lowdown

WHAT IS IT?

Water in solid form, cut into large blocks.

SHAPE

A large cube.

DILUTION

Slow: a large block melts two or three times more slowly than traditional ice cubes, thereby considerably extending the life of a cocktail.

EQUIPMENT

Bread knife
Ice pestle
Ice pick
Ice-making mould with a 5-litre (169oz) capacity.

TEMPERATURE

The outside surface must be around -10°C (14°F).

USES

Cocktails served over ice. Cocktails made in a shaker or mixing glass, with the shaking and mixing times adjusted. A block of ice can be used in any cocktail to which ice cubes are added.

SIZE

About 5cm (2in) square.

STORAGE

Can be kept in an insulated container for several hours.

A DEEPER DIVE

It's relatively easy to track down moulds for making ice blocks to fit into an old-fashioned glass (5-cm/2-in square blocks, or balls 6cm/2½in in diameter). However, the blocks will rarely be perfectly clear, even if they look really impressive.

WHY DOES A BLOCK OF ICE MELT LESS QUICKLY THAN SMALLER PIECES?

Even when they are of equal volume, a large block of ice will melt more slowly than several small blocks because the surface contact with the cocktail is smaller. The thermal changes are therefore less rapid.

HOW TO MAKE A LARGE BLOCK

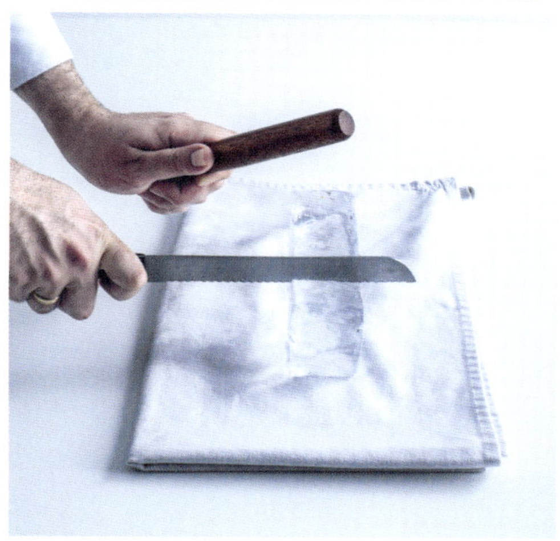

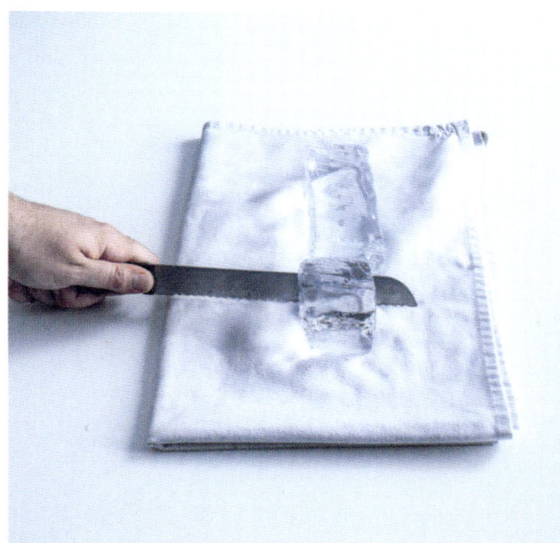

1 Fill a 10-litre (338-oz) ice-making mould, without a cover, with filtered or mineral water and freeze for about 48 hours at a temperature of between -18°C (-0.4°F) and -24°C (11.2F°). Allow twice the amount of time needed for a 5-litre (169-oz) mould. The ice-making mould will slow down the freezing process, pushing air and impurities towards the top as the water turns to ice, giving a crystal-clear result.

2 Leave the ice-making mould at room temperature for 30 minutes.

3 Unmould the block of ice carefully.

4 Using an ice pestle, hit the block several times on the corners where the pure, clear ice stops, to detach the top of the block containing all the impurities.

5 Using an ice pick, mark cutting lines. Placing the blade of a knife on each marked line in turn, hit the back of the knife with the pestle to separate the blocks.

6 Use a knife with a straight, heavy blade to trim the edges straight or to carve the ice to the desired shape.

DECORATIONS

The Lowdown

VISUAL OBJECTIVE

Some cocktails can stand alone because of their colour, texture or choice of glass. However, when these elements don't make a cocktail sufficiently eye-catching, adding a decoration can give it volume and visual weight, while at the same time reflecting the ingredients that have gone into making it. Either way, a decoration gives a cocktail that all-important wow factor.

AROMATIC OBJECTIVE

When drinking, your nose is always close to the glass, and this is when the cocktail can become more seductive. Expressing mint before adding it as a decoration (see page 47, step 2); frosting the rim of the glass with spices; spraying it with absinthe and expressing citrus zest on the glass (see page 46): all of these add a strong, fragrant note to the cocktail, which intensifies and adds complexity upon tasting, while also complementing the cocktail's flavour. Similarly, rubbing the zest over the stem of the glass will delight the taster when their hand, after touching the stem, approaches their nose.

TASTE OBJECTIVE

Some decorations are designed to add that all-important final flourish to the cocktail-drinking experience. For example, salting the rim of a Margarita glass (see page 160) introduces an element that is not part of the cocktail's recipe but that enhances its flavour when enjoyed. Adding a piece of crystallized (candied) ginger to a Penicillin (see page 110) reminds you of the ginger syrup but also adds real pleasure when tasting, while the cherry in a Manhattan (see page 136) matches the cocktail perfectly.

WHOLE FRUITS

WHICH FRUITS CAN BE USED WHOLE?

Physalis, raspberries, blackberries, cherries, small redcurrant sprigs and other fruits of similar size.

WAYS TO USE THEM

Cocktail stick (pick): spear the fruit on a cocktail stick (pick) and put it in the glass.
Position: carefully place fruits on the ice cubes.
Tongs: hold the fruit with a pair of cocktail tongs and drop it into the bottom of the glass without it touching the sides.

TIPS

Choose the most attractive and freshest fruits to place on ice cubes or on the mousse of a cocktail. As a general rule, odd numbers are considered to be more visually pleasing.

CUTTING PIECES OF FRUIT

WHICH FRUITS?

Citrus fruits, pineapple, mango, banana, apple, pear, star fruit, watermelon.

CITRUS FRUITS

1 Cut from the stalk to the base of the citrus fruit.

2 Repeat at an angle of about 45 degrees so that both sides of the flesh are exactly the same size. To arrange one-eighth or one-quarter of a citrus fruit on the rim of the glass, make an incision in the flesh corresponding to the desired position on the glass, without cutting into the zest. It is best visually to make a clean, thin and regular cut.

OTHER FRUITS

Choose a cut that is understated and thick enough to hold the piece of fruit in place, but also thin enough not to be too showy. Usually, pieces of fruit are placed on the ice or a cut is made to position them on the rim of the glass.

CUTTING CITRUS ZEST

WHAT IS ZEST?

Zest is the coloured part of the skin of a citrus fruit and must not be confused with the pith, which is the very bitter white part between the zest and the flesh. It is advisable not to remove any of the pith in order to avoid a pronounced bitterness. Zests are often used to highlight certain characteristics of one or more spirits or to add a citrussy note. They contain the essential oils of the citrus fruit they are pared from.

REMOVAL

With a vegetable shaver or tomato peeler: place it against the rind and remove the zest, using the same movement as you would for peeling a fruit. **With a knife:** the movement must be precise so that you remove just the zest in regular-sized pieces. Put the knife blade against the rind of the fruit and cut away the zest, taking care to apply repeated, constant pressure. Zest removed with a knife will be more brittle when expressed and therefore more difficult to use as a decoration.

TRIMMING

Trim the zest to the desired shape and use the cut pieces to fix the zest on the glass or make a fold.

EXPRESSING CITRUS ZEST

TO EXPRESS

1 Press the zest between your fingers, with the outside facing towards the glass.

2 Also, make sure to rub the zest over the sides and base of the glass to transfer its fragrance to it.

TO FLAMBÉ

1 Heat the outside of the zest with a match for 1 second.

2 Express the zest in the direction of the match flame and above the glass.

3 Drop the zest into the glass.

TIP

In some cases, expressed zests cannot be used for decoration.

FRESH HERBS

WHICH HERBS?

Mint, basil, sage and other soft herbs.

FOR ALL HERBS

1 Always pass the herbs through iced water before using them, as this keeps their vibrant colour and makes them look super fresh.

2 To express a herb, press it once between your hands to release its fragrance, but do so gently to avoid damage.

3 If the cocktail has a straw, always place the herb directly next to the straw so the person enjoying the cocktail can fully enjoy its fragrance.

WHEN USING MINT

Hold the head of a sprig of mint upright, then pinch the base and twist it on itself before placing it in the glass so that it holds this position. It gives the mint a denser head with all the leaves pointing upwards without drooping.

RIMMING THE GLASS

The Lowdown

WHAT IS IT?

A way of frosting the rim of a glass with a ground spice or other flavouring, both for decoration and to add flavour.

NOTE

You can half-rim a glass if you prefer so that the taster gets to choose which side to drink from when served the cocktail.

WHAT POWDERS CAN I USE?

Sugar, salt, nutmeg, powders made from dehydrated fruits, cocoa (chocolate), paprika, mixed spices, flavoured sugar, and more.

TIP

Spices or other powdered ingredients can simply be dusted over cocktails.

AND FOR WHICH COCKTAILS?

The best-known cocktail demonstrating this is the Margarita (see page 160), where the rim of the glass is frosted with fresh lime juice and salt. Frequently used for its visual impact, this technique can also enhance certain notes in a cocktail. The ingredient most commonly used is nutmeg, which is traditionally seen decorating the glasses of Flips and other Nogs, but different spices can also be used.

RIMMING THE GLASS

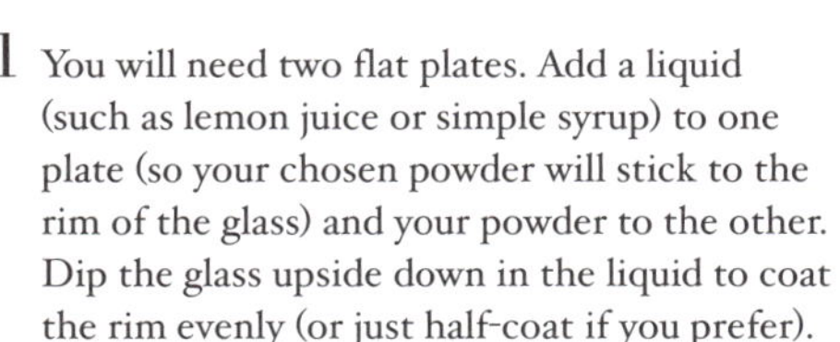

1 You will need two flat plates. Add a liquid (such as lemon juice or simple syrup) to one plate (so your chosen powder will stick to the rim of the glass) and your powder to the other. Dip the glass upside down in the liquid to coat the rim evenly (or just half-coat if you prefer).

2 Lift up the glass and then, in a single, confident movement, stand it upside down on the plate with the powder, so the powder sticks to the dampened rim.

3 Keeping the glass upside down, lift it off the plate and tap it to allow any excess powder to drop off. Turn the glass the right way up and wipe the bowl and stem dry, if necessary.

4 Use it immediately to make the cocktail.

DECORATION

DRAWING WITH BITTERS

The Lowdown

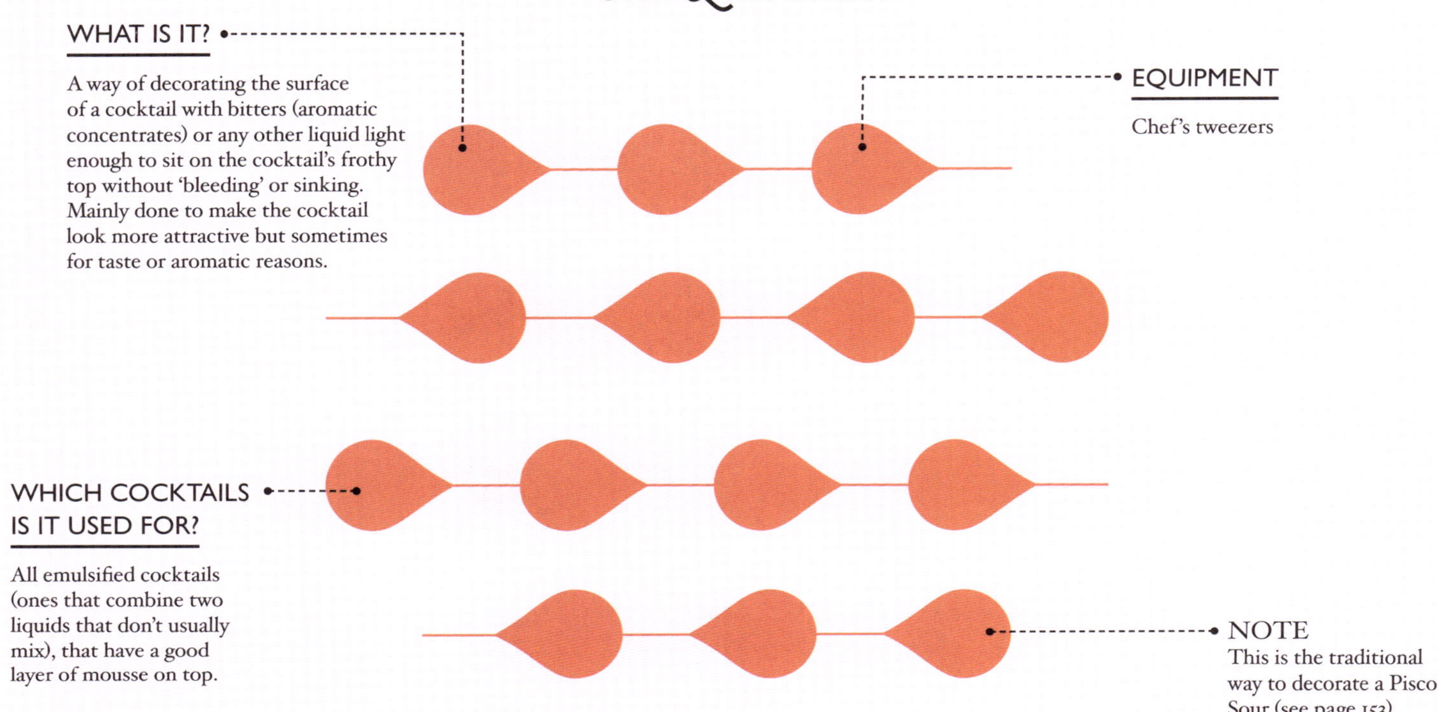

WHAT IS IT?

A way of decorating the surface of a cocktail with bitters (aromatic concentrates) or any other liquid light enough to sit on the cocktail's frothy top without 'bleeding' or sinking. Mainly done to make the cocktail look more attractive but sometimes for taste or aromatic reasons.

EQUIPMENT

Chef's tweezers

WHICH COCKTAILS IS IT USED FOR?

All emulsified cocktails (ones that combine two liquids that don't usually mix), that have a good layer of mousse on top.

NOTE

This is the traditional way to decorate a Pisco Sour (see page 153).

WHAT MAKES THE MOUSSE STAY ON THE COCKTAIL'S SURFACE?

When you emulsify a cocktail, you incorporate air so the mousse becomes less dense than the rest of the cocktail and remains on the surface. The firmer the mousse is, the less quickly it will deflate, meaning the pattern made by the bitters can be seen for longer.

DRAWING WITH BITTERS

CROWN PATTERN

1 Hold the bottle in the hand you most commonly use and tilt it at an angle of 120 degrees, using the index finger of your other hand to hold the bottle steady without it shaking. As drops comes out, move the bottle to make two parallel circles of dots, one inside the other around the edge of the mousse.

2 Using chef's tweezers, join the dots by placing the tips of the tweezers into one dot and gently drawing them to the centre of the one parallel to it. Lift the tweezers out of the mousse, holding them straight. Repeat, connecting the two circles of dots two by two.

3 Place the tips of the tweezers in the mousse where the first two dots meet. Using a steady, single movement, draw the tips through all the points where the pairs of dots meet, without lifting the tweezers out of the mousse. Once you've completed the circle, lift out the tweezers, keeping them straight.

EAR OF CORN PATTERN

Make two parallel lines of dots across the middle of the mousse from one side of the glass to the other. Place the tips of the tweezers into the mousse at the join at the top and middle of the pattern. Using a steady, single movement, draw the tips across all the joins of the other connected dots.

COMMA PATTERN

Let dots flow in a line, moving the bottle so the dots follow the curve of the glass. Place the tips of the tweezers into the mousse in the centre of the first dot. Using a single, steady movement, draw the tips through all the dots.

SINGLE FILTRATION

The Lowdown

WHAT IS IT?

This is passing a drink through a single strainer to remove any non-liquid ingredients from the cocktail.

WHICH COCKTAILS DO I USE IT FOR?

Cocktails served over ice or made in a mixing glass.

EQUIPMENT

Small strainer, pasta strainer or Julep strainer

TIP

Always shake the container well, holding it at an angle of 120 degrees, to make sure you pour out the whole cocktail.

1 Place the strainer on top of the shaker or mixing glass.

2 Hold the handle of the strainer firmly between your index finger and middle finger. Pour while holding the strainer.

DOUBLE

FILTRATION

The Lowdown

WHAT IS IT?

This is passing a drink through a single strainer and then a fine-mesh strainer to remove any non-liquid ingredients from the cocktail.

TIP

Debris often prevents the liquid from draining properly. Remember to tap the strainer with the shaker or a spoon to release the flow. Never tap it on the edge of the glass itself or it may break.

EQUIPMENT

Single strainer
Fine-mesh strainer

WHICH COCKTAILS DO I USE IT FOR?

Cocktails served without ice or mixes using non-liquid ingredients (for example, crushed ice, fresh herbs, pieces of fruit).

NOTE

For preference, use a conical fine-mesh strainer for rapid and efficient filtration.

1 Place the single strainer over the cocktail shaker or mixing glass.

2 Hold the handle of the strainer firmly between your index finger and middle finger as for single filtration.

3 Place the fine-mesh strainer between the serving glass and the shaker.

4 Pour through both strainers to double filter the cocktail.

SETTING UP

The Lowdown

WHAT IS IT?

Assembling the ingredients following the different methods for making a drink.

PREPARATION

A cocktail must be prepared in one go, without a break, otherwise the rate at which it dilutes can't be controlled and, as a result, the quality of the cocktail could suffer. Setting up (all the preparation) must create the perfect conditions before you start making the cocktail itself. Setting up also refers to the environment where you are working both during and after making the cocktail.

MAIN METHODS

In a glass (see page 55): the cocktail is made directly in a serving glass.
In a mixing glass (see page 56): the cocktail is made in a mixing glass and then poured into a serving glass.
Layering (see page 57): the cocktail is made directly in a serving glass but the ingredients are added one at a time, so they remain in separate layers.
Dry shake and shake (see page 58): the cocktail is made in a shaker, being shaken with or without ice to emulsify it, then transferred to a serving glass.
Throwing (see page 59): the cocktail is made in a shaker, then the liquids are 'thrown' from one part of the shaker to the other before serving.

BEFORE

- Clear a workspace and wash your hands.
- Remove the ice from the freezer in advance to ensure it is at optimal temperature (see page 36).
- Get out all the materials and ingredients you are going to need. Check the state of the glasses to avoid any accidents and make sure there is no water in them.
- Put the ingredients that need to be chilled in the refrigerator. Put serving glasses and mixing glasses into the freezer or refrigerator 15 minutes ahead to increase the life of a cocktail, or fill with ice cubes to chill them before using.
- Squeeze any fresh juices you will need.

DURING

- If possible, pour the cheapest ingredients in first to avoid waste in case you make a mistake.
- Take your time to pour the exact quantities you need using a jigger (see page 210).
- Keep your work surface clean as you go along.
- Avoid touching ingredients, ice and the inside of various containers with your hands to avoid the risk of bacterial contamination.

AFTER

- Rinse your equipment in warm water if you need to reuse it; otherwise, wash it.
- Put any ingredients in the refrigerator that need to be kept chilled.
- Clean your work surface.

MAKING A COCKTAIL IN THE GLASS

EQUIPMENT

No specific equipment needed, other than the glass itself.

METHOD

1 Set up what you need, prepare the ingredients and the glass (see page 54).

2 Add the ingredients to the glass in the order indicated and process according to the recipe (for example, Caipirinha, see page 70; Old Fashioned, see page 172; Mojito, see page 178), as cocktails made in a glass each have their own individual quirks.

MAKING A COCKTAIL IN A MIXING GLASS

EQUIPMENT

Mixing glass
Bar spoon
Single strainer or Julep strainer

METHOD

1 Set up what you need, prepare the ingredients and the equipment (see page 54). Pour all the ingredients into a well-chilled mixing glass.

2 Add ice cubes to come at least two fingers above the level of the liquid (see page 215).

3 Stir with the spoon, making small circular movements in the glass (see page 215), for 30–40 seconds (depending on the recipe). Strain into a serving glass using the single strainer or Julep strainer (see page 52).

LAYERING TECHNIQUE

EQUIPMENT

Serving glass
Bar spoon

METHOD

1 Set up what you need, prepare the ingredients and the equipment (see page 54).

2 Pour the first ingredient into the serving glass, according to the recipe.

3 Place the bar spoon in the glass, holding it at a slight angle.

4 Very gently pour the second ingredient into the glass down the long, twisted handle of the spoon, keeping the bowl of the spoon in the liquid.

NOTE

Since the liquids used will have different densities, they must be poured into the glass in the order specified so they remain as separate layers in the glass.

SHAKE & DRY SHAKE

1

2

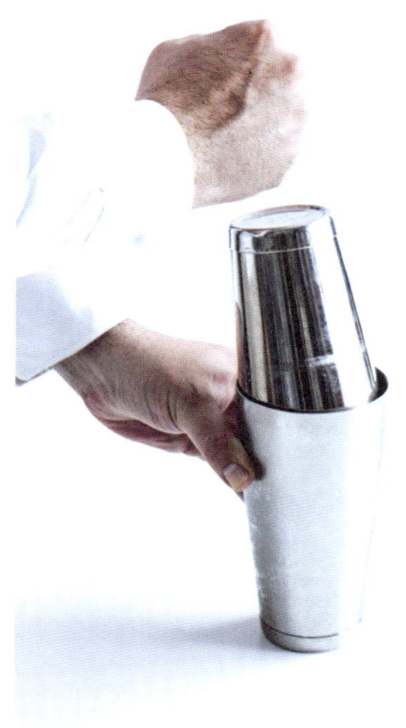

3

EQUIPMENT

Boston shaker (see page 210) or
Parisian shaker (see page 210)

SHAKE

1 Set up what you need, prepare the ingredients and the equipment (see page 54). Check that the shaker is clean and complete. Fill the larger part of the shaker to the brim with ice.

2 Pour the ingredients into the smaller part of the shaker in the order given in the recipe.

3 Pour the contents of the smaller part of the shaker into the larger part or fit the larger part onto the smaller part.

4 Lock the shaker parts together by tapping the smaller part. Shake gently to make sure there are no leaks.

5 Using a rotating motion, shake vigorously from top to bottom, or from right to left, for 10 seconds to blend the ingredients thoroughly.

DRY SHAKE

1 Set up what you need, prepare the ingredients and the equipment (see page 54).

2 Vigorously shake all the ingredients together, without ice, for 5 seconds.

3 Unlock the shaker (see page 215).

4 Pour the contents of the larger part of the shaker into the smaller part, keeping as much distance as possible between the two so as to incorporate air.

NOTE

This type of cocktail must be made in one go, without stopping. As soon as the ingredients are poured in and the shaker is closed, shake immediately, then strain if necessary and serve at once.

THROWING TECHNIQUE

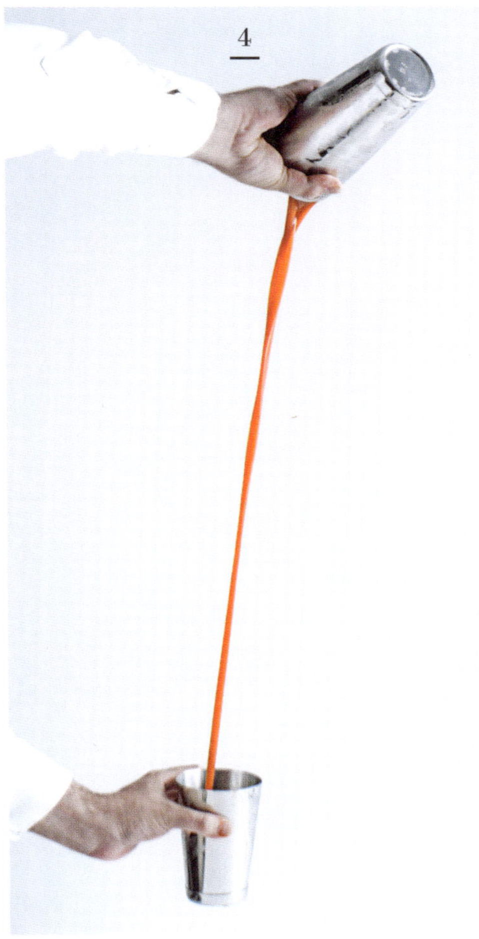

EQUIPMENT

Boston shaker (see page 210) or
Parisian shaker (see page 210)
Bar spoon
Single strainer

1 Set up what you need, prepare the ingredients and the equipment (see page 54). Check that the shaker is clean and complete.

2 Pour all the ingredients into the smaller part of the shaker. If some ingredients are thicker than others, mix them in with the bar spoon to make sure that nothing gets stuck to the sides or the bottom of the shaker (such as puréed fruit or honey).

3 Fill the larger part of the shaker with ice to three fingers from the brim, pour in the cocktail and place the single strainer on top.

4 Next, pour the liquid from the larger part of the shaker into the smaller part, holding the strainer in place to stop the ice cubes from escaping. Try to keep as much distance as possible between the two so as to incorporate plenty of air into the cocktail.

5 Now pour the liquid from the smaller part of the shaker back into the larger part (keep the single strainer on the larger part throughout).

6 Depending on the recipe, repeat this process three or four times.

NOTE

This is a very eye-catching way to make a cocktail but, remember, it does require a bit of practice!
It lets you combine ingredients that are difficult to mix, while simultaneously adding air and diluting the cocktail. It can also be used for the shake or mixing glass techniques to produce frothier cocktails.

CHAPTER 2

COCKTAIL RECIPES

THE ESSENTIALS

MARTINIS

FLIPS

SPIRIT FORWARDS

SOURS

MULES

TIKIS

COLADA

HIGHBALLS

CHAMPAGNE COCKTAILS

BLOODY MARY

The Lowdown

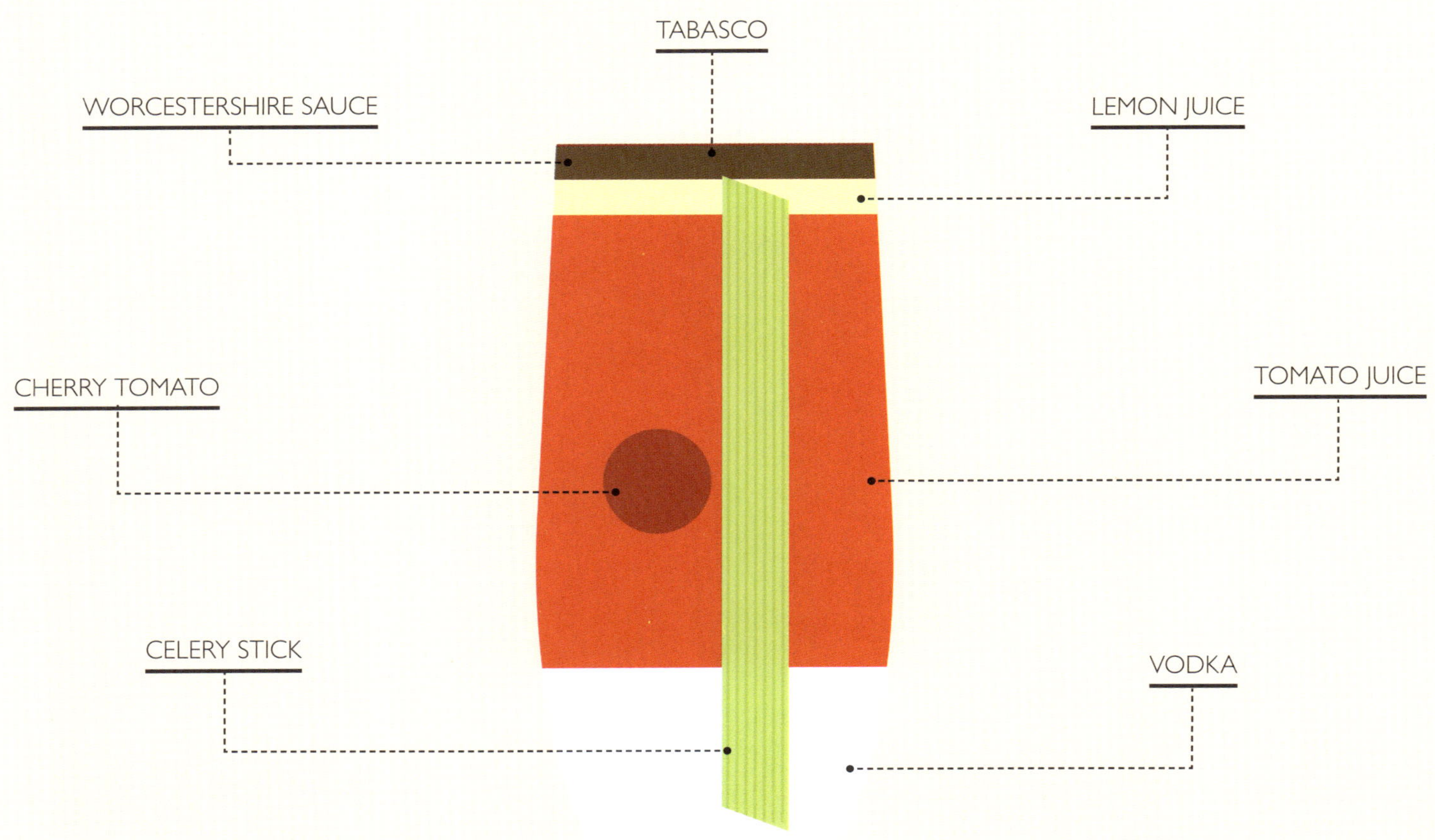

WHAT IS IT?

One of the few long drinks that can be described as salty, this is a mix of vodka and seasoned tomato juice.

FAMILY

Snapper

TYPE

Long drink

ICE FOR SERVING

Cubes

TYPE OF GLASS

Highball

EQUIPMENT

Jigger
Shaker
Bar spoon
Single strainer
Cocktail tweezers

TECHNIQUES TO MASTER

Throwing (see page 59)
Ice cubes (see page 38)

VARIATIONS

Bloody Maria: replace the vodka with the same quantity of tequila.
Red Snapper: replace the vodka with the same quantity of gin.
Red Eye: add an egg yolk to the traditional Bloody Mary mix.
Mocktail: omit the vodka.

SERVES 1

50ml (1 ⅔oz) vodka
120ml (4oz) tomato juice
10ml (2 tsp) lemon juice
10ml (2 tsp) Worcestershire sauce
1 pinch of celery salt
2 grinds of black pepper
1 dash of Tabasco

TO DECORATE

celery stick and 1 cherry tomato

1. Pour all the ingredients into the smaller part of the shaker and mix quickly with the bar spoon.
2. Fill the larger part of the shaker two-thirds full with ice cubes, pour in the cocktail and place the strainer on top.
3. Throw (see page 59) the cocktail four times from the larger part of the shaker to the smaller part.
4. Fill the serving glass to the brim with ice cubes and pour the mixture into it.
5. Add the celery stalk and sit the cherry tomato on the edge of the glass.

AVIATION

The Lowdown

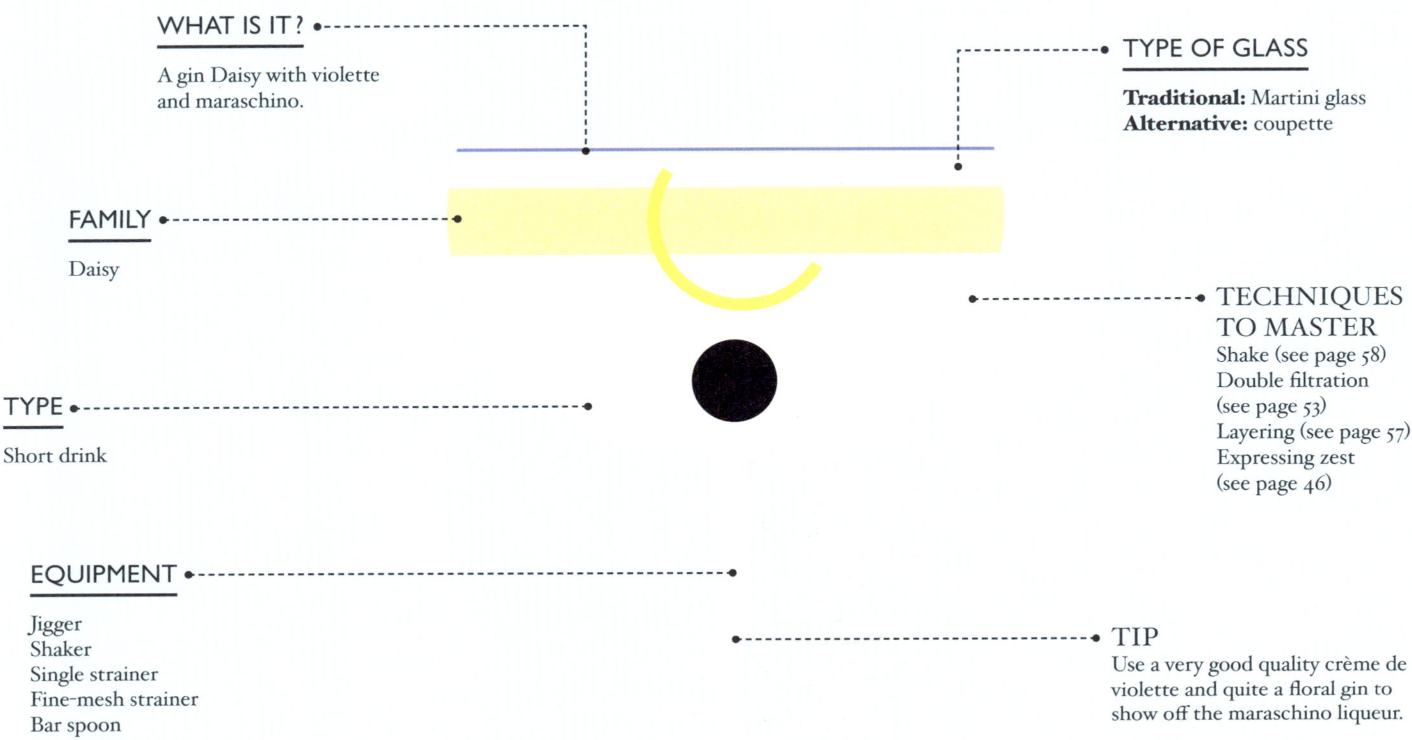

WHAT IS IT?

A gin Daisy with violette and maraschino.

TYPE OF GLASS

Traditional: Martini glass
Alternative: coupette

FAMILY

Daisy

TECHNIQUES TO MASTER

Shake (see page 58)
Double filtration (see page 53)
Layering (see page 57)
Expressing zest (see page 46)

TYPE

Short drink

EQUIPMENT

Jigger
Shaker
Single strainer
Fine-mesh strainer
Bar spoon
Cocktail tweezers

TIP

Use a very good quality crème de violette and quite a floral gin to show off the maraschino liqueur.

SERVES 1

50ml ($1\frac{2}{3}$oz) gin
20ml ($\frac{2}{3}$oz) lemon juice
10ml (2 tsp) maraschino liqueur
1 × 5ml bar spoon crème de violette

TO DECORATE

zest of 1 unwaxed lemon
1 amarena cherry or maraschino cherry

1 Pour all the ingredients, except the crème de violette into the cocktail shaker.

2 Fill the larger part of the shaker to the brim with ice and shake vigorously (see page 58) for 10 seconds.

3 Double filter (see page 53) into the serving glass.

4 Gently add the crème de violette using the spoon to pour it into the centre of the glass to make two distinct layers (see page 57).

5 Express the lemon zest (see page 46) in the centre of the glass and rub it over the rim and the stem of the glass as well.

6 Drop the amarena or maraschino cherry into the glass using the cocktail tweezers.

20TH CENTURY

The Lowdown

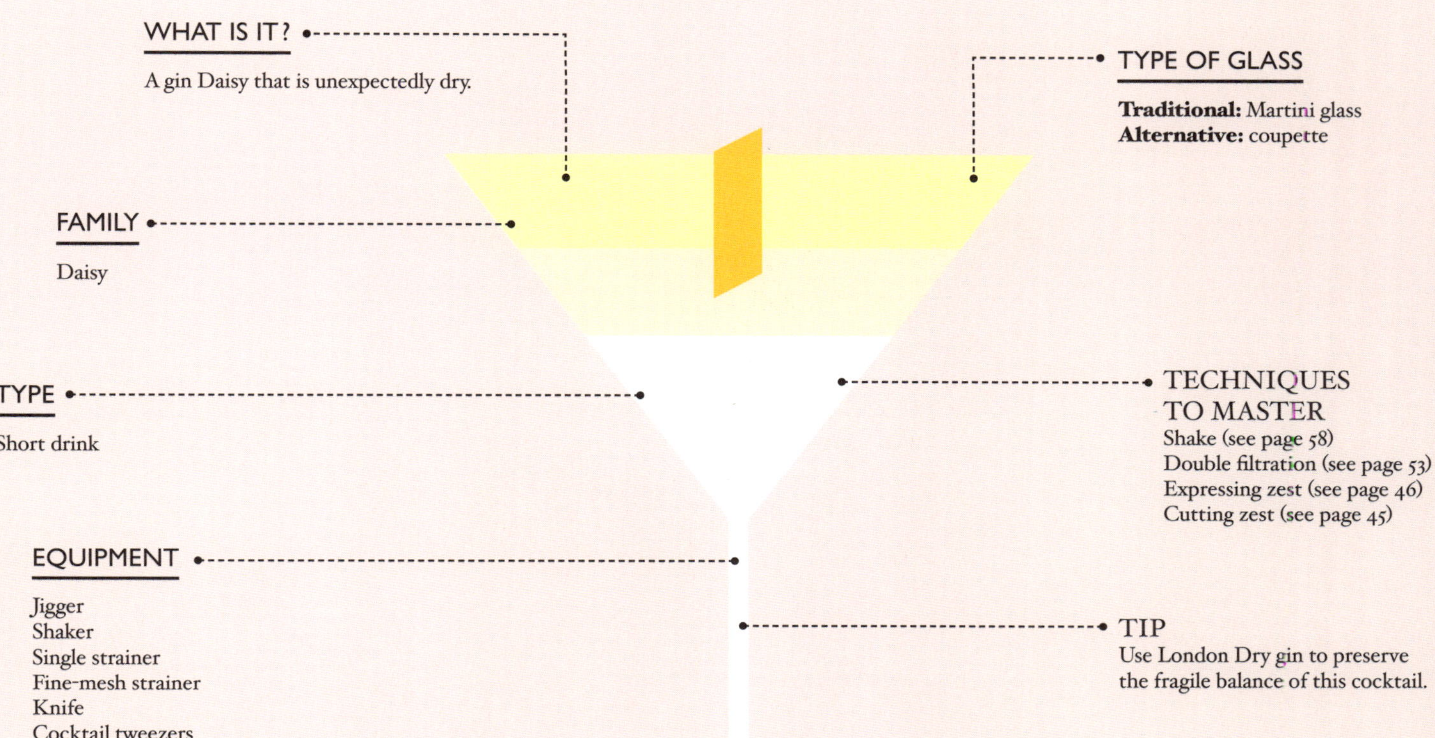

WHAT IS IT?

A gin Daisy that is unexpectedly dry.

TYPE OF GLASS

Traditional: Martini glass
Alternative: coupette

FAMILY

Daisy

TYPE

Short drink

TECHNIQUES TO MASTER

Shake (see page 58)
Double filtration (see page 53)
Expressing zest (see page 46)
Cutting zest (see page 45)

EQUIPMENT

Jigger
Shaker
Single strainer
Fine-mesh strainer
Knife
Cocktail tweezers

TIP

Use London Dry gin to preserve the fragile balance of this cocktail.

SERVES 1

25ml (⅔oz plus 1 tsp) gin
25ml (⅔oz plus 1 tsp) Lillet Blanc
25ml (⅔oz plus 1 tsp) white crème de cacao
25ml (⅔oz plus 1 tsp) lemon juice

TO DECORATE

zest of 1 unwaxed lemon

1 Pour all the ingredients into the cocktail shaker.

2 Fill the larger part of the shaker to the brim with ice and shake vigorously (see page 58) for 10 seconds.

3 Double filter (see page 53) into the serving glass.

4 Express the lemon zest (see page 46) in the centre of the glass and rub it over the rim and the stem of the glass as well.

5 Cut the zest (see page 45) and place it on the rim of the glass using the cocktail tweezers.

GRASSHOPPER

The Lowdown

WHAT IS IT?

A mild, sweet and refreshing after-dinner cocktail.

FAMILY

Trio

TYPE

Short drink

TYPE OF GLASS

Coupette

EQUIPMENT

Jigger
Shaker
Single strainer
Fine-mesh strainer
Cocktail tweezers

TECHNIQUES TO MASTER

Shake (see page 58)
Double filtration (see page 53)

TIP

For a more aerated cocktail, begin by mixing the cream and milk together. Use a pouring cream (which has a higher fat content) rather than single (light) cream, as it will incorporate air better.

Discover

SERVES 1

30ml (1oz) green crème de menthe
30ml (1oz) white crème de cacao
15ml (½oz) full-fat milk (whole milk)
15ml (½oz) double (heavy) cream

TO DECORATE

1 mint leaf

1. Pour all the ingredients into the cocktail shaker.
2. Fill the larger part of the shaker to the brim with ice and shake vigorously (see page 58) for 10 seconds.
3. Double filter (see page 53) into the serving glass.
4. Place the mint leaf upright in the centre of the glass using the cocktail tweezers.

BLOOD &

SAND

The Lowdown

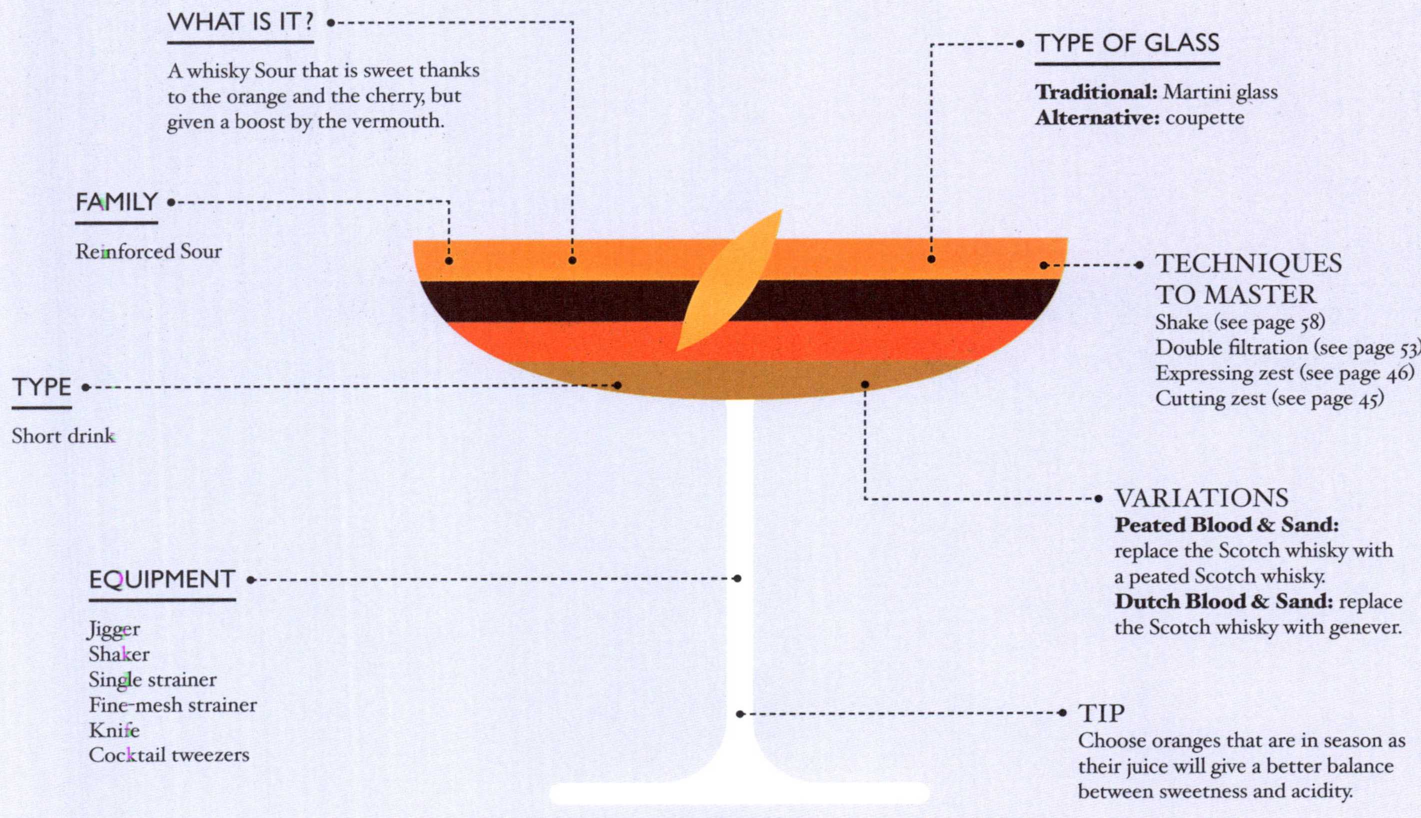

WHAT IS IT?

A whisky Sour that is sweet thanks to the orange and the cherry, but given a boost by the vermouth.

TYPE OF GLASS

Traditional: Martini glass
Alternative: coupette

FAMILY

Reinforced Sour

TECHNIQUES TO MASTER

Shake (see page 58)
Double filtration (see page 53)
Expressing zest (see page 46)
Cutting zest (see page 45)

TYPE

Short drink

VARIATIONS

Peated Blood & Sand: replace the Scotch whisky with a peated Scotch whisky.
Dutch Blood & Sand: replace the Scotch whisky with genever.

EQUIPMENT

Jigger
Shaker
Single strainer
Fine-mesh strainer
Knife
Cocktail tweezers

TIP

Choose oranges that are in season as their juice will give a better balance between sweetness and acidity.

SERVES 1

25ml (⅔oz plus 1 tsp) Scotch whisky
25ml (⅔oz plus 1 tsp) red vermouth
25ml (⅔oz plus 1 tsp) cherry liqueur, Heering style
25ml (⅔oz plus 1 tsp) orange juice

TO DECORATE

zest of 1 unwaxed orange

1 Pour all the ingredients into the cocktail shaker.

2 Fill the larger part of the shaker to the brim with ice and shake vigorously (see page 58) for 10 seconds.

3 Double filter (see page 53) into the serving glass.

4 Express the orange zest (see page 46) in the centre of the glass and rub it over the rim and the stem as well.

5 Cut the zest (see page 45) and curve so it can sit over the rim of the glass.

CHARLIE
CHAPLIN

The Lowdown

SERVES 1

25ml (⅔oz plus 1 tsp) apricot brandy
25ml (⅔oz plus 1 tsp) sloe gin
25ml (⅔oz plus 1 tsp) lime juice

1 Pour all the ingredients into the cocktail shaker.

2 Fill the larger part of the shaker to the brim with ice and shake vigorously (see page 58) for 10 seconds.

3 Double filter (see page 53) into the serving glass.

CAIPIRINHA

The Lowdown

WHAT IS IT?

The national cocktail of Brazil. Very refreshing, it is a mix of cachaça, lime and sugar.

FAMILY

Caipirinha

TYPE

Short drink

ICE FOR SERVING

Crushed ice

TYPE OF GLASS

Single Old Fashioned or goblet

EQUIPMENT

Jigger
Knife
Muddler
Bar spoon
2 reuseable or biodegradable straws
Cocktail tweezers

TECHNIQUES TO MASTER

Making a cocktail in a glass (see page 55)
Using a muddler (see page 214)
Crushed ice (see page 39)

VARIATIONS

Caiproska: replace the cachaça with the same quantity of vodka.

ALTERNATIVE

Muddle lots of red fruits and exotic fruits (for example, raspberries, blackcurrants, blackberries, strawberries, mango, pineapple, lychees) with the pieces of lime or replace the simple syrup with a flavoured syrup, to create an infinite number of combinations.

TIP

Choose unwaxed limes for preference. See Nectars, purées and fruit juices (page 32).

Discover

SERVES 1

25ml (⅔oz plus 1 tsp) simple syrup
3 lime wedges (each ⅛ of a lime)
50ml (1⅔oz) cachaça
10ml (2 tsp) lime juice

TO DECORATE

lime wedge (⅛ of a lime)

1 Pour the syrup into the serving glass.

2 Add the lime wedges.

3 Using the muddler (see page 214), crush the lime wedges to a pulp.

4 Add the cachaça and lime juice.

5 Half fill the glass with crushed ice (see page 39).

6 Stir everything vigorously with the bar spoon for 5 seconds.

7 Cover the contents of the glass completely with crushed ice.

8 Place two straws in the glass and, using the cocktail tweezers, sit the remaining lime wedge next to them.

CORPSE

REVIVER Nº2

The Lowdown

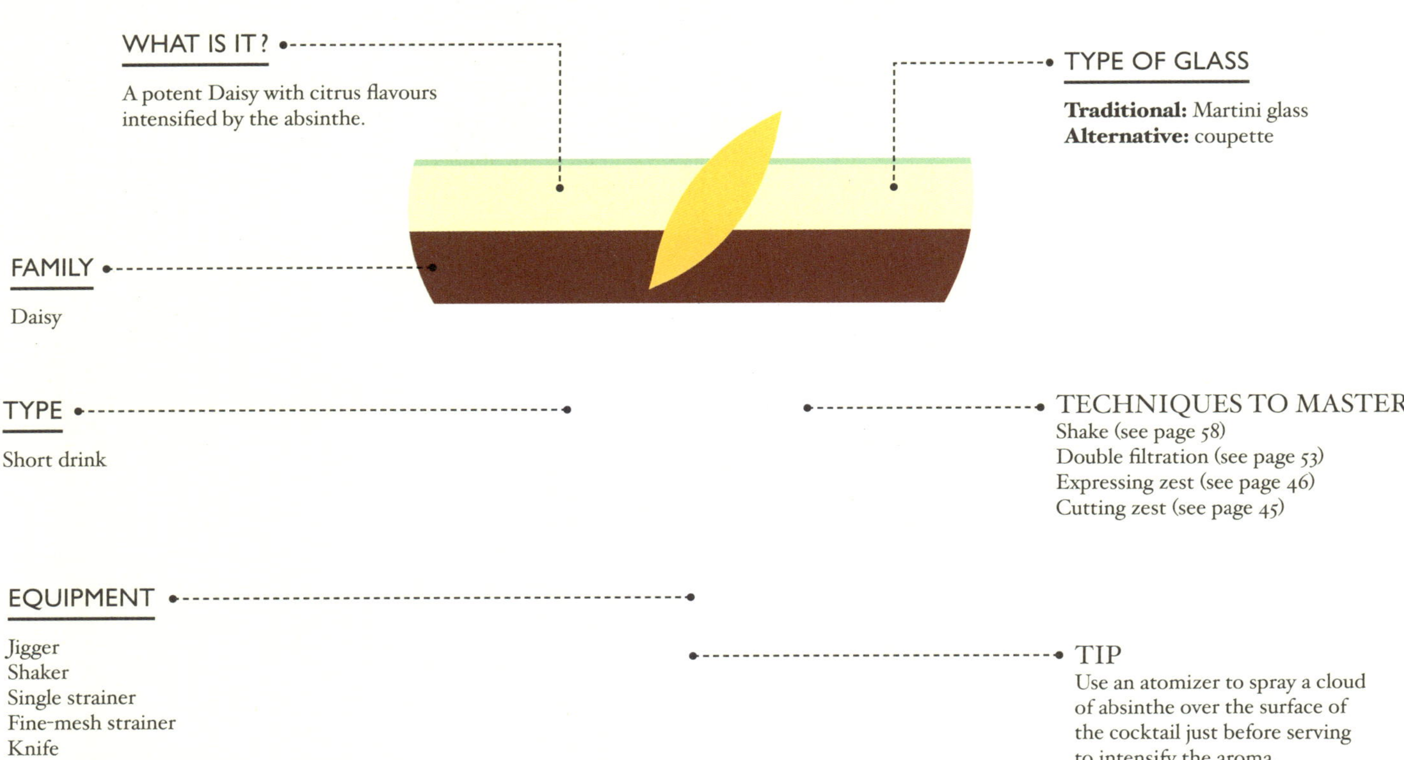

WHAT IS IT?

A potent Daisy with citrus flavours intensified by the absinthe.

TYPE OF GLASS

Traditional: Martini glass
Alternative: coupette

FAMILY

Daisy

TYPE

Short drink

TECHNIQUES TO MASTER

Shake (see page 58)
Double filtration (see page 53)
Expressing zest (see page 46)
Cutting zest (see page 45)

EQUIPMENT

Jigger
Shaker
Single strainer
Fine-mesh strainer
Knife
Cocktail tweezers

TIP

Use an atomizer to spray a cloud of absinthe over the surface of the cocktail just before serving to intensify the aroma.

SERVES 1

25ml (⅔oz plus 1 tsp) gin
25ml (⅔oz plus 1 tsp) Cocchi Americano Bianco or Lillet Blanc
25ml (⅔oz plus 1 tsp) Cointreau
25ml (⅔oz plus 1 tsp) lemon juice
1 dash of absinthe

TO DECORATE

zest of 1 unwaxed lemon

1. Pour all the ingredients into the shaker.
2. Fill the larger part of the shaker to the brim with ice and shake vigorously (see page 58) for 10 seconds.
3. Double filter (see page 53) into the serving glass.
4. Express the lemon zest (see page 46) in the centre of the glass and rub it over the rim and the stem as well.
5. Cut the zest (see page 45) and place it over the rim of the glass using the cocktail tweezers.

LAST WORD

The Lowdown

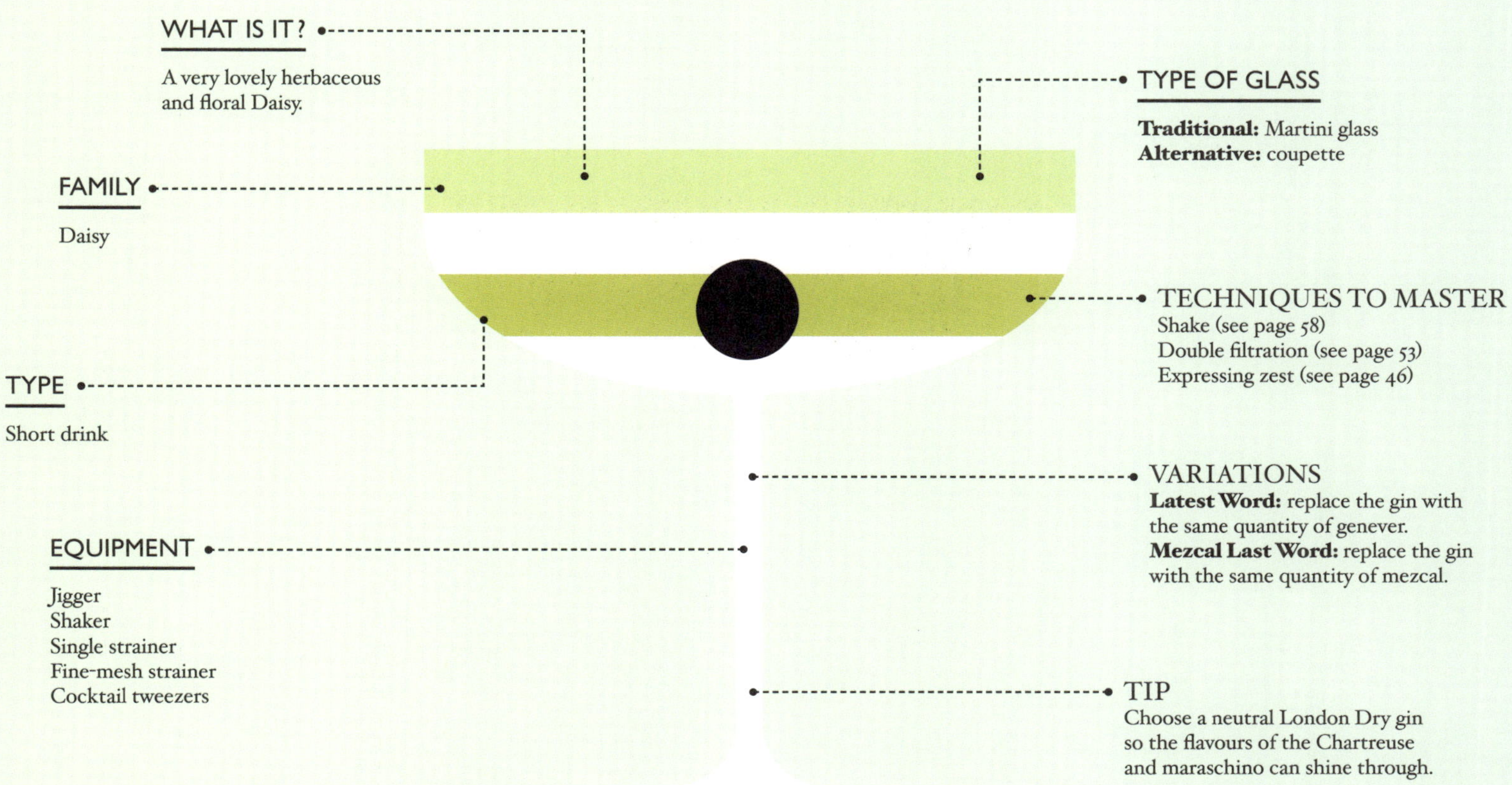

WHAT IS IT?

A very lovely herbaceous and floral Daisy.

FAMILY

Daisy

TYPE

Short drink

EQUIPMENT

Jigger
Shaker
Single strainer
Fine-mesh strainer
Cocktail tweezers

TYPE OF GLASS

Traditional: Martini glass
Alternative: coupette

TECHNIQUES TO MASTER

Shake (see page 58)
Double filtration (see page 53)
Expressing zest (see page 46)

VARIATIONS

Latest Word: replace the gin with the same quantity of genever.
Mezcal Last Word: replace the gin with the same quantity of mezcal.

TIP

Choose a neutral London Dry gin so the flavours of the Chartreuse and maraschino can shine through.

SERVES 1

25ml (⅔oz plus 1 tsp) gin
25ml (⅔oz plus 1 tsp) green Chartreuse
25ml (⅔oz plus 1 tsp) maraschino liqueur
25ml (⅔oz plus 1 tsp) lime juice

TO DECORATE

zest of 1 unwaxed lemon
1 amarena cherry

1 Pour all the ingredients into the shaker.

2 Fill the larger part of the shaker to the brim with ice and shake vigorously (see page 58) for 10 seconds.

3 Double filter (see page 53) into the serving glass.

4 Express the lemon zest (see page 46) in the centre of the glass and rub it over the rim and the stem as well.

5 Place a cherry at the bottom of the glass using the cocktail tweezers.

COSMOPOLITAN

The Lowdown

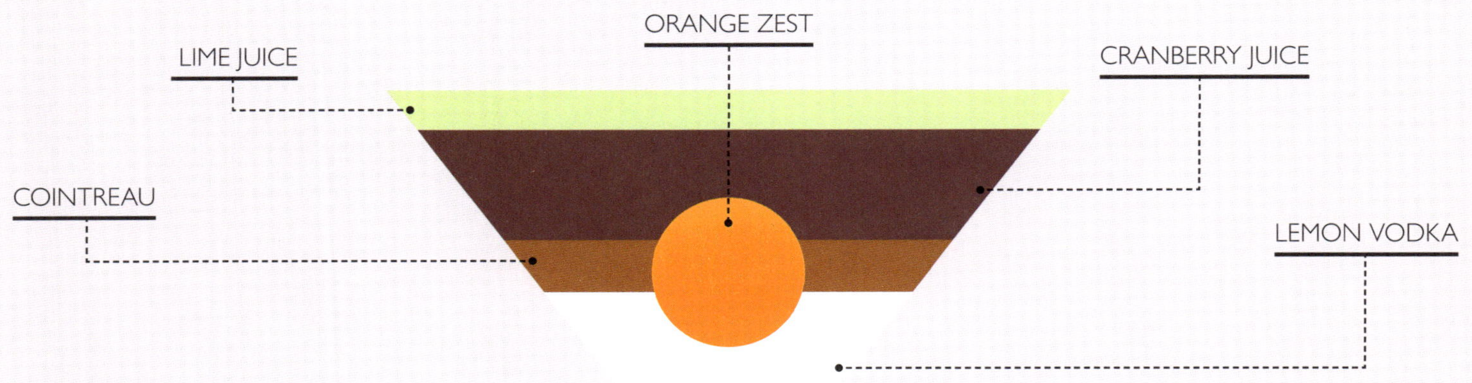

WHAT IS IT?

A subtly balanced cocktail when made perfectly.

FAMILY

Daisy

TYPE

Short drink

TYPE OF GLASS

Traditional: Martini glass
Alternative: coupette

EQUIPMENT

Jigger
Shaker
Single strainer
Fine-mesh strainer
Knife
Matches

TECHNIQUES TO MASTER

Shake (see page 58)
Double filtration (see page 53)
Cutting zest (see page 45)
Expressing zest and singeing (see page 46)

TIP

Always use unwaxed oranges so that the essential oils in the zest can add fragrance to the cocktail. To make lemon vodka, express the zest of two unwaxed lemons into the measure of vodka.

Discover

SERVES 1

45ml (1½oz) lemon vodka
15ml (½oz) Cointreau
30ml (1oz) cranberry juice
10ml (2 tsp) lime juice

TO DECORATE

1 unwaxed orange

1. Pour all the ingredients into the shaker.
2. Fill the larger part of the shaker to the brim with ice and shake vigorously (see page 58) for 10 seconds.
3. Double filter into the serving glass (see page 53).
4. Cut a round of zest from the orange (see page 45).
5. Heat the outside of the zest with a match for 1 second.
6. Express the zest (see page 46) in the direction of the match flame and above the glass.
7. Drop the zest into the glass.

LONG ISLAND

ICED TEA

The Lowdown

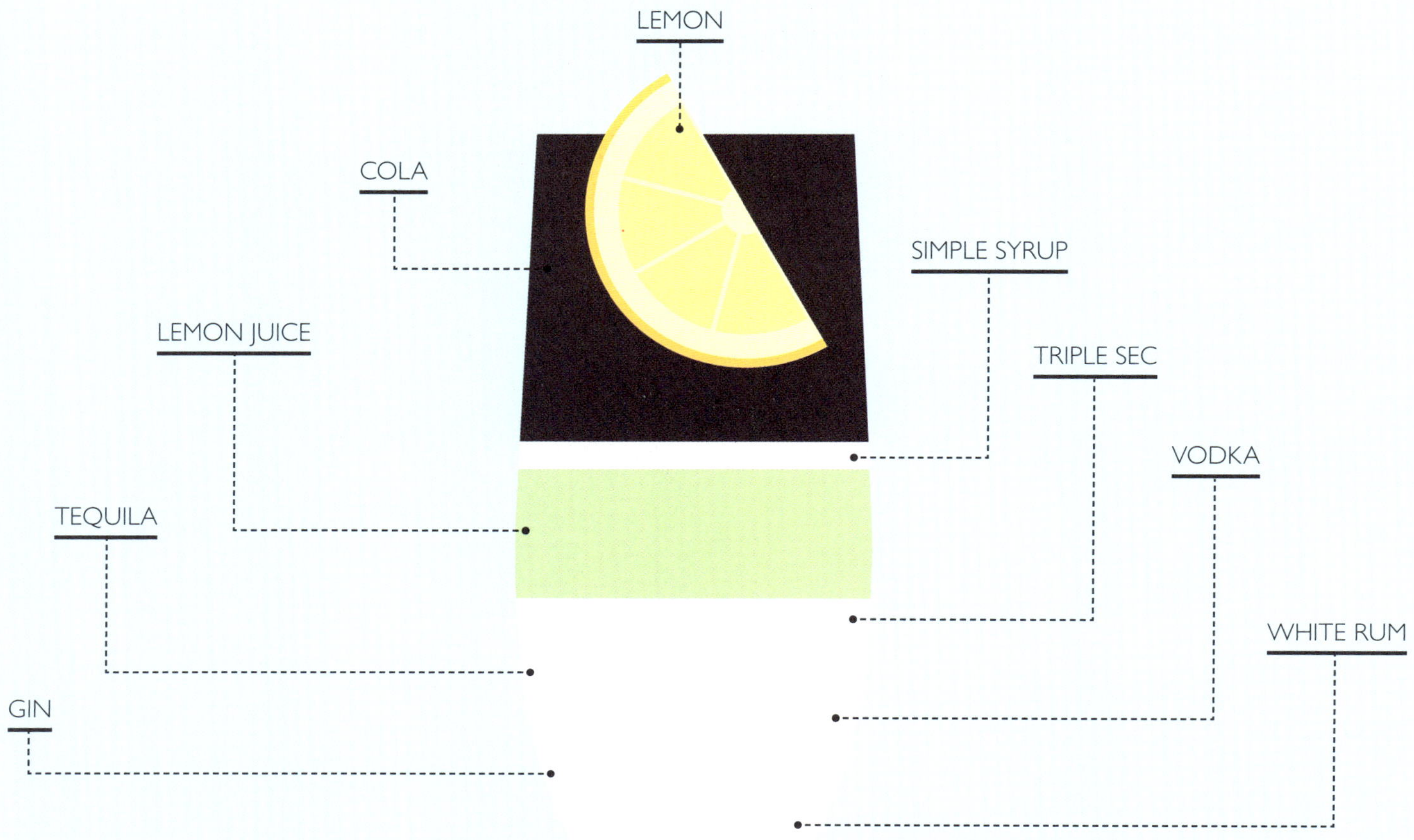

WHAT IS IT?

A sparkling and tangy blockbuster mix of clear spirits that's not for the faint hearted!

FAMILY

Long Island Iced Tea

TYPE

Long drink

ICE FOR SERVING

Cubes

TYPE OF GLASS

Traditional: tumbler
Alternative: highball

EQUIPMENT

Jigger
Shaker
Single strainer
Bar spoon

TECHNIQUES TO MASTER

Shake (see page 58)
Single filtration (see page 52)

VARIATIONS

Italian Iced Tea: pour in 10ml (2 tsp) Galliano when you've finished making the cocktail.
Perfect Iced Tea: replace the triple sec with Chambord and the cola with Champagne.

TIP

Always choose a cola without added sweeteners, as they react badly with alcohol and have a more acidic pH.

Discover

SERVES 1

10ml (2 tsp) white rum
10ml (2 tsp) gin
10ml (2 tsp) vodka
10ml (2 tsp) tequila
10ml (2 tsp) triple sec
25ml (⅔oz plus 1 tsp) lemon juice
5ml (1 tsp) simple syrup
60ml (2oz) cola

TO DECORATE

lemon wedge (⅛ of a lemon)

1. Pour all the ingredients except the cola into the shaker.
2. Fill the larger part of the shaker to the brim with ice and shake vigorously (see page 58) for 10 seconds.
3. Single filter (see page 52) into the serving glass.
4. Fill the glass with ice cubes.
5. Add the cola.
6. Stir briskly with the bar spoon.
7. Sit the lemon wedge on the ice and against the rim of the glass.

B52

The Lowdown

WHAT IS IT?

Quite a sweet shot that catches fire like nothing you've ever seen!

FAMILY

Shot

TYPE

Shot

TYPE OF GLASS

Traditional: shot glass
Alternative: stemmed shot glass

EQUIPMENT

Jigger
Bar spoon
Chef's blow torch or gas lighter

TECHNIQUES TO MASTER
Layering (see page 57)

TIP
Make sure the bottles of alcohol and the glass are at room temperature so the triple sec ignites easily.

SERVES 1

10ml (2 tsp) coffee liqueur
10ml (2 tsp) Irish cream liqueur
10ml (2 tsp) triple sec

1 Pour the coffee liqueur into the glass.

2 Place the spoon in the glass so it touches the surface of the coffee liqueur.

3 Bring the pouring spout of the bottle of cream liqueur as close as possible to the twisted handle of the spoon.

4 Tilt the bottle of cream liqueur at an angle of 90 degrees and pour for 2 seconds (see page 57).

5 Repeat with the triple sec.

6 Ignite the triple sec with the blow torch or gas lighter.

7 Drink in one go through a straw, beginning at the bottom of the glass.

8 Once you have finished the cocktail, remember to turn the glass upside down to avoid any accidents with the hot glass.

IRISH COFFEE

The Lowdown

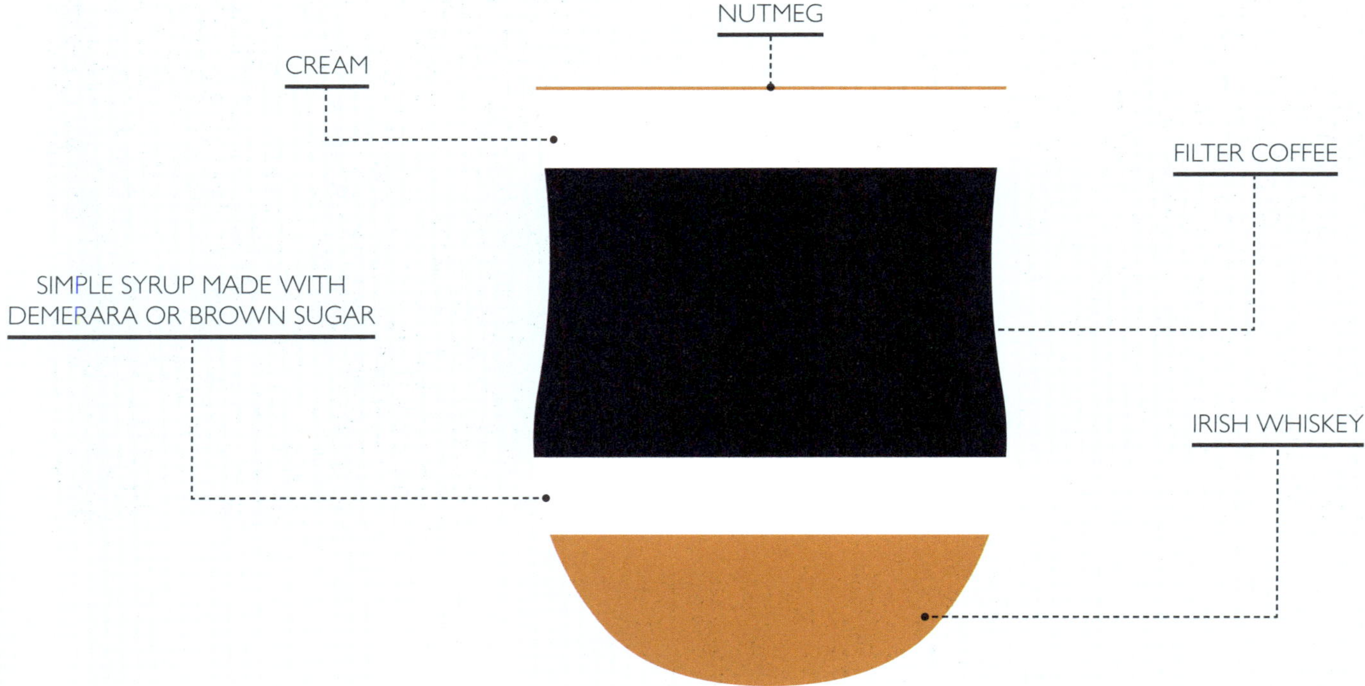

WHAT IS IT?

A hot cocktail that is a genuine one-off.

TYPE

Long drink

TYPE OF GLASS

Traditional: hot toddy
Alternative: large coffee cup

EQUIPMENT

Jigger
Bar spoon
Nutmeg grater

TECHNIQUES TO MASTER

Making a cocktail in a glass (see page 55)
Layering (see page 57)

TIP

Mix the coffee and syrup together before you start to fully appreciate the drink's robust flavour.

VARIATIONS

The whiskey can be replaced with the same quantity of another brown spirit, such as Cognac, rum or bourbon.

SERVES 1

40ml (1⅓oz) Irish whiskey
20ml (⅔oz) simple syrup made with demerara or brown sugar
75ml (2⅓oz plus 1 tsp) hot filter coffee
25ml (⅔oz plus 1 tsp) pouring cream (30% fat)

TO DECORATE

freshly grated nutmeg

1. Warm the serving glass and pour the whiskey and the syrup into it.
2. Pour in the hot coffee and mix quickly with the bar spoon.
3. Place the spoon in the glass so it touches the surface of the coffee (see page 57) and carefully pour in the cream so it forms a layer on top.
4. Grate nutmeg evenly over the top of the cream.

BALTIMORE

EGGNOG

The Lowdown

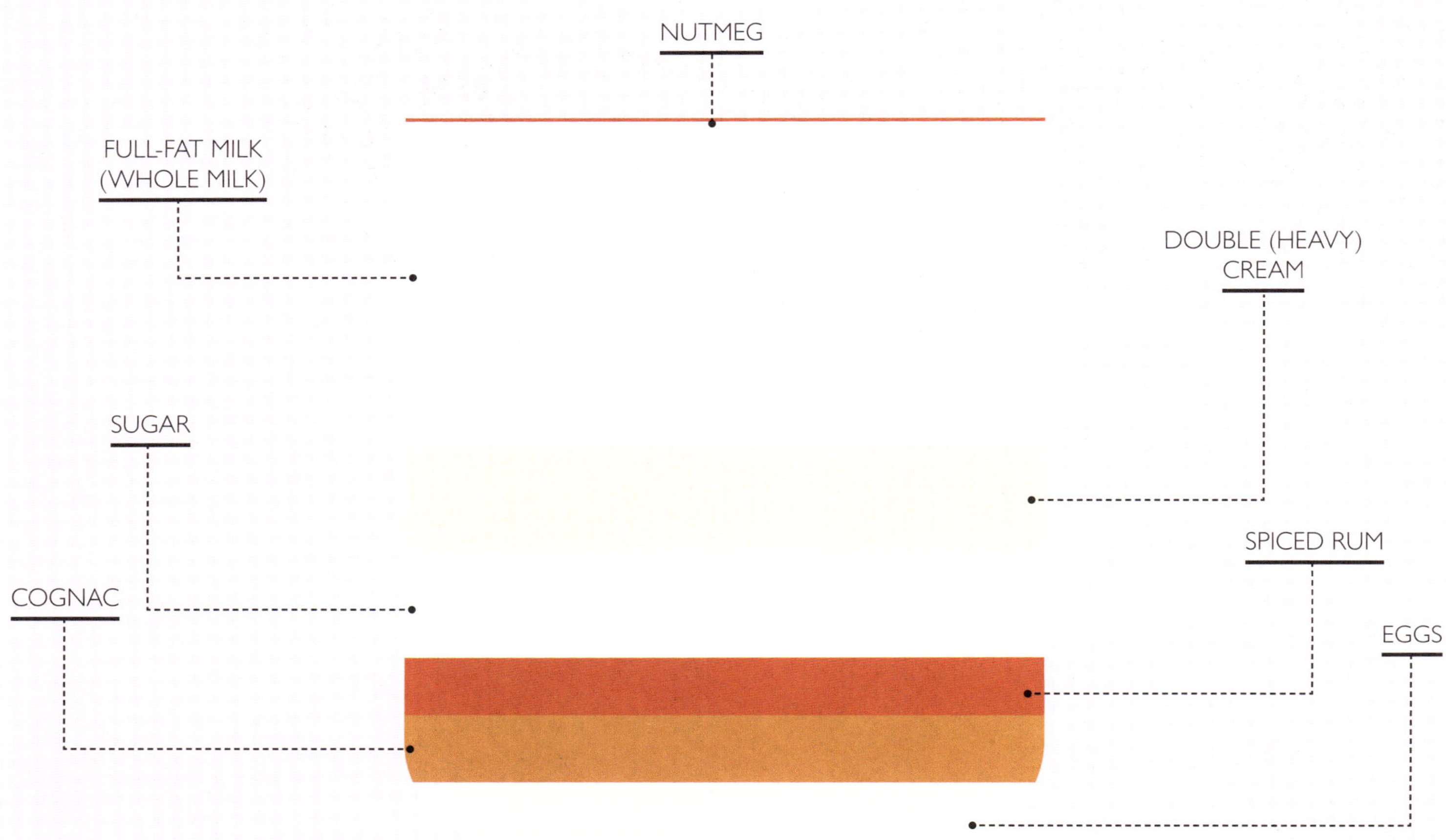

WHAT IS IT?

A drink of milk and eggs that should be made in advance. It's traditionally drunk at New Year celebrations.

FAMILY

Nog

TYPE

Eggnog

TYPE OF GLASS

Mug, coffee cup, goblet, simple Old Fashioned

EQUIPMENT

Measuring glass
Scales
Whisk
2 mixing bowls
Spatula
Nutmeg grater

VARIATIONS

The Cognac can be replaced with the same quantity of another brown spirit, such as whisky, rum or bourbon. The nutmeg can be replaced with ground cloves, cinnamon or star anise.

ALTERNATIVE

Mocktail: omit the alcohol and use 400ml (13½oz) of a flavoured syrup (hazelnut, cookie, almond) and half quantity of both the sugar and eggs.

TIP

The quality of your chosen spirit will greatly affect the final result.

STORAGE

Seven days in the refrigerator. Shake well before serving.

MAKES ENOUGH FOR 20 × 150ML (5OZ) GLASSES

12 eggs
500g (1lb 2oz) caster (superfine) sugar
500ml (17oz) double (heavy) cream
1.5 litres (51oz) full-fat (whole) milk
250ml (8½oz) spiced rum
350ml (12oz) Cognac
1 pinch of salt
1 × 5ml bar spoon of freshly grated nutmeg

TO DECORATE

freshly grated nutmeg

How to make Baltimore Eggnog

1 Separate the eggs and whisk the yolks with the sugar until pale, thick and creamy.

2 Gradually whisk in the cream in a thin, steady stream.

3 Next, add the milk, followed by the rum and Cognac.

4 Whisk the egg whites with the salt and nutmeg until they form stiff peaks.

5 Carefully fold the whisked whites into the mixture.

6 Transfer to bottles and chill in the refrigerator for 4 hours before serving, dusted with freshly grated nutmeg.

NEGRONI

The Lowdown

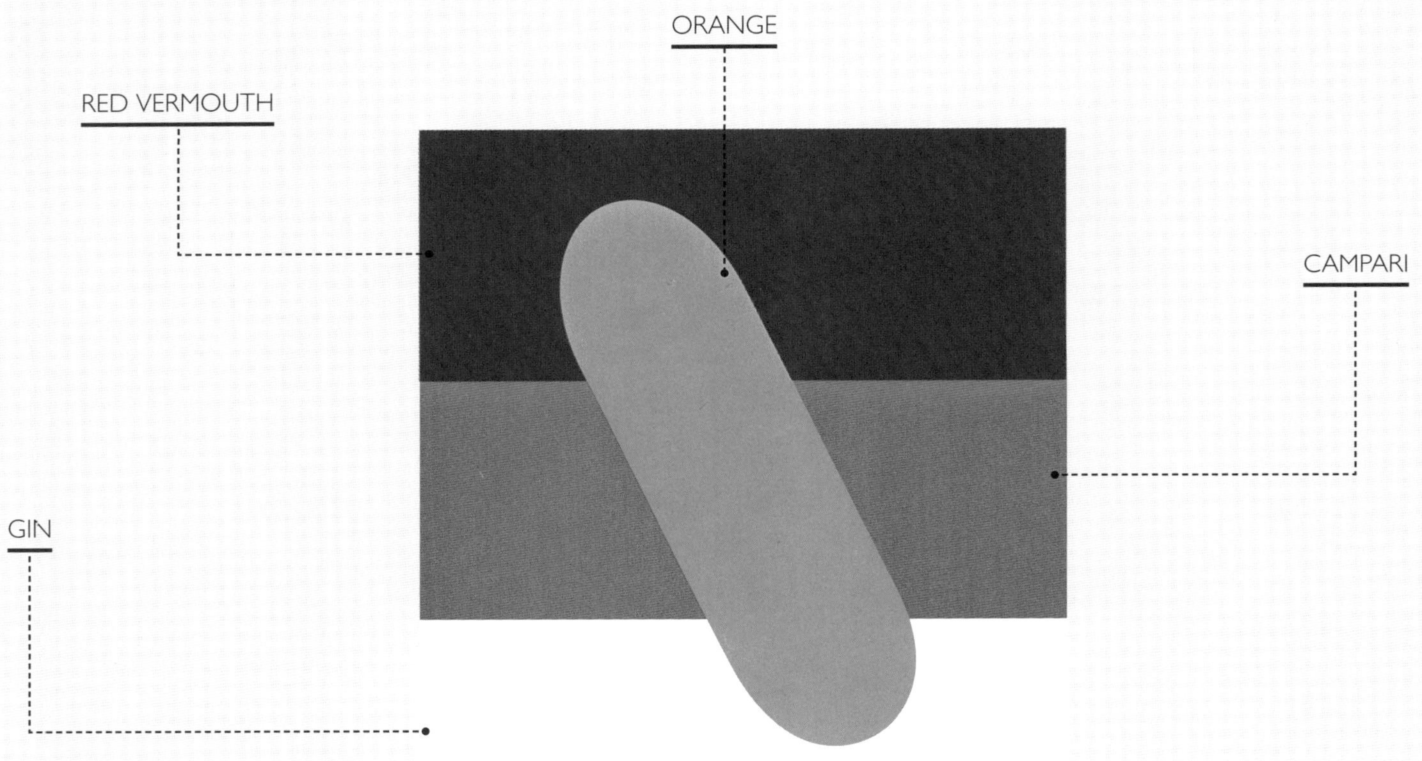

WHAT IS IT?

The No 1 classic bitter cocktail. Thanks to the simple way it is made, it can be adapted in an infinite number of ways.

FAMILY

Ladder

TYPE

Short drink

ICE FOR SERVING

Cubes or block

TYPE OF GLASS

Old Fashioned

EQUIPMENT

Jigger
Mixing glass
Bar spoon
Single strainer or Julep strainer
Knife
Cocktail tweezers

TECHNIQUES TO MASTER

Ice cubes/block of ice (see page 36)
Making a cocktail in a mixing glass (see page 56)
Single filtration (see page 52)
Expressing zest (see page 46)
Cutting zest (see page 45)

VARIATIONS

Boulevardier: see page 146.
Rabo-de-Gallo: replace the gin with the same quantity of cachaça.
Mezcal Negroni: replace the gin with the same quantity of mezcal.
Negroni Sbagliato: replace the gin with the same quantity of prosecco.

TIP

How you decorate the cocktail is up to you as it's all about personal taste. An orange slice will add a refreshing touch, while the zest will be drier.

SERVES 1

25ml (⅔oz plus 1 tsp) gin
25ml (⅔oz plus 1 tsp) Campari
25ml (⅔oz plus 1 tsp) red vermouth

TO DECORATE

zest of 1 unwaxed orange or 1 orange slice

1 Pour all the ingredients into the mixing glass, which should be well chilled.

2 Add ice to come about two fingers above the liquid.

3 Mix for 40 seconds.

4 Taste to check the dilution is perfect, mixing a little more if necessary.

5 Single filter (see page 52) into the serving glass.

6 Add a block of ice or ice cubes to reach the brim of the glass (see page 36).

7 Express the orange zest (see page 46) in the centre of the glass, then rub it over the rim.

8 Cut the zest (see page 45) and place inside the glass using the cocktail tweezers or sit an orange slice inside the glass, along the rim, again using the cocktail tweezers.

BRANDY

ALEXANDER

The Lowdown

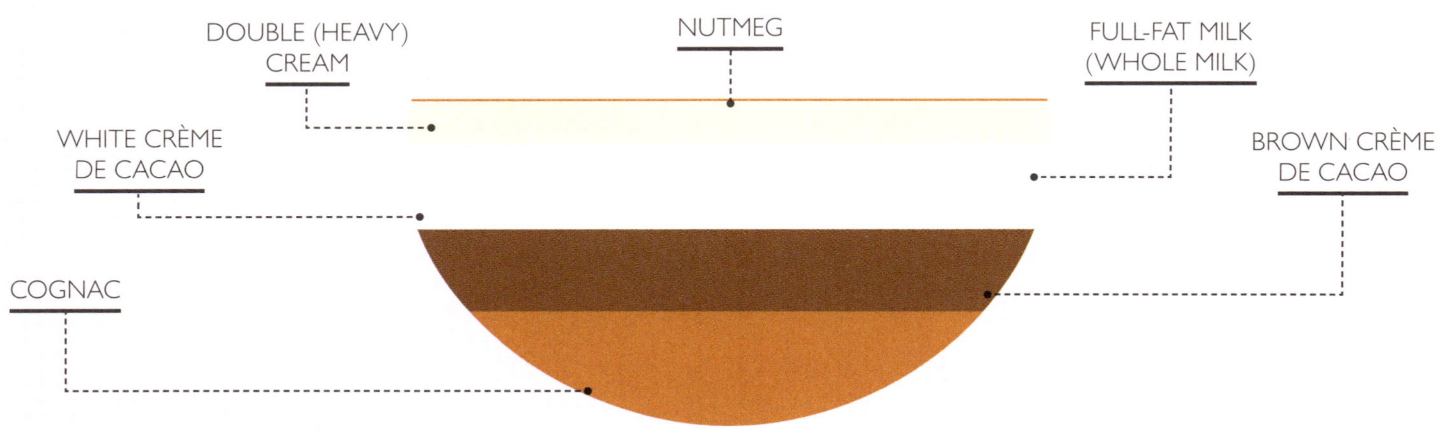

WHAT IS IT?

A cocktail served as a digestif with a simple balance that is very easy to adapt.

FAMILY

Trio

TYPE

Short drink

TYPE OF GLASS

Traditional: Martini glass
Alternative: coupette

EQUIPMENT

Jigger
Shaker
Single strainer
Fine-mesh strainer
Nutmeg grater

TECHNIQUES TO MASTER

Shake (see page 58)
Double filtration (see page 53)

TIP

Choose a VSOP Cognac, which will give the cocktail more body.

VARIATION

Just about anything is possible as long as you stick to the balance of one-third 40% ABV (80 proof) spirit, blended with one-third cream liqueur and one-third double (heavy) cream.

ALTERNATIVE

Cherry Alexander: 30ml (1oz) vodka, 30ml (1oz) cherry liqueur (for example Heering), 15ml (½oz) full-fat (whole) milk and 15ml (½oz) double (heavy) cream.

SERVES 1

30ml (1oz) Cognac
20ml (⅔oz) brown crème de cacao
10ml (2 tsp) white crème de cacao
15ml (½oz) full-fat (whole) milk
15ml (½oz) double (heavy) cream

TO DECORATE

freshly grated nutmeg

1 Pour all the ingredients into the shaker.

2 Fill the larger part of the shaker to the brim with ice and shake (see page 58) vigorously for 10 seconds.

3 Double filter (see page 53) into the serving glass.

4 Grate nutmeg evenly over the top of the cocktail.

SIDECAR

The Lowdown

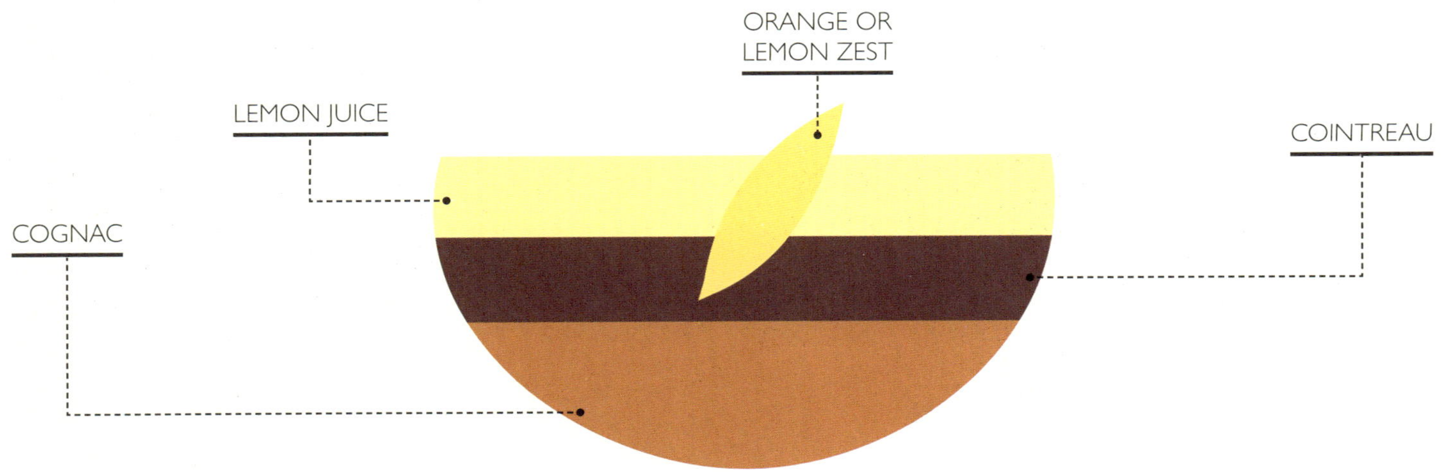

WHAT IS IT?

A Daisy that can be very indulgent thanks to its perfect balance.

FAMILY

Daisy

TYPE

Short drink

TYPE OF GLASS

Traditional: Martini glass
Alternative: coupette

EQUIPMENT

Jigger
Shaker
Single strainer
Fine-mesh strainer
Knife
Cocktail tweezers

TECHNIQUES TO MASTER

Shake (see page 58)
Double filtration (see page 53)
Expressing zest (see page 46)
Cutting zest (see page 45)

VARIATIONS

Between the Sheets: replace 25ml (⅔oz plus 1 tsp) Cognac with 25ml (½oz) white rum.
Chelsea Sidecar: replace the Cognac with the same quantity of gin.
Deauville: replace 25ml (⅔oz plus 1 tsp) Cognac with 25ml (⅔oz plus 1 tsp) Calvados.

TIP

Choose a VSOP Cognac, which will give the cocktail more body.
Orange zest will deliver some roundness to the cocktail, while lemon zest will bring out its acidic and dry notes.

SERVES 1

50ml (1⅔oz) Cognac
25ml (⅔oz plus 1 tsp) Cointreau
25ml (⅔oz plus 1 tsp) lemon juice

TO DECORATE

zest of 1 unwaxed lemon or orange

1. Pour all the ingredients into the shaker.
2. Fill the larger part of the shaker to the brim with ice and shake (see page 58) vigorously for 10 seconds.
3. Double filter (see page 53) into the serving glass.
4. Express the orange or lemon zest (see page 46) in the centre of the glass, then rub it over the rim and stem of the glass.
5. Cut the zest (see page 45) and sit it on the rim of the glass using the cocktail tweezers.

SINGAPORE

SLING

The Lowdown

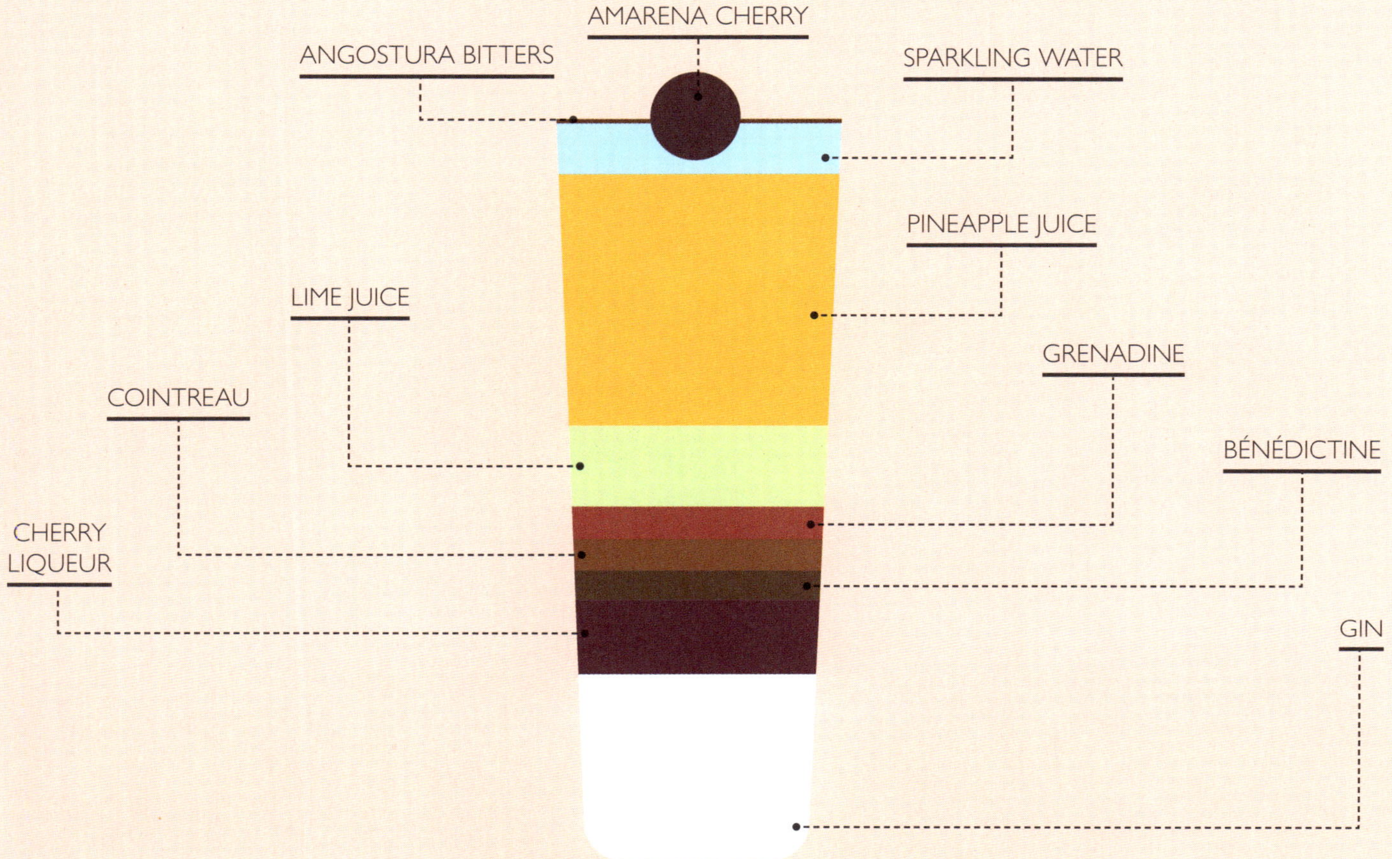

WHAT IS IT?

A long drink that never goes out of style and is enjoyed for its balance and complexity.

FAMILY

Sling

TYPE

Long drink

ICE FOR SERVING

Cubes

TYPE OF GLASS

Traditional: sling
Alternative: highball

EQUIPMENT

Jigger
Shaker
Single strainer
Cocktail stick (pick)

TECHNIQUES TO MASTER

Ice cubes/block of ice (see page 36)
Shake (see page 58)
Single filtration (see page 52)

VARIATIONS

Saigon: 45ml (1½oz) gin, 25ml (⅔oz plus 1 tsp) ginger and lemongrass cordial, 15ml (½oz) honey vodka, 10ml (2 tsp) passion fruit liqueur, 25ml (⅔oz plus 1 tsp) lime juice, 30ml (1oz) pineapple juice, 2 dashes Peychaud's bitters.
Basil Bramble Sling: 60ml (2oz) gin, 45ml (1½oz) lemon juice, 15ml (½oz) simple syrup, 15ml (½oz) crème de mûre (blackberry liqueur), 7 fresh basil leaves.

TIP

Choose a pineapple juice made from 100% freshly squeezed juice to add richness and perfect balance.

Discover

SERVES 1

30ml (1oz) gin
15ml (½oz) cherry liqueur (for example, Heering)
5ml (1 tsp) Bénédictine
5ml (1 tsp) Cointreau
5ml (1 tsp) grenadine
15ml (½oz) lime juice
50ml (1⅔oz) pineapple juice
1 dash of Angostura bitters
10ml (2 tsp) sparkling water

TO DECORATE

1 amarena cherry

1. Pour all the ingredients into the shaker, apart from the sparkling water.
2. Fill the larger part of the shaker to the brim with ice and shake (see page 58) vigorously for 10 seconds.
3. Single filter (see page 52) into the serving glass.
4. Add ice to the brim.
5. Add the sparkling water.
6. Skewer the cherry onto the cocktail stick (pick) and place upright in the glass so the cherry sits on the rim.

BASIL SMASH

The Lowdown

WHAT IS IT?

A very refreshing Smash.

FAMILY

Smash

TYPE

Short drink

ICE FOR SERVING

Cubes

TYPE OF GLASS

Traditional: single rocks glass
Alternative: goblet

EQUIPMENT

Jigger
Shaker
Single strainer
Fine-mesh strainer
Cocktail tweezers

TECHNIQUES TO MASTER

Ice cubes/block of ice (see page 36)
Shake (see page 58)
Double filtration (see page 53)

TIP

Briefly plunge the basil for decoration in iced water before serving.

VARIATION

You can create many different Smashes by replacing the gin with other spirits and the basil with the same amount of mint. For example, you could make whiskey smash, Scotch whisky smash, bourbon smash or tequila smash.

Discover

SERVES 1

50ml (1⅔oz) gin
25ml (⅔oz plus 1 tsp) simple syrup
25ml (⅔oz plus 1 tsp) lemon juice
7 basil leaves

TO DECORATE

1 attractive basil sprig

1 Pour all the ingredients into the shaker.

2 Fill the larger part of the shaker to the brim with ice and shake (see page 58) vigorously for 10 seconds.

3 Fill the serving glass to the brim with ice cubes (see page 38) and double filter (see page 53) the cocktail into it.

4 Balance the basil sprig on top of the cocktail.

CLOVER CLUB

The Lowdown

WHAT IS IT?

A creamy Sour that is dry and fruity.

FAMILY

Reinforced Sour

TYPE

Short drink

TYPE OF GLASS

Traditional: coupette
Alternative: goblet

EQUIPMENT

Jigger
Shaker
Single strainer
Fine-mesh strainer
Knife
Cocktail tweezers

TECHNIQUES TO MASTER

Dry shake (see page 58)
Throwing (see page 59)
Shake (see page 58)
Double filtration (see page 53)
Expressing zest (see page 46)
Cutting zest (see page 45)

VARIATION

Replace the egg white with the same weight of aquafaba.

TIPS

Press fresh raspberries when they are in season and mix the juice with an equal amount of sugar to make the best raspberry syrup ever (but remember it will only keep for one day in the refrigerator). Choose a London Dry gin for its strong juniper flavour to enhance the aromatic palette this cocktail offers.

Discover

SERVES 1

50ml (1⅔oz) gin
10ml (2 tsp) raspberry syrup
20ml (⅔oz) lemon juice
1 egg white or 30ml (1oz) aquafaba

TO DECORATE

zest of 1 unwaxed lemon
1 raspberry

1. Pour all the ingredients into the shaker.
2. Dry shake (see page 58) vigorously for 5 seconds without adding any ice.
3. Throw the mix from the larger part of the shaker to the smaller part to incorporate air into it (see page 59).
4. Fill the larger part of the shaker to the brim with ice and shake (see page 58) vigorously for 10 seconds.
5. Double filter (see page 53) into the serving glass.
6. Express the lemon zest (see page 46) into the centre of the glass, then rub it over the rim and stem of the glass.
7. Cut the zest (see page 45) and rest it on the rim of the glass using the cocktail tweezers. Using the tweezers, place the raspberry in the centre of the glass, with the cavity left by the hull uppermost, so it floats on the mousse.

WHITE LADY

The Lowdown

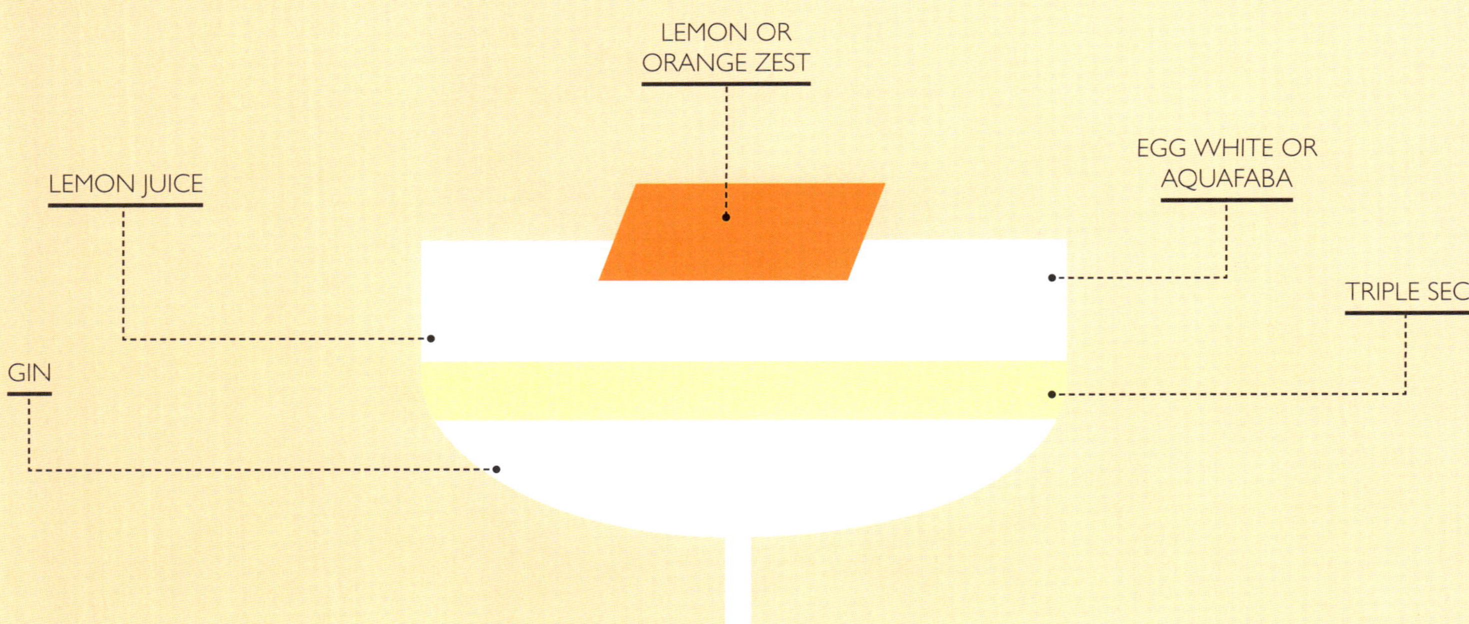

WHAT IS IT?

A very straightforward, well-balanced Daisy with tangy notes.

FAMILY

Daisy

TYPE

Short drink

TYPE OF GLASS

Traditional: coupette
Alternative: goblet

EQUIPMENT

Jigger
Shaker
Single strainer
Fine-mesh strainer
Knife
Cocktail tweezers

TECHNIQUES TO MASTER

Dry shake (see page 58)
Throwing (see page 59)
Shake (see page 58)
Double filtration (see page 53)
Expressing zest (see page 46)
Cutting zest (see page 45)

ALTERNATIVE

Replace the egg white with the same weight of aquafaba.

VARIATION

Pink Lady: add 15ml (½oz) Applejack (apple brandy) or 30&40 Double Jus and 10ml (2 tsp) grenadine in place of the triple sec.

TIP

A very floral gin can add a final flourish to this cocktail. Orange zest adds roundness to the flavour, while lemon zest will bring out more acidic and dry notes.

Discover

SERVES 1

50ml (1⅔oz) gin
25ml (⅔oz plus 1 tsp) triple sec
25ml (⅔oz plus 1 tsp) lemon juice
1 egg white

TO DECORATE

zest of 1 unwaxed lemon or orange

1 Pour all the ingredients into the shaker.

2 Dry shake (see page 58) vigorously for 5 seconds without adding any ice.

3 Throw the mix from the larger part of the shaker to the smaller part to incorporate air into it (see page 59).

4 Fill the larger part of the shaker to the brim with ice and shake (see page 58) vigorously for 10 seconds.

5 Double filter (see page 53) into the serving glass.

6 Express the lemon or orange zest (see page 46) in the centre of the glass, then rub it over the rim and stem of the glass.

7 Cut the zest (see page 45) and drape it over the rim of the glass using the cocktail tweezers.

SOUTHSIDE

The Lowdown

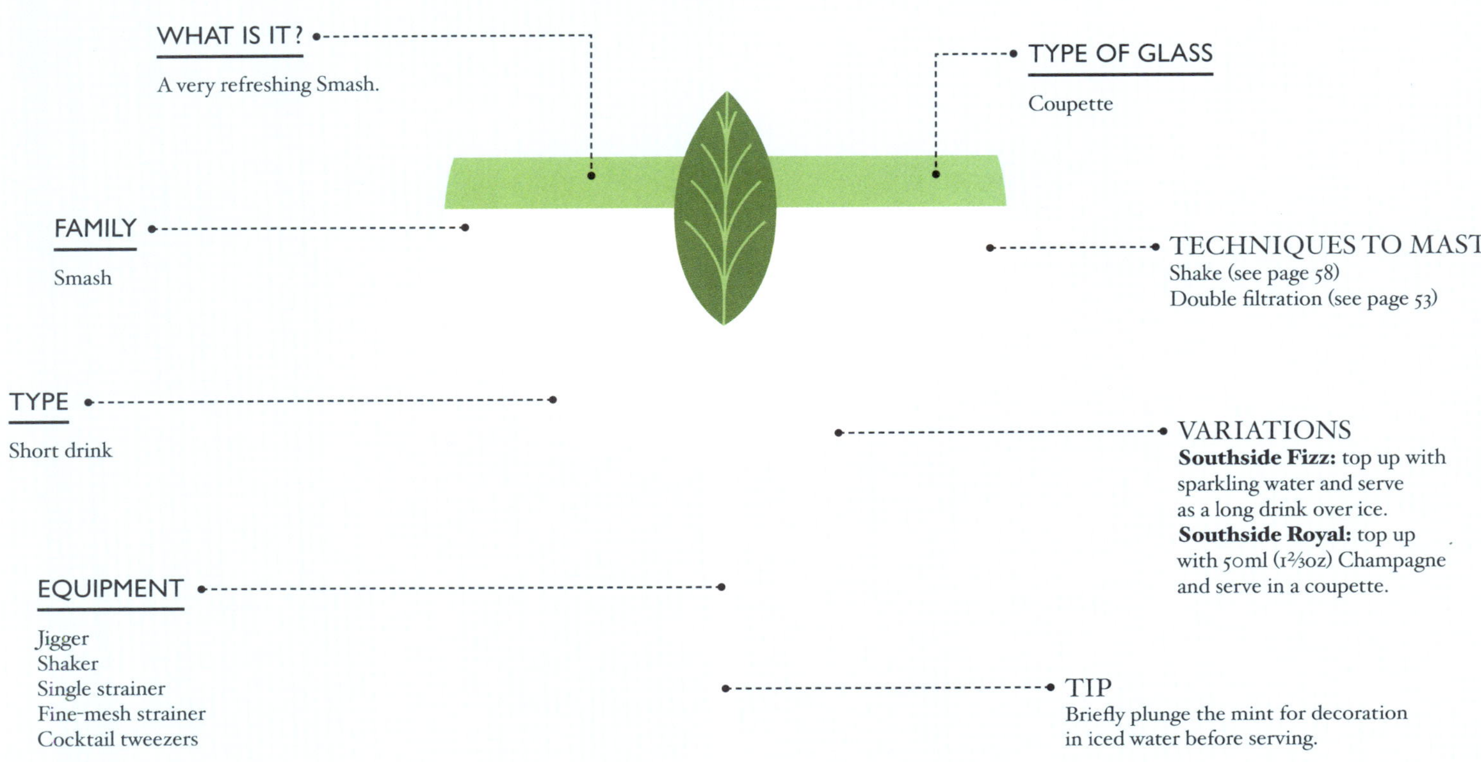

WHAT IS IT?

A very refreshing Smash.

TYPE OF GLASS

Coupette

FAMILY

Smash

TECHNIQUES TO MASTER

Shake (see page 58)
Double filtration (see page 53)

TYPE

Short drink

VARIATIONS

Southside Fizz: top up with sparkling water and serve as a long drink over ice.
Southside Royal: top up with 50ml (1⅔oz) Champagne and serve in a coupette.

EQUIPMENT

Jigger
Shaker
Single strainer
Fine-mesh strainer
Cocktail tweezers

TIP

Briefly plunge the mint for decoration in iced water before serving.

SERVES 1

50ml (1⅔oz) gin
25ml (⅔oz plus 1 tsp) simple syrup
25ml (⅔oz plus 1 tsp) lime juice
7 mint leaves

TO DECORATE

1 attractive mint leaf

1 Pour all the ingredients into the shaker.

2 Fill the larger part of the shaker to the brim with ice and shake (see page 58) vigorously for 10 seconds.

3 Double filter (see page 53) into the serving glass.

4 Balance the mint leaf for decoration upright between the edge of the glass and the cocktail.

MARY PICKFORD

The Lowdown

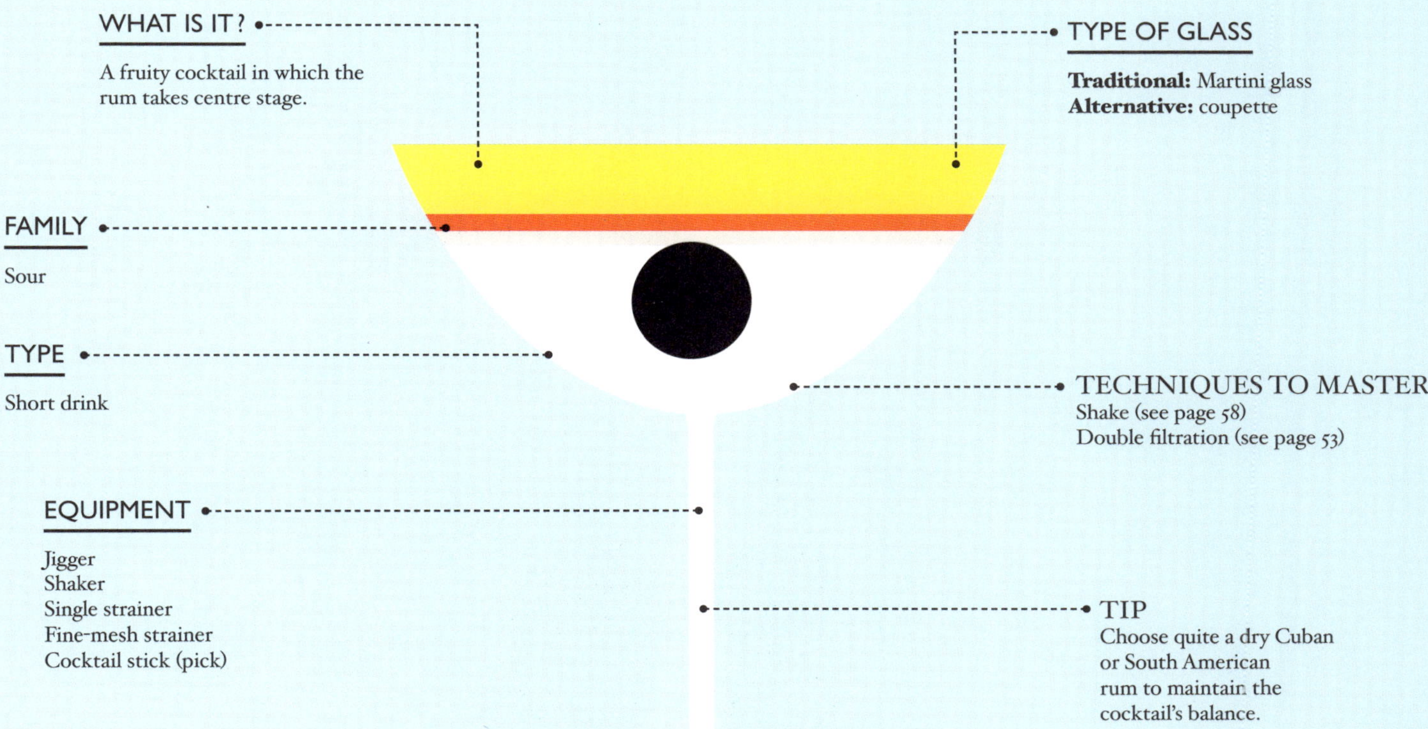

WHAT IS IT?

A fruity cocktail in which the rum takes centre stage.

TYPE OF GLASS

Traditional: Martini glass
Alternative: coupette

FAMILY

Sour

TYPE

Short drink

TECHNIQUES TO MASTER

Shake (see page 58)
Double filtration (see page 53)

EQUIPMENT

Jigger
Shaker
Single strainer
Fine-mesh strainer
Cocktail stick (pick)

TIP

Choose quite a dry Cuban or South American rum to maintain the cocktail's balance.

SERVES 1

50ml (1⅔oz) white rum
7.5ml (1½ tsp) maraschino liqueur
7.5ml (1½ tsp) grenadine
30ml (1oz) pineapple juice

TO DECORATE

1 amarena cherry

1 Pour all the ingredients into the shaker.

2 Fill the larger part of the shaker to the brim with ice and shake (see page 58) vigorously for 10 seconds.

3 Double filter (see page 53) into the serving glass.

4 Skewer the cherry on the cocktail stick (pick) and rest the stick (pick) against the side of the glass with the cherry in the cocktail.

BRAMBLE

The Lowdown

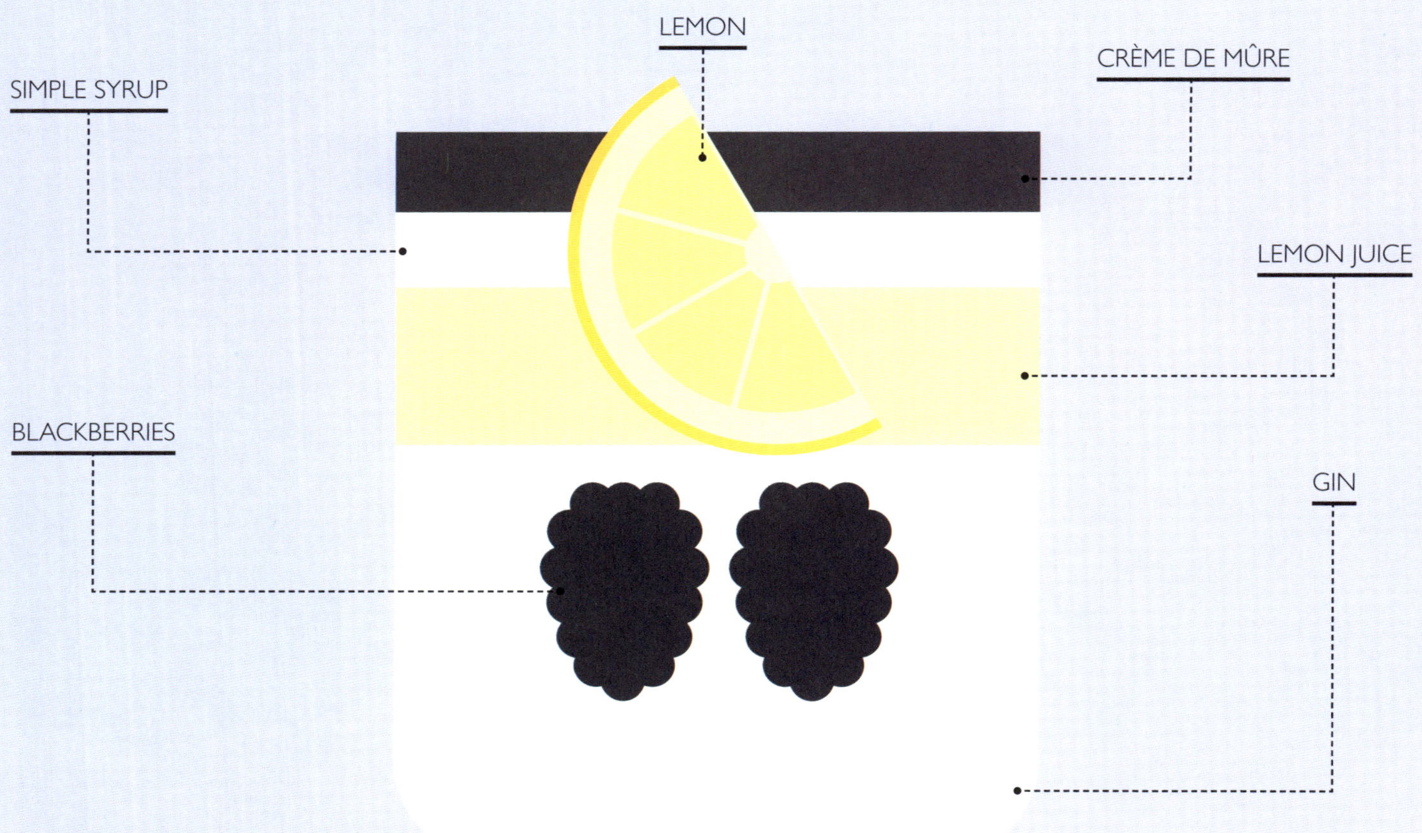

WHAT IS IT ?

A Daisy that's fruity and very refreshing.

FAMILY

Daisy

TYPE

Short drink

ICE FOR SERVING

Crushed

TYPE OF GLASS

Traditional: single Old Fashioned
Alternative: goblet

EQUIPMENT

Jigger
Shaker
Single strainer
Biodegradable or reusable straw
Cocktail tweezers

TECHNIQUES TO MASTER

Shake (see page 58)
Single filtration (see page 52)
Crushed ice (see page 39)

TIP

Choose a peppery gin as it will enhance the crème de mûre perfectly.

Discover

SERVES 1

50ml (1⅔oz) gin
20ml (⅔oz) lemon juice
10ml (2 tsp) simple syrup
15ml (½oz) crème de mûre (blackberry liqueur)

TO DECORATE

lemon wedge (⅛ of a lemon)
2–4 blackberries

1 Pour all the ingredients except the crème de mûre into the smaller part of the shaker.

2 Fill the larger part of the shaker to the brim with ice. Shake (see page 58) vigorously for 5 seconds.

3 Single filter (see page 52) into the serving glass.

4 Fill the glass to the brim with crushed ice (see page 39), packing it down well so it forms a dome (see page 214).

5 Very gently pour the crème de mûre in a thin stream randomly all over the crushed ice.

6 Add the straw to the glass. Using the cocktail tweezers, position the lemon wedge and the blackberries on top of the ice close to the straw.

FOG CUTTER

The Lowdown

WHAT IS IT?

A powerful and complex Tiki.

FAMILY

Tiki

TYPE

Long drink

TYPE OF GLASS

Traditional: sling
Alternative: highball

EQUIPMENT

Jigger
Shaker
Single strainer
Cocktail stick (pick)

TECHNIQUES TO MASTER

Shake (see page 58)
Single filtration (see page 52)
Expressing mint (see page 47)
Twisting mint (see page 47)

VARIATION

Fog Cutter Bramble Style: omit the triple sec, orange juice and orgeat syrup and replace the lemon juice with lime juice. Just as you would for a Bramble, shake all the ingredients and filter into a single rocks glass, then fill with crushed ice and pour over 15ml (½oz) of cherry liqueur (for example, Heering) in a thin stream.

TIP

Choose very sweet oranges as their juice will prolong the flavour and bring the ingredients together beautifully in this delicately balanced cocktail.

Discover

SERVES 1

30ml (1oz) white rum
15ml (½oz) Cognac
15ml (½oz) gin
15ml (½oz) dry Curaçao
15ml (½oz) fortified Spanish wine, such as amontillado sherry
25ml (⅔oz plus 1 tsp) orgeat syrup (see page 31)
45ml (1½oz) orange juice
30ml (1oz) lemon juice

TO DECORATE

1 mint sprig
½ orange slice
1 amarena cherry

1 Pour all the ingredients into the shaker.

2 Fill the larger part of the shaker to the brim with ice and shake (see page 58) vigorously for 10 seconds.

3 Fill the serving glass to the brim with ice cubes and single filter (see page 52) the cocktail into it.

4 Express the mint (see step 2, page 47), rolling it up on itself (see page 47) and tucking it in the glass between the ice cubes.

5 Place the half orange slice on one side of the mint. Skewer the cherry on the cocktail stick (pick) and place it on the other side.

TOREADOR

The Lowdown

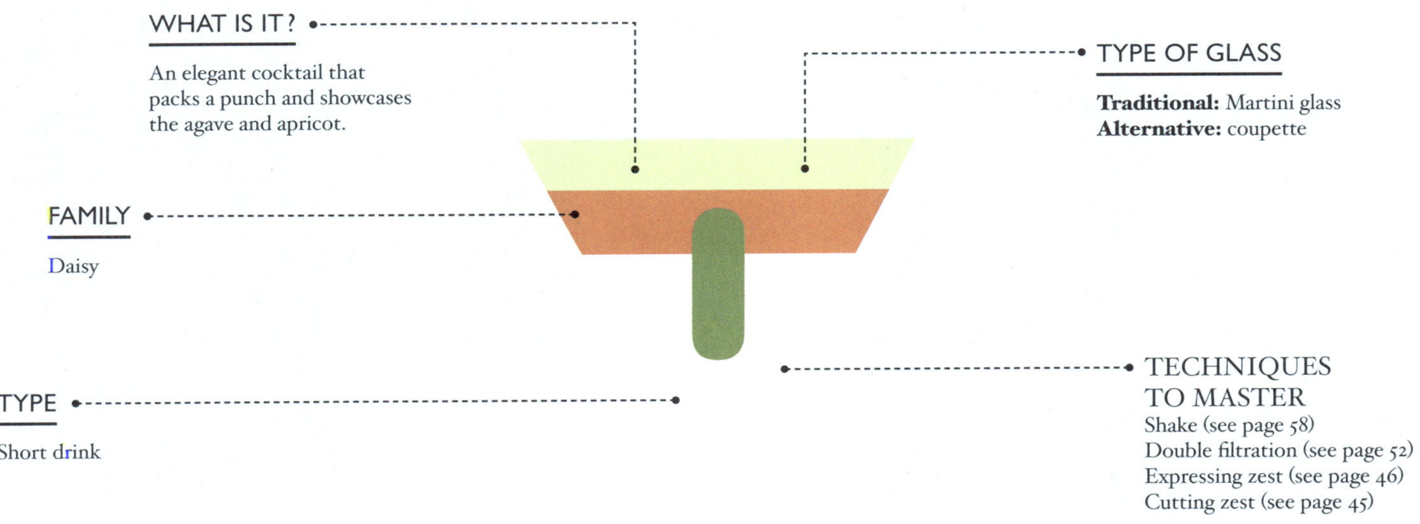

WHAT IS IT?

An elegant cocktail that packs a punch and showcases the agave and apricot.

TYPE OF GLASS

Traditional: Martini glass
Alternative: coupette

FAMILY

Daisy

TYPE

Short drink

TECHNIQUES TO MASTER

Shake (see page 58)
Double filtration (see page 52)
Expressing zest (see page 46)
Cutting zest (see page 45)

EQUIPMENT

Jigger
Shaker
Single strainer
Fine-mesh strainer
Knife
Cocktail tweezers

TIP

The tequila used for this cocktail will make a world of difference: a silver or joven tequila will produce a light and fresh-tasting cocktail, while a 'rested' (reposado) tequila will bring plenty of body and roundness.

SERVES 1

50ml (1⅔oz) tequila
20ml (⅔oz) apricot brandy
20ml (⅔oz) lime juice

TO DECORATE

zest of 1 unwaxed lime

1. Pour all the ingredients into the shaker.
2. Fill the larger part of the shaker to the brim with ice and shake (see page 58) vigorously for 10 seconds.
3. Double filter (see page 53) into the serving glass.
4. Express the zest (see page 46) in the centre of the glass, then rub it over the rim and stem of the glass.
5. Cut the zest (see page 45) and, using the cocktail tweezers, place it over the rim of the glass.

NAKED & FAMOUS

The Lowdown

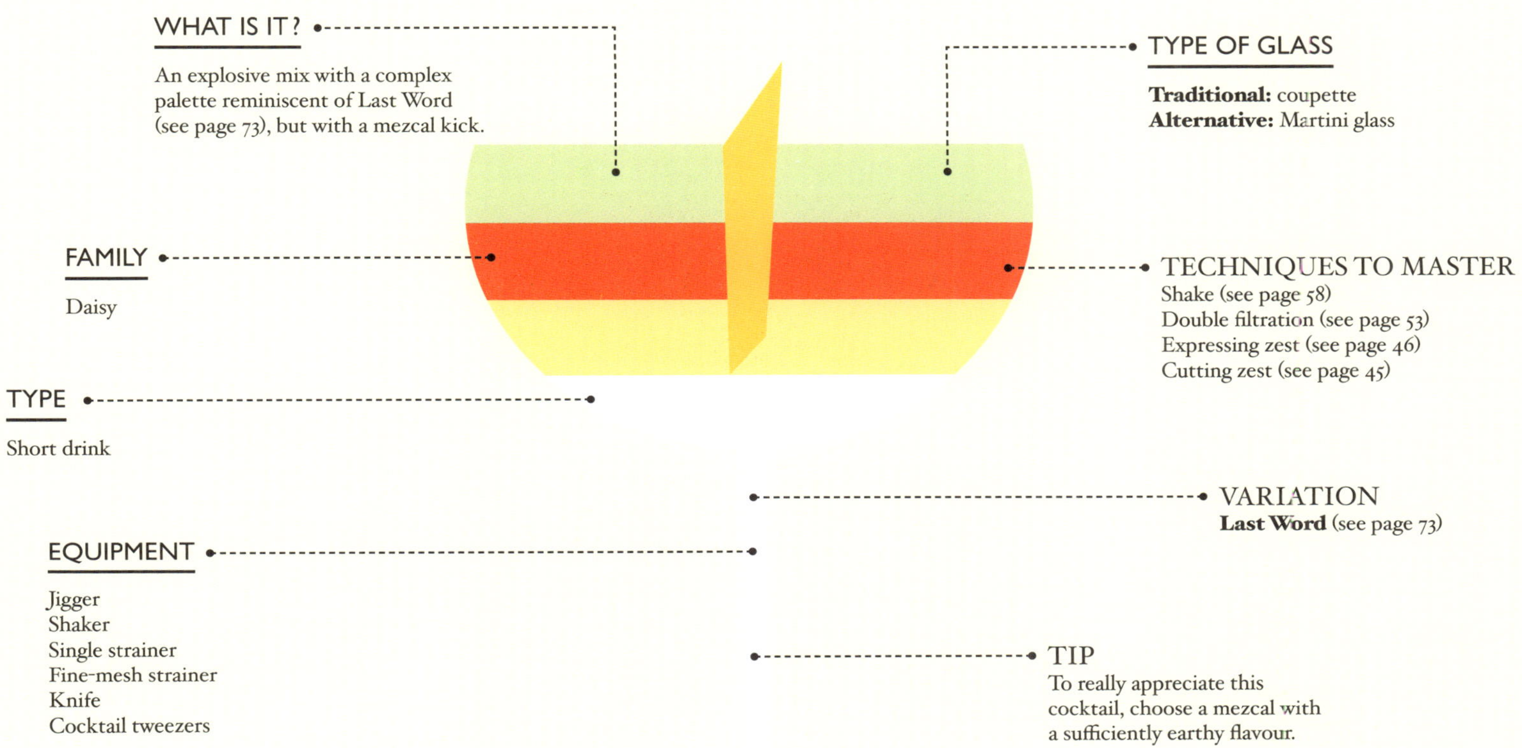

WHAT IS IT?
An explosive mix with a complex palette reminiscent of Last Word (see page 73), but with a mezcal kick.

TYPE OF GLASS
Traditional: coupette
Alternative: Martini glass

FAMILY
Daisy

TECHNIQUES TO MASTER
Shake (see page 58)
Double filtration (see page 53)
Expressing zest (see page 46)
Cutting zest (see page 45)

TYPE
Short drink

VARIATION
Last Word (see page 73)

EQUIPMENT
Jigger
Shaker
Single strainer
Fine-mesh strainer
Knife
Cocktail tweezers

TIP
To really appreciate this cocktail, choose a mezcal with a sufficiently earthy flavour.

SERVES 1
25ml (⅔oz plus 1 tsp) tequila
25ml (⅔oz plus 1 tsp) yellow Chartreuse
25ml (⅔oz plus 1 tsp) Aperol
25ml (⅔oz plus 1 tsp) lime juice

TO DECORATE
zest of 1 unwaxed lime

1 Pour all the ingredients into the shaker.

2 Fill the larger part of the shaker to the brim with ice and shake (see page 58) vigorously for 10 seconds.

3 Double filter (see page 53) into the serving glass.

4 Express the zest (see page 46) in the centre of the glass, then rub it over the rim and stem of the glass.

5 Cut the zest (see page 45) and place it on the rim of the glass, using the cocktail tweezers.

PAPER PLANE

The Lowdown

WHAT IS IT?

A complex Daisy thanks to the addition of an amaro.

TYPE OF GLASS

Traditional: Martini glass
Alternative: coupette

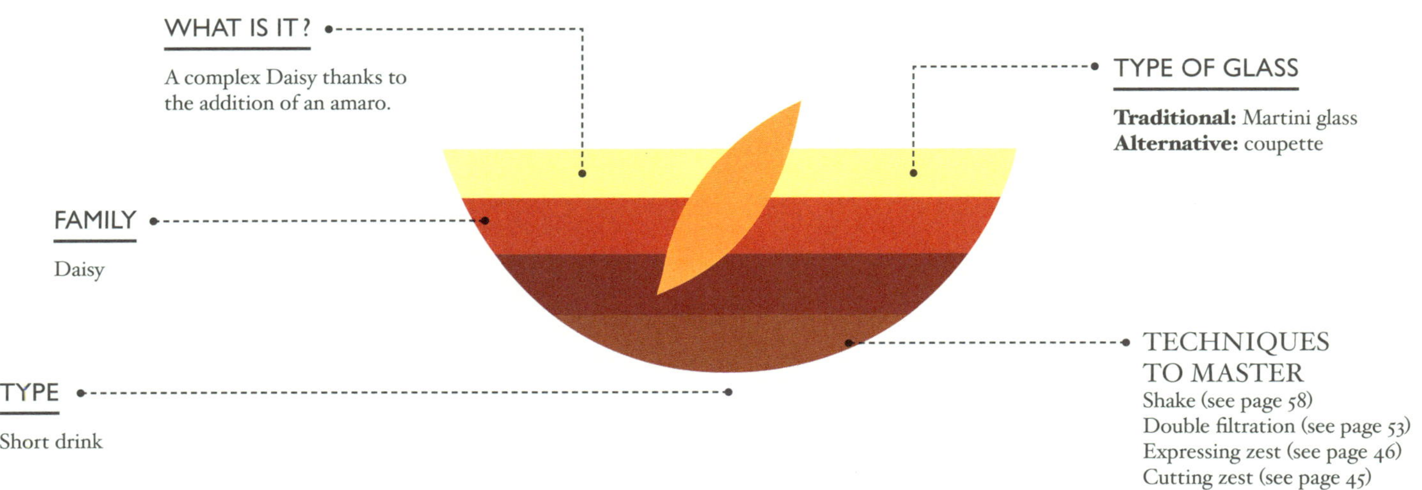

FAMILY

Daisy

TECHNIQUES TO MASTER

Shake (see page 58)
Double filtration (see page 53)
Expressing zest (see page 46)
Cutting zest (see page 45)

TYPE

Short drink

EQUIPMENT

Jigger
Shaker
Single strainer
Fine-mesh strainer
Knife
Cocktail tweezers

TIP

The way this cocktail is structured means you can vary your mix by picking an atypical bourbon or a different amaro, without running the risk of altering its balance.

SERVES 1

25ml (⅔oz plus 1 tsp) bourbon
25ml (⅔oz plus 1 tsp) Amaro Nonino
25ml (⅔oz plus 1 tsp) Aperol
25ml (⅔oz plus 1 tsp) lemon juice

TO DECORATE

zest of 1 unwaxed orange

1 Pour all the ingredients into the shaker.

2 Fill the larger part of the shaker to the brim with ice and shake (see page 58) vigorously for 10 seconds.

3 Double filter (see page 53) into the serving glass.

4 Express the zest (see page 46) in the centre of the glass, then rub it over the rim and stem of the glass.

5 Cut the zest (see page 45) and place it on the rim of the glass, using the cocktail tweezers.

OLD PAL

The Lowdown

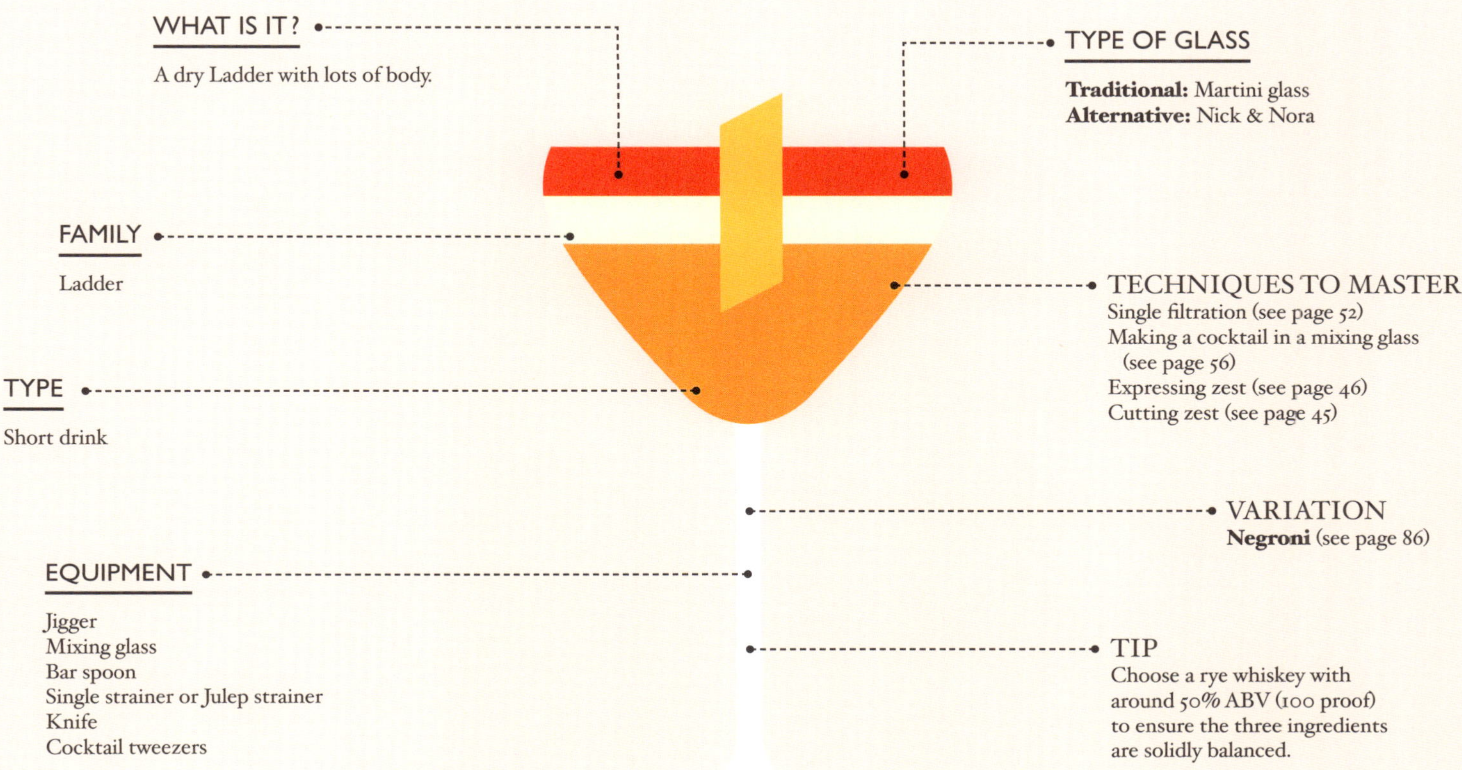

WHAT IS IT?
A dry Ladder with lots of body.

TYPE OF GLASS
Traditional: Martini glass
Alternative: Nick & Nora

FAMILY
Ladder

TECHNIQUES TO MASTER
Single filtration (see page 52)
Making a cocktail in a mixing glass (see page 56)
Expressing zest (see page 46)
Cutting zest (see page 45)

TYPE
Short drink

VARIATION
Negroni (see page 86)

EQUIPMENT
Jigger
Mixing glass
Bar spoon
Single strainer or Julep strainer
Knife
Cocktail tweezers

TIP
Choose a rye whiskey with around 50% ABV (100 proof) to ensure the three ingredients are solidly balanced.

SERVES 1

40ml (1 ⅓oz) rye whiskey
20ml (⅔oz) dry or extra-dry vermouth
20ml (⅔oz) Campari

TO DECORATE

zest of 1 unwaxed lemon

1. Pour all the ingredients into a well-chilled mixing glass.
2. Add ice to come to around two fingers above the liquid.
3. Mix (see page 56) for 40 seconds.
4. Taste to check that the dilution is perfect, mixing a little more if necessary.
5. Filter (see page 52) into the serving glass.
6. Express the zest (see page 46) in the centre of the glass, then rub it over the rim of the glass.
7. Cut the zest (see page 45) and, using the cocktail tweezers, lay it over the rim of the glass.

PENICILLIN

The Lowdown

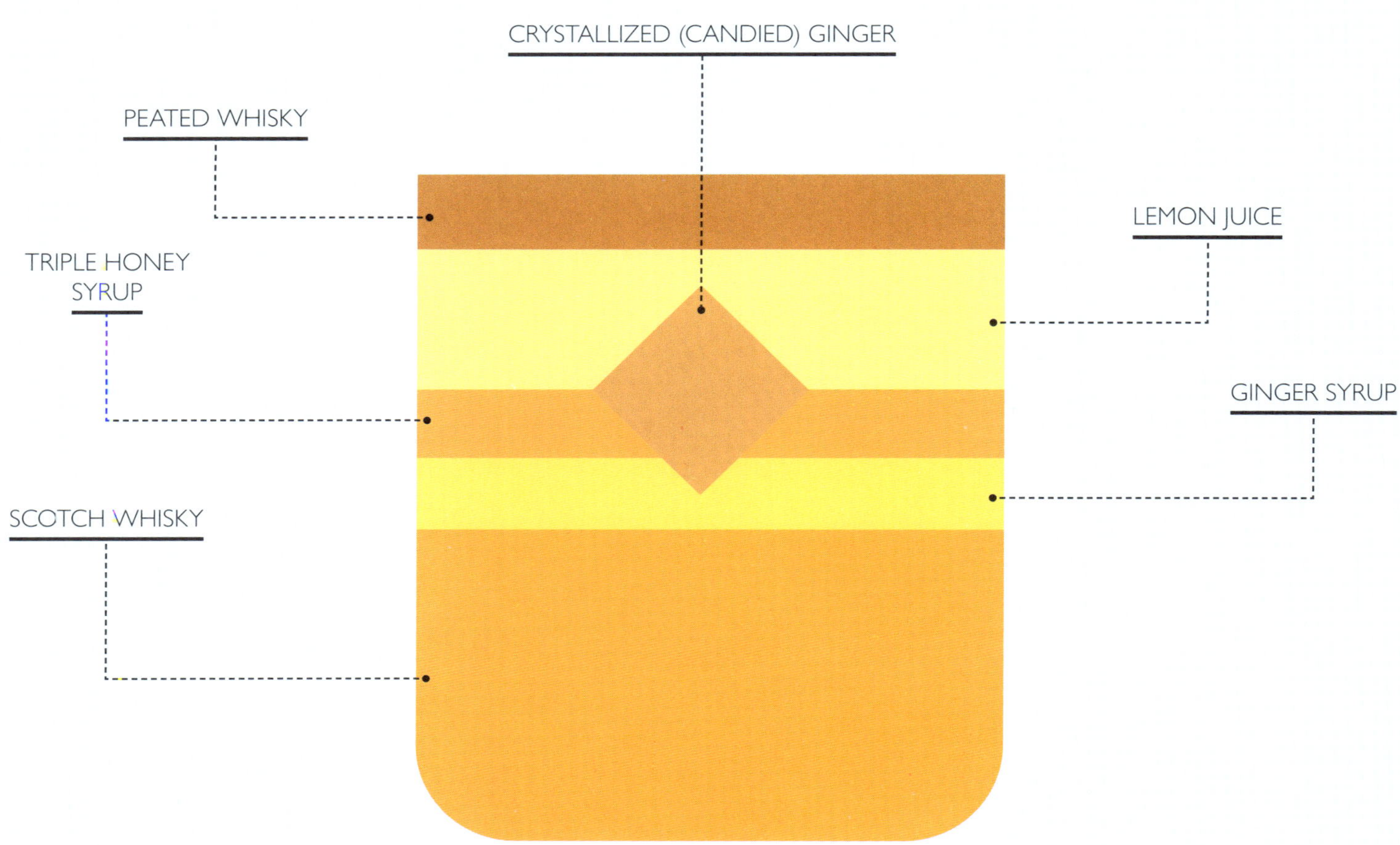

WHAT IS IT?

A Sour that is complex, peaty and very elegant.

FAMILY

Ladder

TYPE

Short drink

ICE FOR SERVING

Cubes

TYPE OF GLASS

Traditional: double Old Fashioned
Alternative: goblet

EQUIPMENT

Jigger
Shaker
Single strainer
Bar spoon
Cocktail stick (pick)

TECHNIQUES TO MASTER

Syrup (see page 30)
Shake (see page 58)
Single filtration (see page 52)
Layering (see page 57)
Ice cubes/block of ice (see page 36)

VARIATION

Medicina Latina: Use tequila instead of Scotch whisky, lime instead of lemon and a heaped teaspoon of mezcal in place of the peated whisky float.

Discover

SERVES 1

40ml (1⅓oz) Scotch whisky
10ml (2 tsp) ginger syrup
10ml (2 tsp) triple honey syrup (see page 30)
20ml (⅔oz) lemon juice
10ml (2 tsp) peated whisky

TO DECORATE

1 piece of crystallized (candied) ginger

1 Pour all the ingredients (except the peated whisky) into the shaker.

2 Fill the larger part of the shaker to the brim with ice and shake (see page 58) vigorously for 10 seconds.

3 Fill the serving glass with ice cubes or a block of ice (see page 36) and filter the cocktail into it.

4 Place the bar spoon in the glass so it touches the top of the liquid and carefully pour the peated whisky down the twisted handle of the spoon on top of the cocktail (see page 57).

5 Skewer the piece of crystallized (candied) ginger on a cocktail stick (pick) and place it upright against the inside of the glass.

BROWN DERBY

The Lowdown

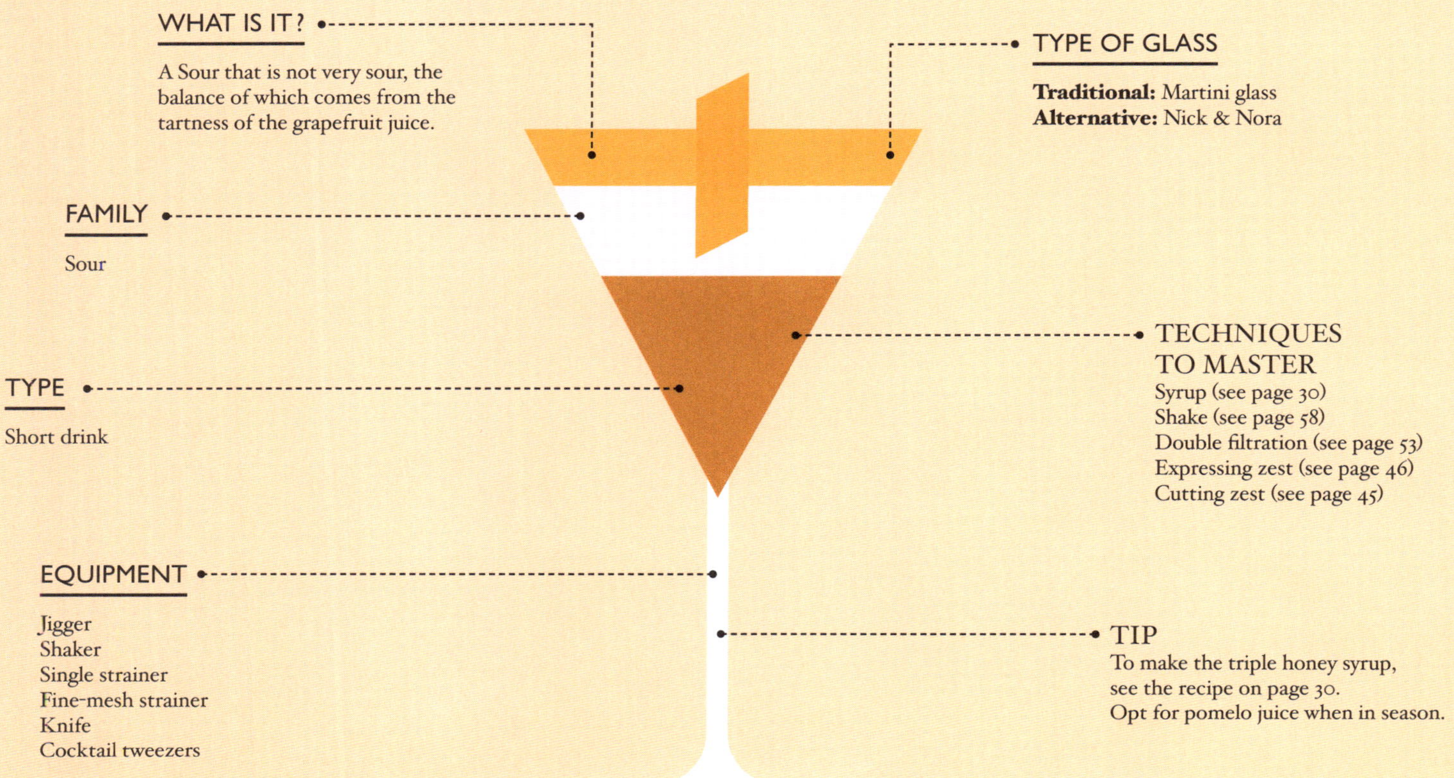

WHAT IS IT?

A Sour that is not very sour, the balance of which comes from the tartness of the grapefruit juice.

TYPE OF GLASS

Traditional: Martini glass
Alternative: Nick & Nora

FAMILY

Sour

TECHNIQUES TO MASTER

Syrup (see page 30)
Shake (see page 58)
Double filtration (see page 53)
Expressing zest (see page 46)
Cutting zest (see page 45)

TYPE

Short drink

EQUIPMENT

Jigger
Shaker
Single strainer
Fine-mesh strainer
Knife
Cocktail tweezers

TIP

To make the triple honey syrup, see the recipe on page 30.
Opt for pomelo juice when in season.

SERVES 1

50ml (1⅔oz) bourbon
25ml (⅔oz plus 1 tsp) grapefruit juice
15ml (½oz) triple honey syrup (see page 30)

TO DECORATE

zest of 1 unwaxed grapefruit

1. Pour all the ingredients into the shaker.
2. Fill the larger part of the shaker to the brim with ice and shake (see page 58) vigorously for 10 seconds.
3. Double filter (see page 53) into the serving glass.
4. Express the zest (see page 46) in the centre of the glass, then rub it over the rim and stem of the glass.
5. Cut the zest (see page 45) and, using the cocktail tweezers, place it on the rim of the glass.

ROME WITH A VIEW

The Lowdown

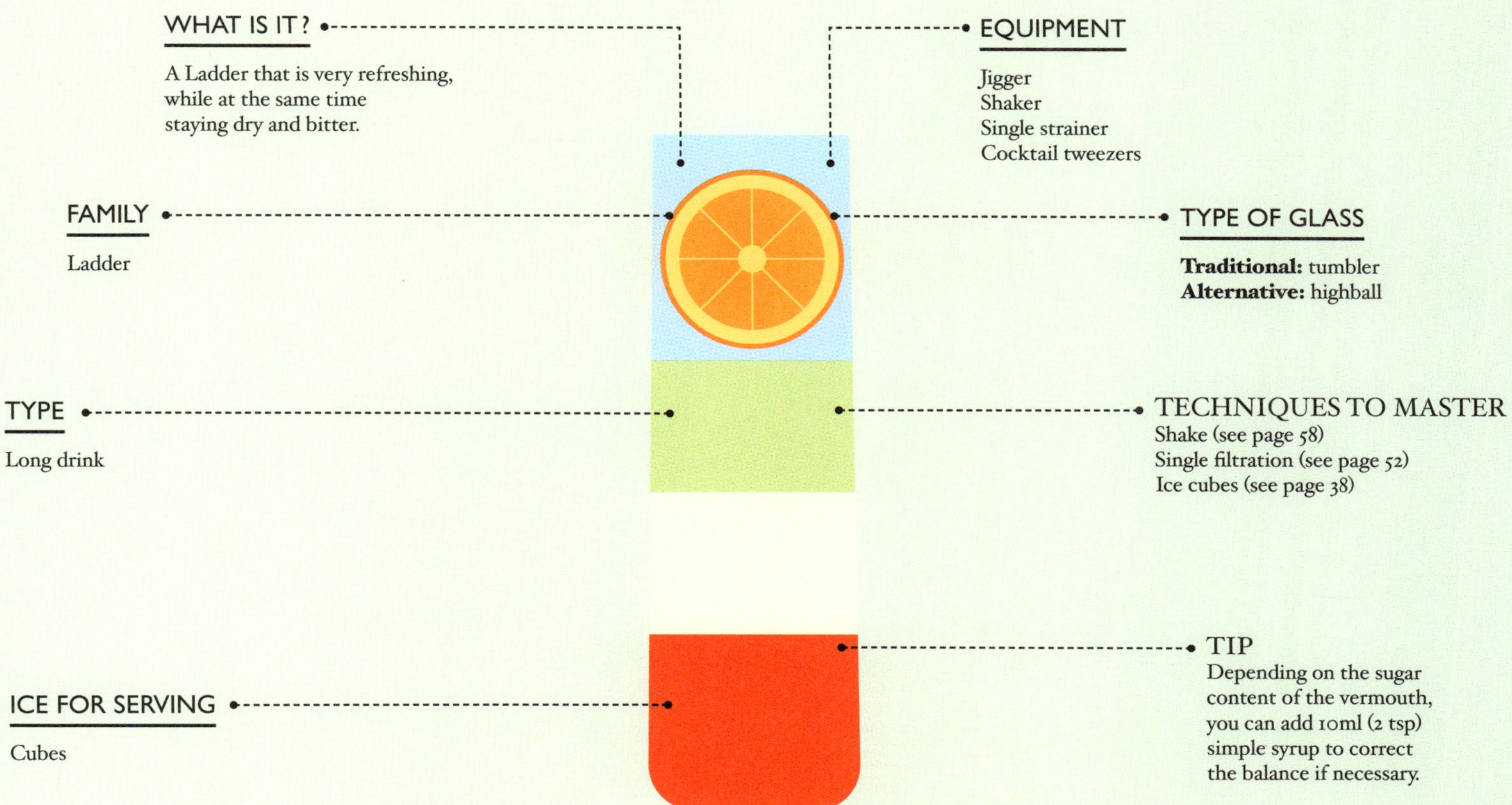

SERVES 1

30ml (1oz) Campari
30ml (1oz) dry or extra-dry vermouth
30ml (1oz) lime juice
60ml (2oz) sparkling water, plus extra to top up

TO DECORATE

1 orange slice

1. Pour all the ingredients into the shaker.
2. Fill the larger part of the shaker to the brim with ice and shake (see page 58) vigorously for 10 seconds.
3. Single filter (see page 52) into the serving glass.
4. Fill the glass to the brim with ice cubes.
5. Add enough sparkling water to come to two fingers below the rim.
6. Using the cocktail tweezers, slide the orange slice between the ice cubes and the side of the glass, then turn it round the glass a few times.

BAMBOO

The Lowdown

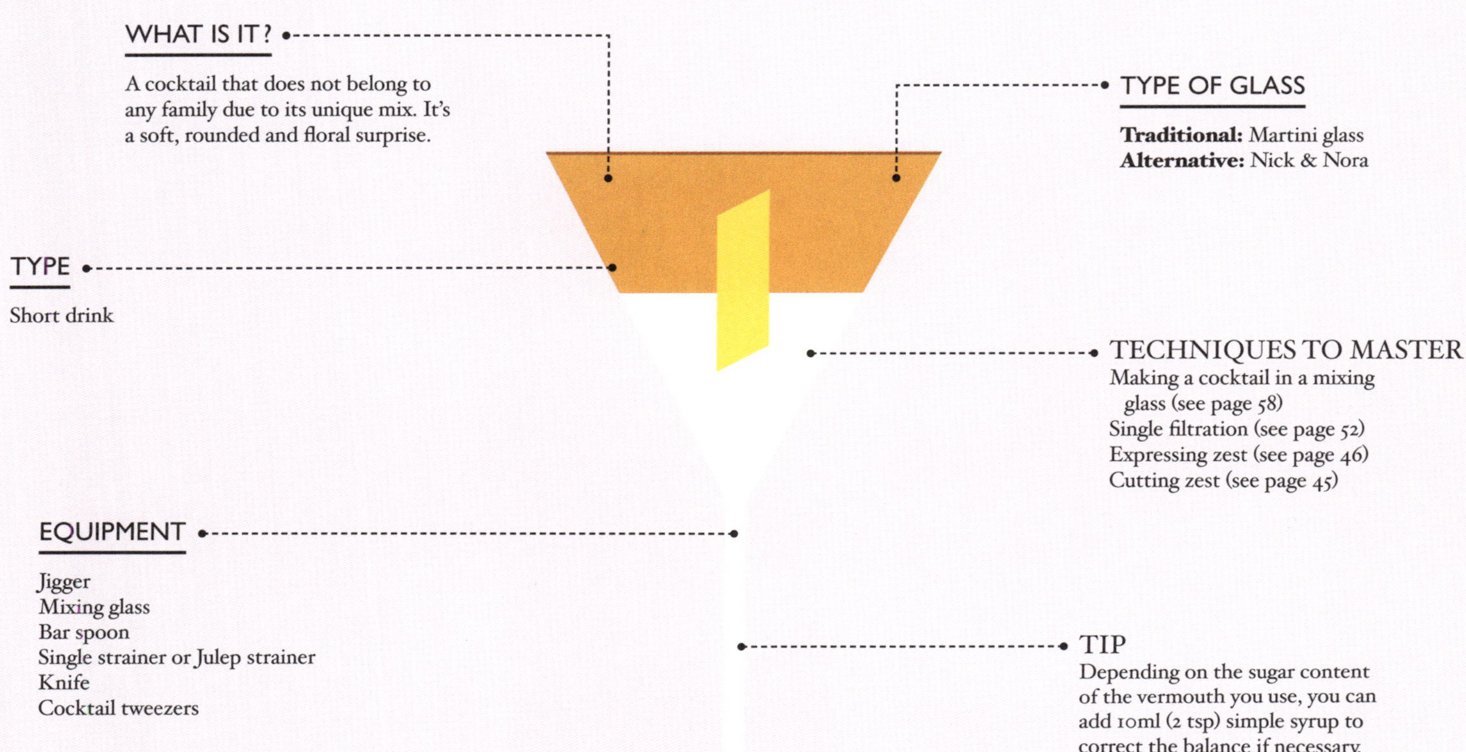

WHAT IS IT?

A cocktail that does not belong to any family due to its unique mix. It's a soft, rounded and floral surprise.

TYPE OF GLASS

Traditional: Martini glass
Alternative: Nick & Nora

TYPE

Short drink

TECHNIQUES TO MASTER

Making a cocktail in a mixing glass (see page 58)
Single filtration (see page 52)
Expressing zest (see page 46)
Cutting zest (see page 45)

EQUIPMENT

Jigger
Mixing glass
Bar spoon
Single strainer or Julep strainer
Knife
Cocktail tweezers

TIP

Depending on the sugar content of the vermouth you use, you can add 10ml (2 tsp) simple syrup to correct the balance if necessary.

SERVES 1

45ml (1½oz) dry or extra-dry vermouth
45ml (1½oz) fortified Spanish wine, such as fino sherry
2 dashes of orange bitters

TO DECORATE

zest of 1 unwaxed lemon

1. Pour all the ingredients into the mixing glass, which should be well chilled.
2. Add ice to come to about two fingers above the liquid.
3. Mix (see page 56) for 40 seconds.
4. Taste to check the dilution is perfect, mixing a little more if necessary.
5. Single filter (see page 52) into the serving glass.
6. Express the zest (see page 46) in the centre of the glass, then rub it over the rim and stem of the glass.
7. Cut the zest (see page 45) and, using the cocktail tweezers, place it inside the glass so it rests on the rim.

BLACK RUSSIAN

The Lowdown

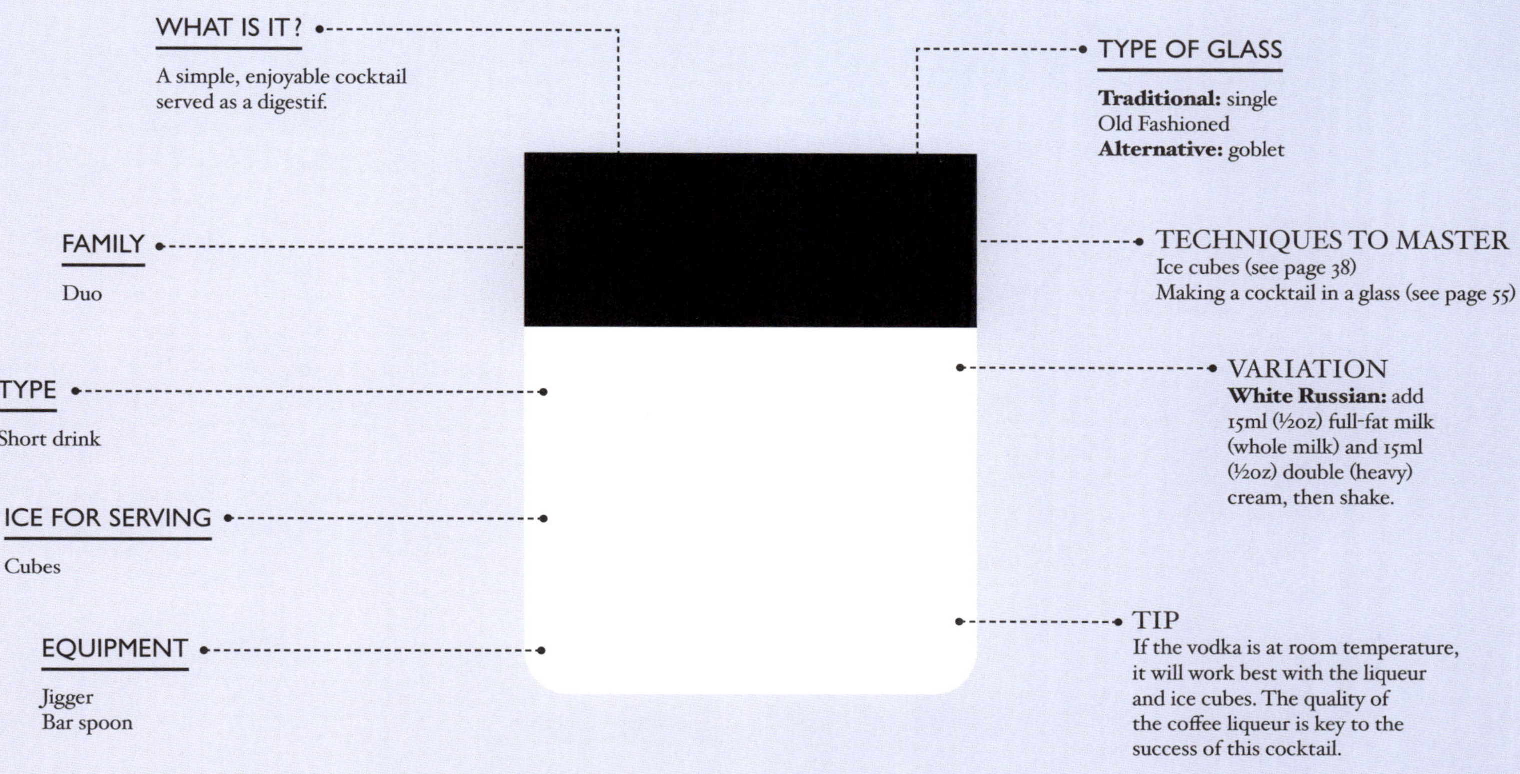

WHAT IS IT?
A simple, enjoyable cocktail served as a digestif.

TYPE OF GLASS
Traditional: single Old Fashioned
Alternative: goblet

FAMILY
Duo

TECHNIQUES TO MASTER
Ice cubes (see page 38)
Making a cocktail in a glass (see page 55)

TYPE
Short drink

VARIATION
White Russian: add 15ml (½oz) full-fat milk (whole milk) and 15ml (½oz) double (heavy) cream, then shake.

ICE FOR SERVING
Cubes

EQUIPMENT
Jigger
Bar spoon

TIP
If the vodka is at room temperature, it will work best with the liqueur and ice cubes. The quality of the coffee liqueur is key to the success of this cocktail.

SERVES 1

50ml (1⅔oz) vodka
25ml (⅔oz plus 1 tsp) coffee liqueur

1. Fill the serving glass to the brim with ice cubes or add a block of ice (see page 36) and pour in the ingredients.
2. Mix with the bar spoon for 25 seconds.
3. Add more ice cubes if necessary.

ADONIS

The Lowdown

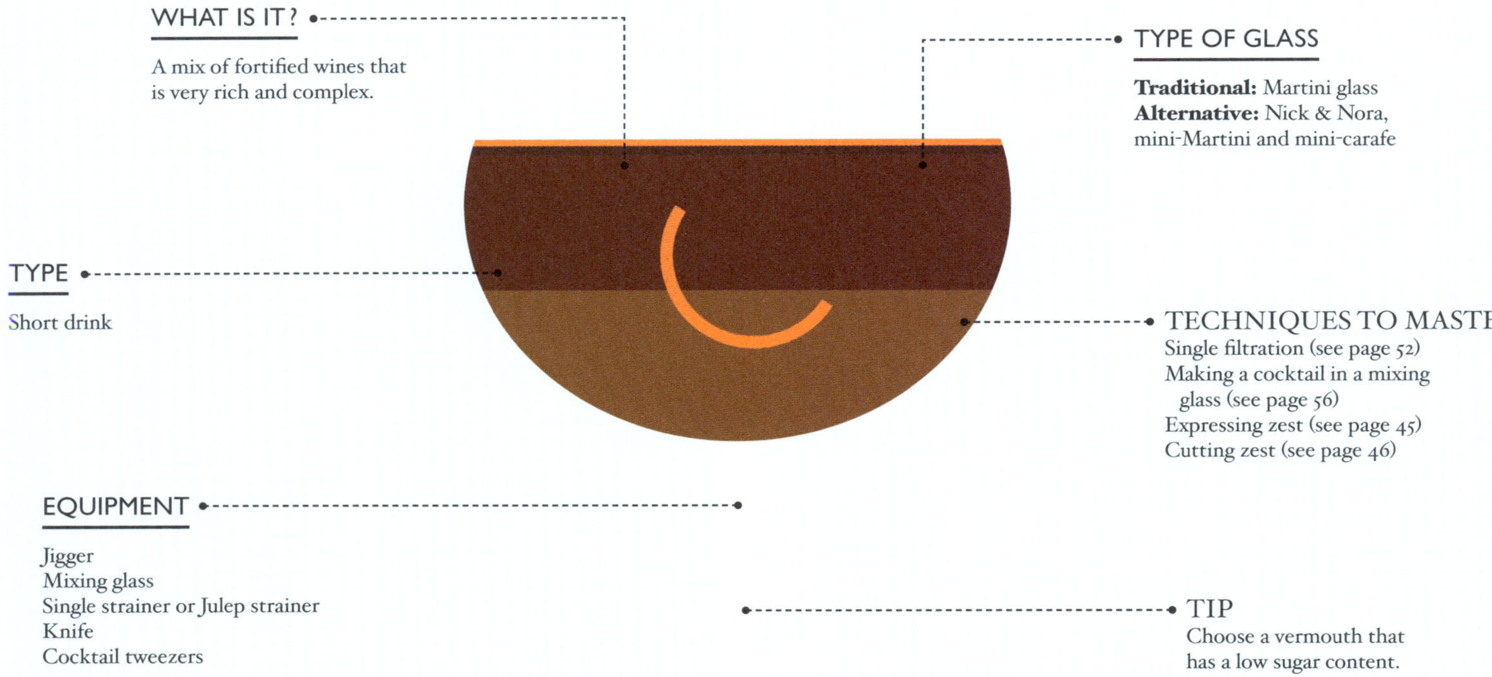

WHAT IS IT?

A mix of fortified wines that is very rich and complex.

TYPE OF GLASS

Traditional: Martini glass
Alternative: Nick & Nora, mini-Martini and mini-carafe

TYPE

Short drink

TECHNIQUES TO MASTER

Single filtration (see page 52)
Making a cocktail in a mixing glass (see page 56)
Expressing zest (see page 45)
Cutting zest (see page 46)

EQUIPMENT

Jigger
Mixing glass
Single strainer or Julep strainer
Knife
Cocktail tweezers

TIP

Choose a vermouth that has a low sugar content.

SERVES 1

45ml (1½oz) fino sherry
45ml (1½oz) red vermouth
2 dashes of orange bitters
2 dashes of Angostura bitters

TO DECORATE

zest of 1 unwaxed orange

1. Pour all the ingredients into the mixing glass, which should be well chilled.
2. Add ice to come to about two fingers above the liquid.
3. Mix (see page 56) for 40 seconds.
4. Taste to check the dilution is perfect, mixing a little more if necessary.
5. Single filter (see page 52) into the serving glass.
6. Express the zest (see page 46) in the centre of the glass, then rub it over the rim and stem of the glass.
7. Cut the zest (see page 45) and, using the cocktail tweezers, sit it on the rim of the glass.

CHRYSANTHEMUM

The Lowdown

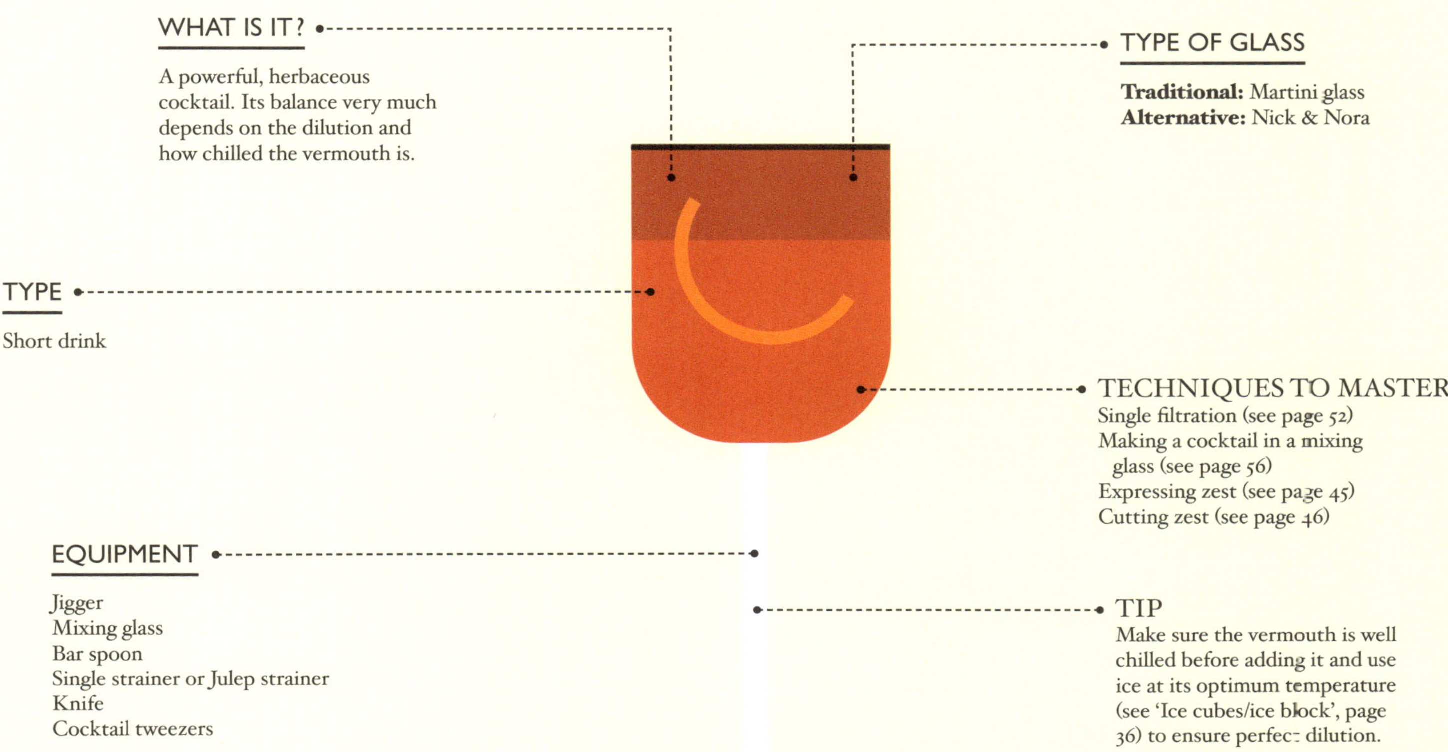

WHAT IS IT?

A powerful, herbaceous cocktail. Its balance very much depends on the dilution and how chilled the vermouth is.

TYPE OF GLASS

Traditional: Martini glass
Alternative: Nick & Nora

TYPE

Short drink

TECHNIQUES TO MASTER

Single filtration (see page 52)
Making a cocktail in a mixing glass (see page 56)
Expressing zest (see page 45)
Cutting zest (see page 46)

EQUIPMENT

Jigger
Mixing glass
Bar spoon
Single strainer or Julep strainer
Knife
Cocktail tweezers

TIP

Make sure the vermouth is well chilled before adding it and use ice at its optimum temperature (see 'Ice cubes/ice block', page 36) to ensure perfect dilution.

SERVES 1

50ml (1⅔oz) dry or extra-dry vermouth
25ml (⅔oz plus 1 tsp) Bénédictine
2 dashes of absinthe

TO DECORATE

zest of 1 unwaxed orange

1 Pour all the ingredients into the mixing glass, which should be well chilled.

2 Add ice to come to about two fingers above the liquid.

3 Mix (see page 56) for 40 seconds.

4 Taste to check the dilution is perfect, mixing a little more if necessary.

5 Single filter (see page 52) into the serving glass.

6 Express the zest (see page 46) in the centre of the glass, then rub it over the rim and stem of the glass.

7 Cut a long strip of zest (see page 45) and, using the cocktail tweezers, place the zest over the rim of the glass so that it curls into the drink.

CHAMPS-ÉLYSÉES

The Lowdown

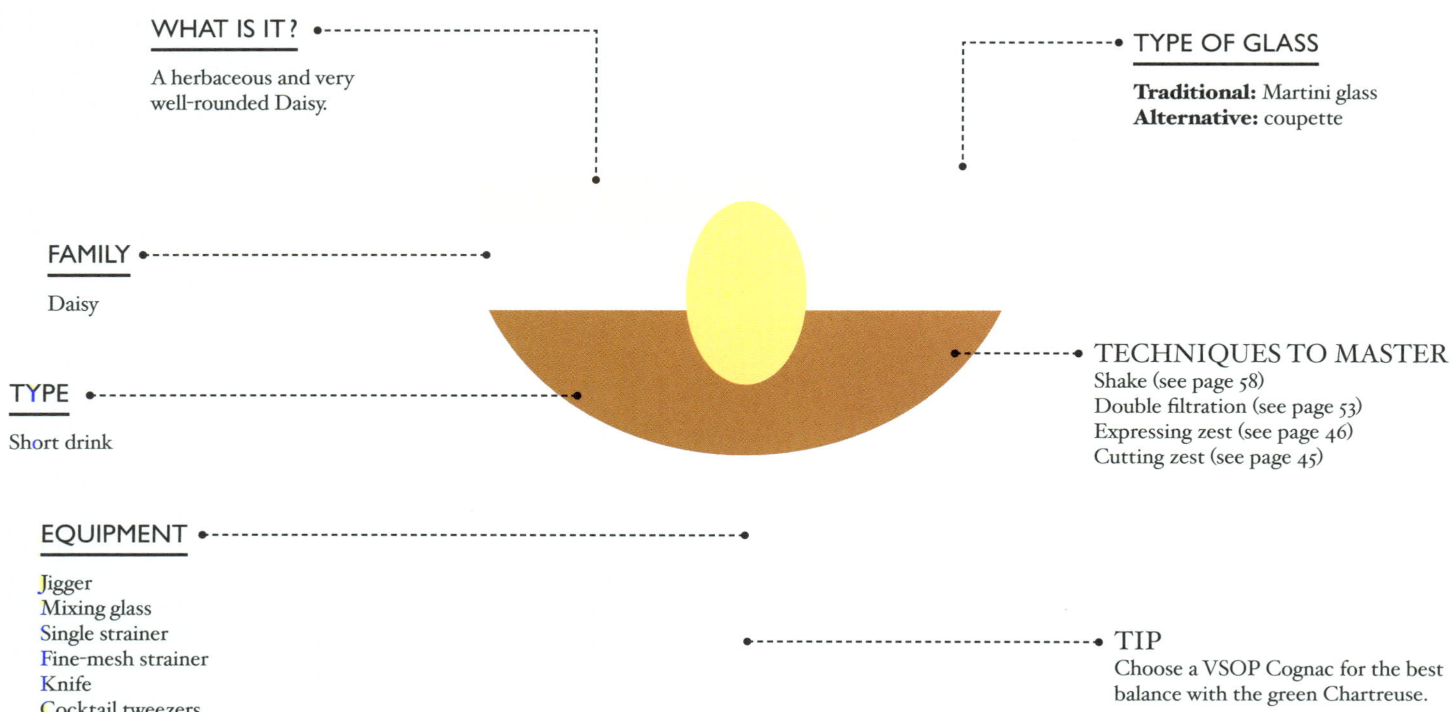

WHAT IS IT?

A herbaceous and very well-rounded Daisy.

TYPE OF GLASS

Traditional: Martini glass
Alternative: coupette

FAMILY

Daisy

TECHNIQUES TO MASTER

Shake (see page 58)
Double filtration (see page 53)
Expressing zest (see page 46)
Cutting zest (see page 45)

TYPE

Short drink

EQUIPMENT

Jigger
Mixing glass
Single strainer
Fine-mesh strainer
Knife
Cocktail tweezers

TIP

Choose a VSOP Cognac for the best balance with the green Chartreuse.

SERVES 1

50ml (1⅔oz) Cognac
25ml (⅔oz plus 1 tsp) green Chartreuse
20ml (⅔oz) lemon juice
10ml (2 tsp) simple syrup
1 dash of Angostura bitters

TO DECORATE

zest of 1 unwaxed lemon

1. Pour all the ingredients into the shaker.
2. Fill the larger part of the shaker to the brim with ice and shake (see page 58) vigorously for 10 seconds.
3. Double filter (see page 53) into the serving glass.
4. Express the zest (see page 46) in the centre of the glass, then rub it over the rim and stem of the glass.
5. Cut the zest (see page 45) and, using the cocktail tweezers, balance it on the rim of the glass.

JAPANESE

COCKTAIL

The Lowdown

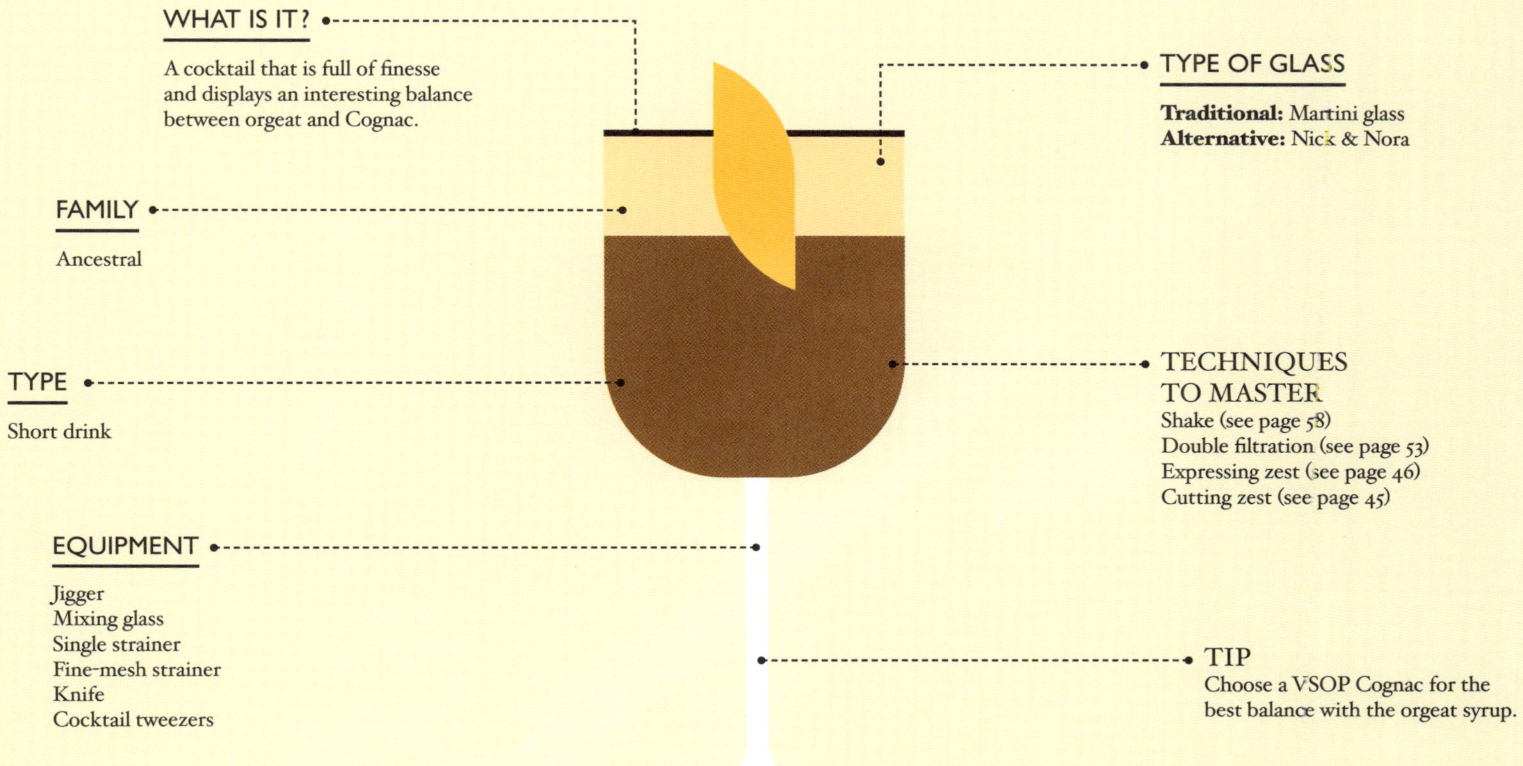

WHAT IS IT?

A cocktail that is full of finesse and displays an interesting balance between orgeat and Cognac.

FAMILY

Ancestral

TYPE

Short drink

EQUIPMENT

Jigger
Mixing glass
Single strainer
Fine-mesh strainer
Knife
Cocktail tweezers

TYPE OF GLASS

Traditional: Martini glass
Alternative: Nick & Nora

TECHNIQUES TO MASTER

Shake (see page 58)
Double filtration (see page 53)
Expressing zest (see page 46)
Cutting zest (see page 45)

TIP

Choose a VSOP Cognac for the best balance with the orgeat syrup.

SERVES 1

50ml ($1\frac{2}{3}$oz) Cognac
25ml ($\frac{2}{3}$oz plus 1 tsp) orgeat syrup
2 dashes of Angostura bitters

TO DECORATE

zest of 1 unwaxed lemon

1. Pour all the ingredients into the shaker.
2. Fill the larger part of the shaker to the brim with ice and shake (see page 58) vigorously for 10 seconds.
3. Double filter (see page 53) into the serving glass.
4. Express the zest (see page 46) in the centre of the glass, then rub it over the rim and stem of the glass.
5. Cut the zest (see page 45) and, using the cocktail tweezers, balance it on the rim of the glass.

TI' PUNCH

The Lowdown

WHAT IS IT?

Iconic in Réunion, French Guiana and the French-speaking Caribbean islands, this is one of the few cocktails served at room temperature.

TYPE

Short drink

TYPE OF GLASS

Traditional: single Old Fashioned
Alternative: goblet

EQUIPMENT

Jigger
Muddler
Bar spoon

TECHNIQUES TO MASTER

Muddling (see page 214)
Making a cocktail in a serving glass (see page 55)

VARIATION

Very enjoyable when made with honey syrup instead of simple syrup. Can be served over ice.

TIP

You can make the cocktail with white or amber rum, whichever you prefer. The type of sugar used will make all the different to the end result.
The cocktail is traditionally drunk at room temperature but add a few ice cubes if you wish.

SERVES 1

20ml (⅔oz) simple syrup
1 × 5ml bar spoon brown, muscovado or demerara sugar
3 unwaxed lime wedges (each ⅛ of a lime)
50ml (1⅔oz) rhum agricole

1. Pour the syrup into the serving glass and add the brown sugar.
2. Add the lime wedges.
3. Muddle (see page 214) until the lime flesh is reduced to a pulp.
4. Mix with the bar spoon until everything forms a kind of smooth paste.
5. Add the rum slowly and carefully, stirring until you have a smooth liquid.

DRY MARTINI

The Lowdown

WHAT IS IT?

A dry cocktail that has become iconic.

FAMILY

Martini

TYPE

Short drink

TYPE OF GLASS

Traditional: Martini glass
Alternative: mini-Martini glass and mini-carafe

EQUIPMENT

Jigger
Mixing glass
Bar spoon
Single strainer or Julep strainer
Knife
Cocktail tweezers
Cocktail stick (pick)

TECHNIQUES TO MASTER

Making a cocktail in a mixing glass (see page 56)
Single filtration (see page 52)
Expressing zest (see page 46)
Cutting zest (see page 45)

VARIATIONS

Extra dry: use 5ml (1 tsp) vermouth.
Wet Martini: use 45ml (1½oz) gin or vodka, 30ml (1oz) vermouth.
Marguerite: use 35ml (1oz plus 1 tsp) gin, 35ml (1oz plus 1 tsp) extra-dry vermouth, 1 dash of orange bitters.
Bronx: use 45ml (1½oz) gin, 15ml (½oz) red vermouth, 15ml (½oz) dry or extra-dry vermouth, 20ml (⅔oz) orange juice.

TIP

Choose a gin or vodka with a high enough level of alcohol (more than 45% ABV/90 proof) to produce a cocktail that fully expresses balance. Put the bottle of spirit in the freezer well before you need it and keep the vermouth in the refrigerator.

Discover

SERVES 1

60ml (2oz) gin or vodka
15ml (½oz) dry or extra-dry vermouth

TO DECORATE

zest of 1 unwaxed lemon or a green olive

1 Pour the ingredients into the mixing glass, which must be well chilled.

2 Add ice to come to about two fingers above the liquid.

3 Mix (see page 56) for 40 seconds.

4 Taste to check the dilution is perfect, mixing a little more if necessary.

5 Single filter (see page 52) into the serving glass.

6 Express the zest (see page 46) in the centre of the glass and then rub it over the rim. Cut the zest (see page 45) and place it over the rim of the glass using the cocktail tweezers. Alternatively, skewer the olive on the cocktail stick (pick) and place it in the glass.

DIRTY MARTINI

The Lowdown

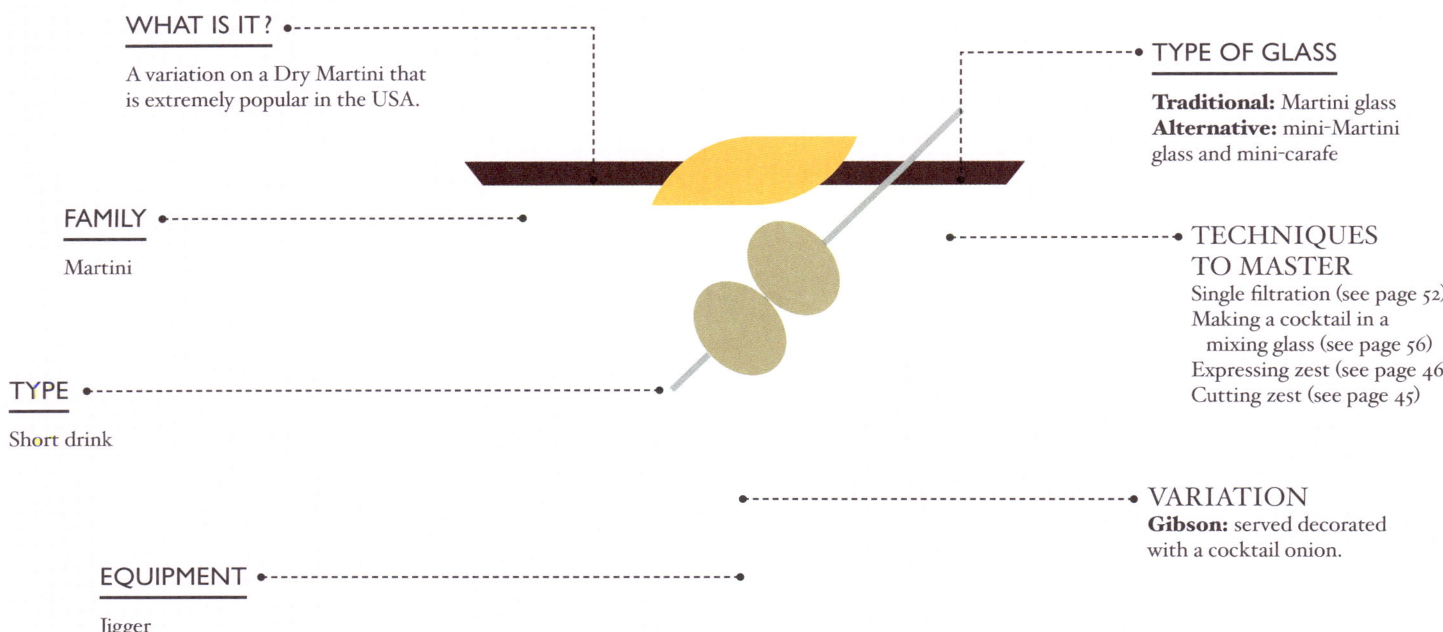

WHAT IS IT?

A variation on a Dry Martini that is extremely popular in the USA.

FAMILY

Martini

TYPE

Short drink

EQUIPMENT

Jigger
Mixing glass
Bar spoon
Single strainer or Julep strainer
Cocktail stick (pick)

TYPE OF GLASS

Traditional: Martini glass
Alternative: mini-Martini glass and mini-carafe

TECHNIQUES TO MASTER

Single filtration (see page 52)
Making a cocktail in a mixing glass (see page 56)
Expressing zest (see page 46)
Cutting zest (see page 45)

VARIATION

Gibson: served decorated with a cocktail onion.

TIP

See Dry Martini (see page 122). Choose large green olives. The quality of the brine they are pickled in and its salt content will determine how good the cocktail is.

SERVES 1

60ml (2oz) gin or vodka
15ml (½oz) dry or extra-dry vermouth
2 × 5ml bar spoons of brine from the olive jar (depending on its flavour and salt content)

TO DECORATE

zest of 1 unwaxed lemon
1 green olive

1. Pour the ingredients into the mixing glass, which must be well chilled.
2. Add ice to come to about two fingers above the liquid.
3. Mix (see page 56) for 40 seconds.
4. Taste to check the dilution is perfect, mixing a little more if necessary.
5. Single filter (see page 52) into the serving glass.
6. Express the zest (see page 46) in the centre of the glass and then rub it over the rim. Skewer the olive on the cocktail stick (pick) and place it in the glass.

APPLE MARTINI

The Lowdown

SERVES 1

60ml (2oz) vodka
20ml (⅔oz) apple liqueur

TO DECORATE

½ apple slice

1. Pour the ingredients into the shaker.
2. Fill the larger part of the shaker to the brim with ice and shake (see page 58) vigorously for 10 seconds.
3. Double filter (see page 53) into the serving glass.
4. Sit the half slice of apple (see page 44) on the rim of the glass, using the cocktail tweezers.

ESPRESSO

MARTINI

The Lowdown

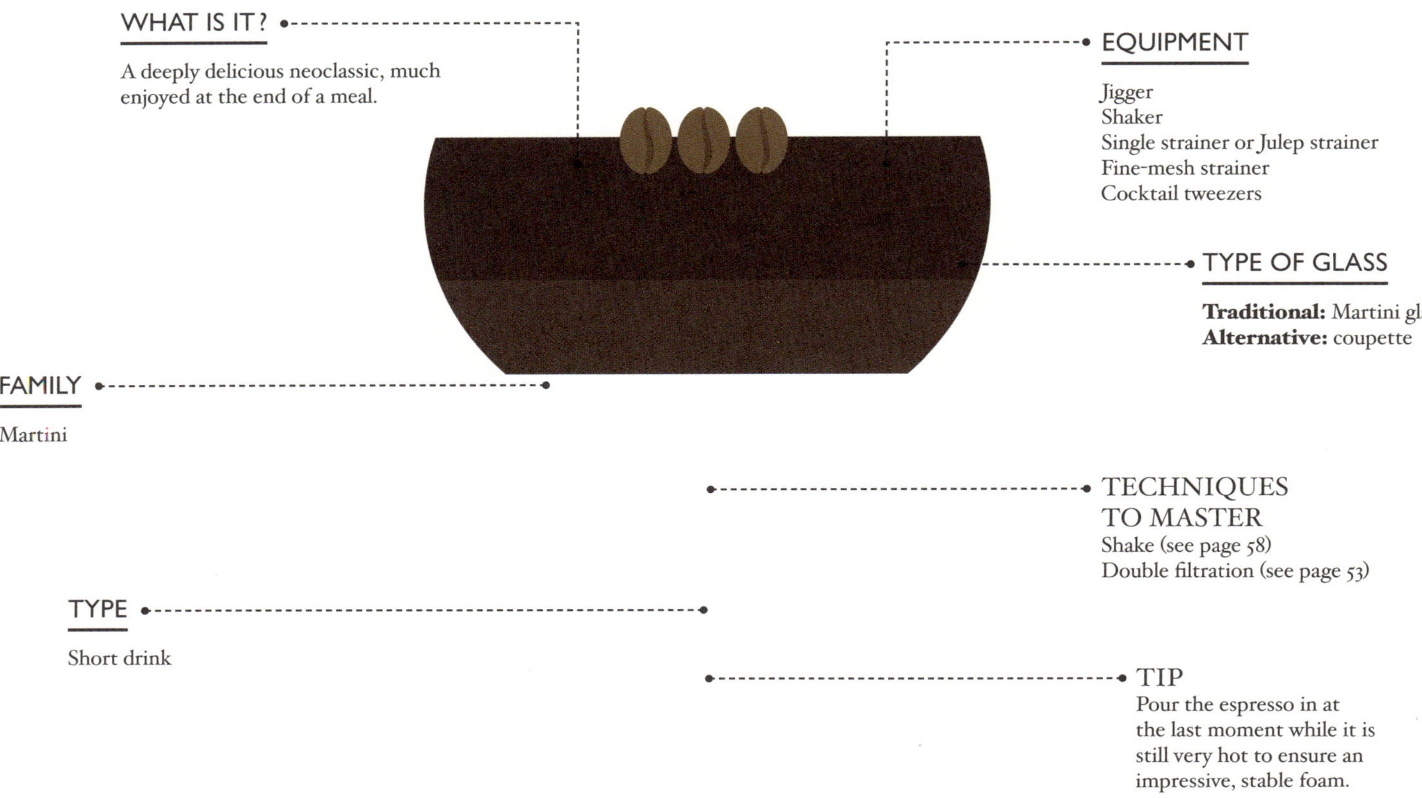

SERVES 1

50ml (1⅔oz) vodka
15ml (½oz) coffee liqueur
1 hot, freshly made espresso

TO DECORATE

3 coffee beans

1. Pour the ingredients, except the espresso, into the shaker.
2. Fill the larger part of the shaker to the brim with ice and pour the coffee over it. Shake (see page 58) vigorously for 10 seconds.
3. Double filter (see page 53) into the serving glass.
4. Using the cocktail tweezers, sit the 3 coffee beans on top, grouped together but not in the centre.

LEMON DROP

The Lowdown

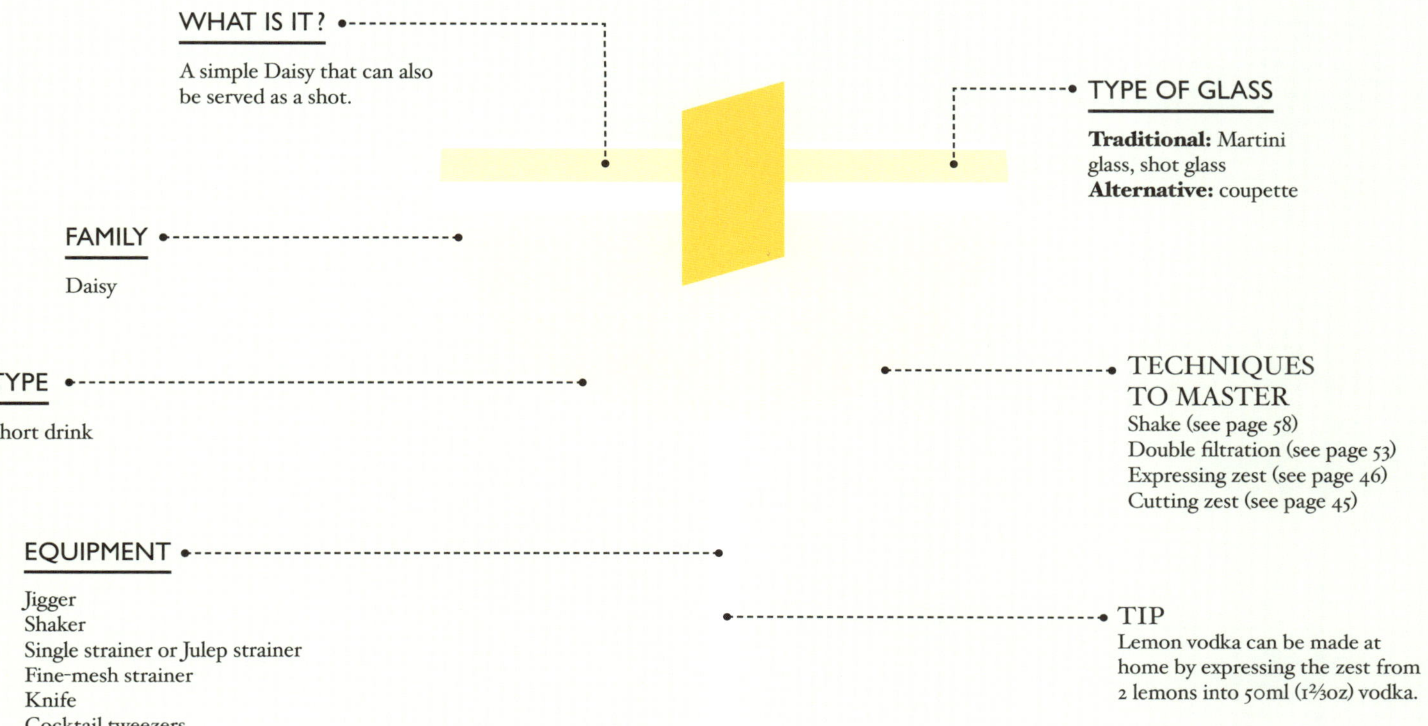

WHAT IS IT?

A simple Daisy that can also be served as a shot.

TYPE OF GLASS

Traditional: Martini glass, shot glass
Alternative: coupette

FAMILY

Daisy

TYPE

Short drink

TECHNIQUES TO MASTER

Shake (see page 58)
Double filtration (see page 53)
Expressing zest (see page 46)
Cutting zest (see page 45)

EQUIPMENT

Jigger
Shaker
Single strainer or Julep strainer
Fine-mesh strainer
Knife
Cocktail tweezers

TIP

Lemon vodka can be made at home by expressing the zest from 2 lemons into 50ml (1⅔oz) vodka.

SERVES 1

50ml (1⅔oz) lemon vodka (see 'Tip')
10ml (2 tsp) triple sec
15ml (½oz) lemon juice
1 × 5ml bar spoon simple syrup

TO DECORATE

zest of 1 unwaxed lemon

1. Pour all the ingredients into the shaker.
2. Fill the larger part of the shaker to the brim with ice. Shake (see page 58) vigorously for 10 seconds.
3. Double filter (see page 53) into the serving glass.
4. Express the zest (see page 46) in the centre of the glass and then rub it over the rim and stem.
5. Cut the zest (see page 45) and, using the cocktail tweezers, place it over the rim of the glass.

PORNSTAR

MARTINI

The Lowdown

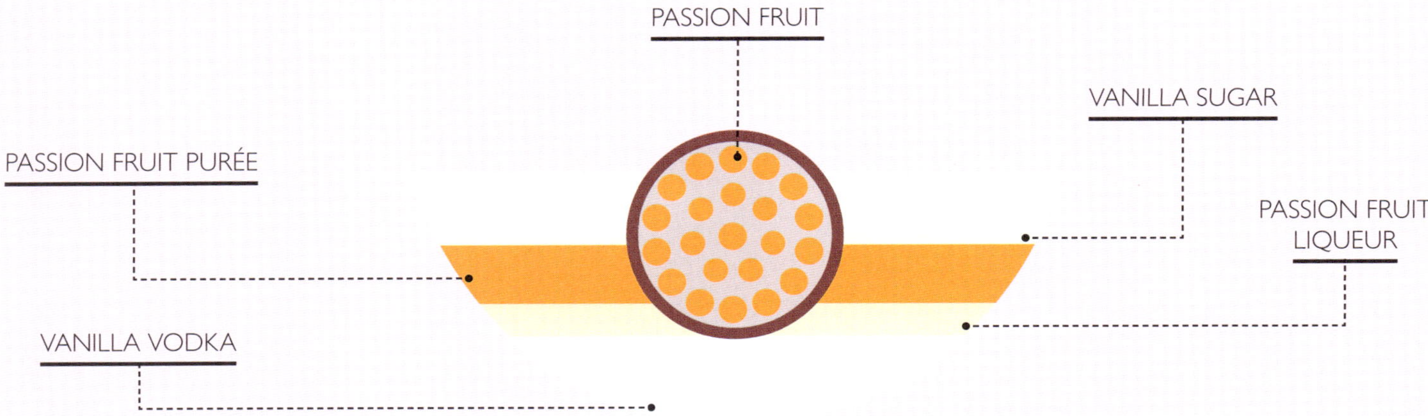

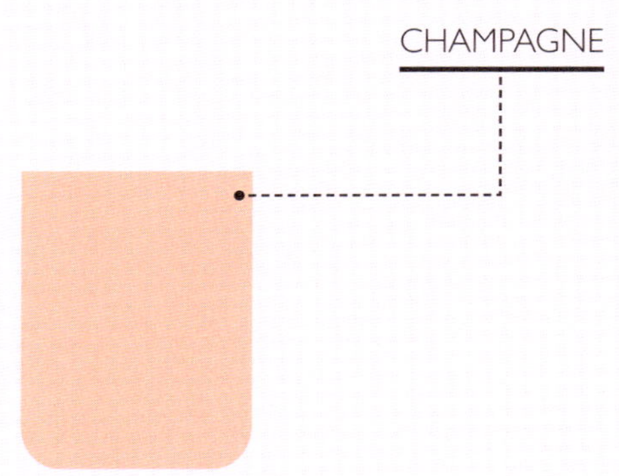

WHAT IS IT?

A Martini with a fruity flavour and an interesting way of being served.

FAMILY

Martini

TYPE

Short drink

TYPE OF GLASS

Traditional: Martini glass + shot glass
Alternative: coupette + shot glass

EQUIPMENT

Jigger
Bar spoon
Shaker
Single strainer or Julep strainer
Fine-mesh strainer
Cocktail tweezers

TECHNIQUES TO MASTER

Shake (see page 58)
Double filtration (see page 53)

VARIATIONS

The passion fruit purée can be replaced with the fruit from a whole passion fruit.

TIP

To make vanilla vodka at home, infuse half a vanilla pod (vanilla bean) in a 700ml (24oz) bottle of vodka for 8 hours.

Discover

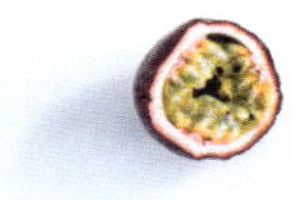

SERVES 1

45ml (1½oz) vanilla vodka (see 'Tip')
15ml (½oz) passion fruit liqueur
30ml (1oz) passion fruit purée
2 × 5ml bar spoons vanilla sugar
30ml (1oz) Champagne

TO DECORATE

½ passion fruit

1 Pour the ingredients, except the Champagne, into the shaker.

2 Fill the larger part of the shaker to the brim with ice and shake (see page 58) vigorously for 10 seconds.

3 Double filter (see page 53) into the serving glass.

4 Place the passion fruit half in the centre of the glass, cut-side up, using the cocktail tweezers.

5 Serve the Champagne alongside in the shot glass.

BREAKFAST

MARTINI

The Lowdown

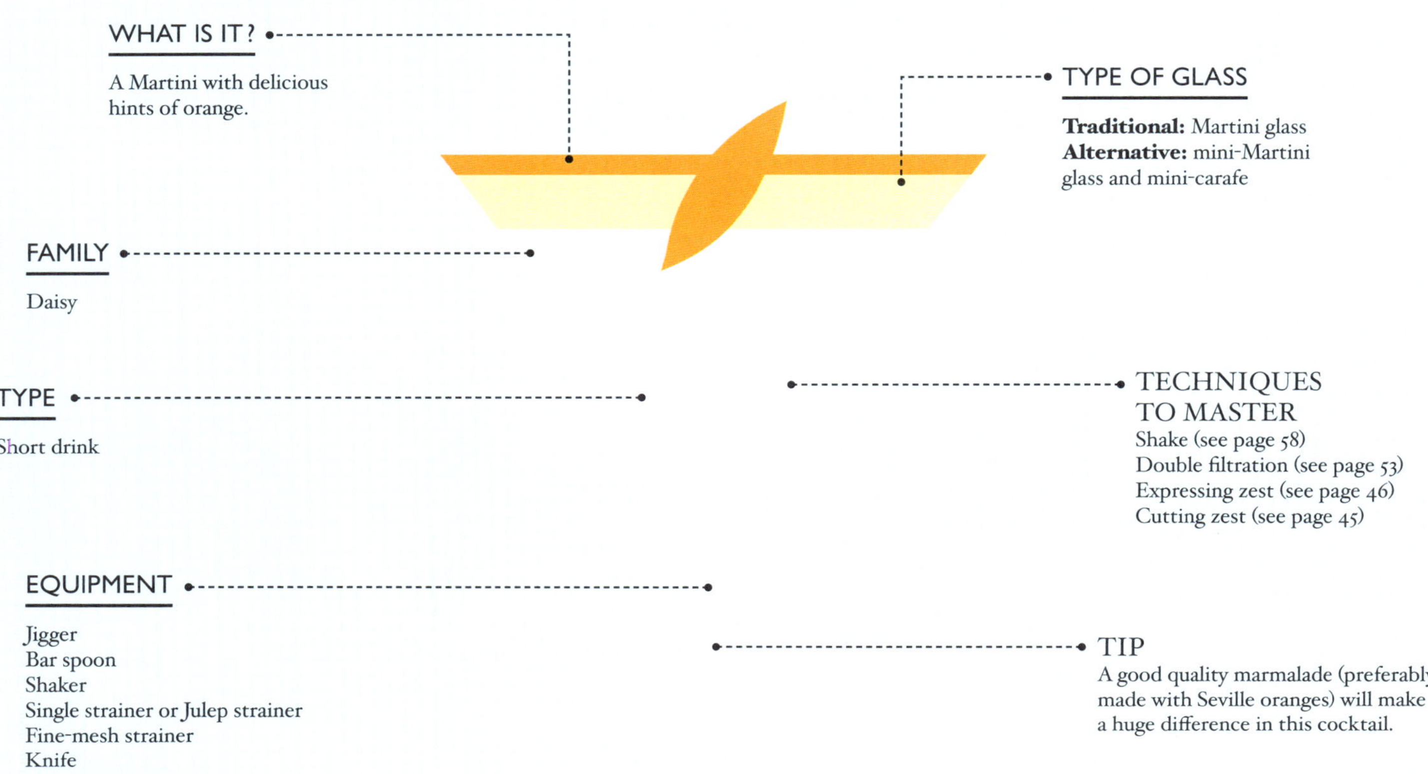

WHAT IS IT?

A Martini with delicious hints of orange.

TYPE OF GLASS

Traditional: Martini glass
Alternative: mini-Martini glass and mini-carafe

FAMILY

Daisy

TYPE

Short drink

TECHNIQUES TO MASTER

Shake (see page 58)
Double filtration (see page 53)
Expressing zest (see page 46)
Cutting zest (see page 45)

EQUIPMENT

Jigger
Bar spoon
Shaker
Single strainer or Julep strainer
Fine-mesh strainer
Knife
Cocktail tweezers

TIP

A good quality marmalade (preferably made with Seville oranges) will make a huge difference in this cocktail.

SERVES 1

15ml (½oz) lemon juice
1 × 5ml bar spoon orange marmalade
60ml (2oz) gin
15ml (½oz) triple sec

TO DECORATE

zest of 1 unwaxed orange

1 Pour the lemon juice into the bottom part of the shaker, add the marmalade and mix with the bar spoon until smooth.

2 Pour the rest of the ingredients into the shaker.

3 Fill the larger part of the shaker to the brim with ice and shake (see page 58) vigorously for 10 seconds.

4 Double filter (see page 53) into the serving glass.

5 Express the zest (see page 46) in the centre of the glass and then rub it over the rim and stem of the glass.

6 Cut the zest (see page 45) and, using the cocktail tweezers, place it over the rim of the glass.

FRENCH MARTINI

The Lowdown

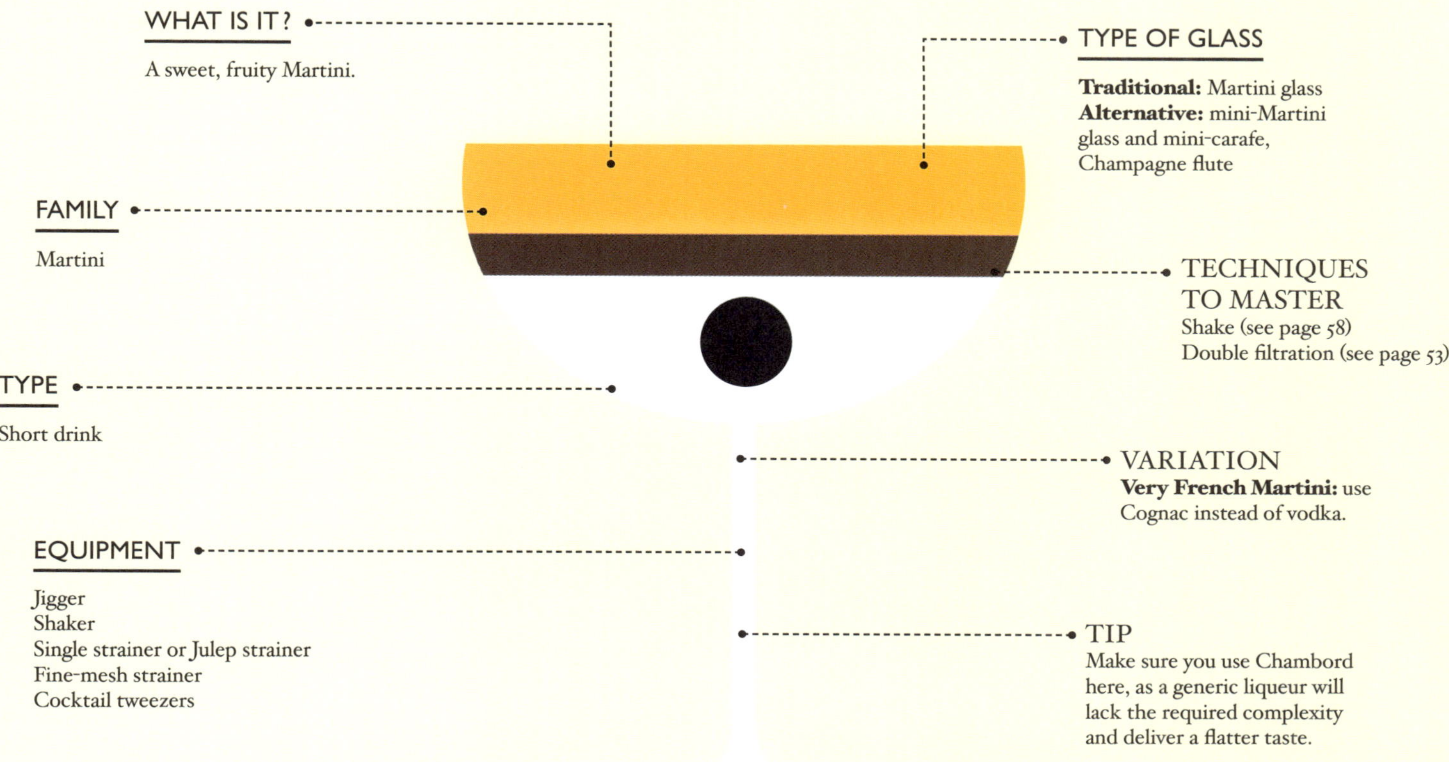

SERVES 1

60ml (2oz) vodka
15ml (½oz) black raspberry liqueur, such as Chambord
45ml (1½oz) pineapple juice

TO DECORATE

1 amarena cherry
wedge of fresh pineapple

1 Pour all the ingredients into the shaker.

2 Fill the larger part of the cocktail shaker with ice and shake (see page 58) vigorously for 10 seconds.

3 Double filter (see page 53) into the serving glass.

4 Using the cocktail tweezers, drop the cherry into the glass. Decorate the rim of the glass with a wedge of fresh pineapple.

GIMLET

The Lowdown

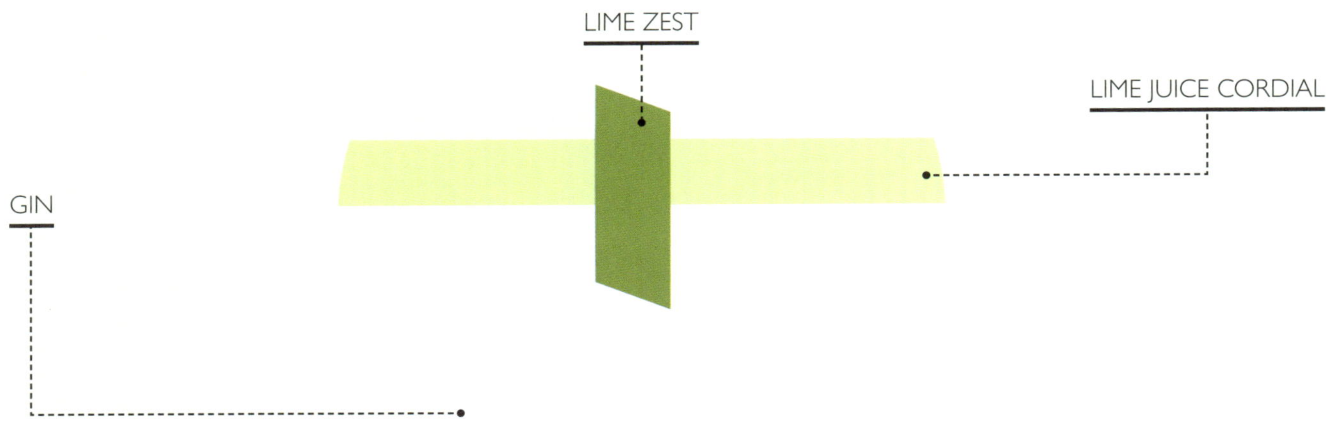

WHAT IS IT?

A tart cocktail made with just two ingredients.

FAMILY

Martini

TYPE

Short drink

TYPE OF GLASS

Traditional: Martini glass
Alternative: mini-Martini glass and mini-carafe

EQUIPMENT

Jigger
Shaker
Single strainer or Julep strainer
Fine-mesh strainer
Knife
Cocktail tweezers

TECHNIQUES TO MASTER

Shake (see page 58)
Double filtration (see page 53)
Expressing zest (see page 46)
Cutting zest (see page 45)

TIP

The aromatic profile of your chosen gin will determine the fragrance and taste of this cocktail.

Discover

SERVES 1

60ml (2oz) gin
15ml (½oz) lime juice cordial

TO DECORATE

zest of 1 unwaxed lime

1 Pour the ingredients into the shaker.

2 Fill the larger part of the shaker to the brim with ice and shake (see page 58) vigorously for 10 seconds.

3 Double filter (see page 53) into the serving glass.

4 Express the zest (see page 46) in the centre of the glass and then rub it over the rim and stem of the glass.

5 Cut the zest (see page 45) and, using the cocktail tweezers, curl the zest over the rim of the glass.

FLIP

The Lowdown

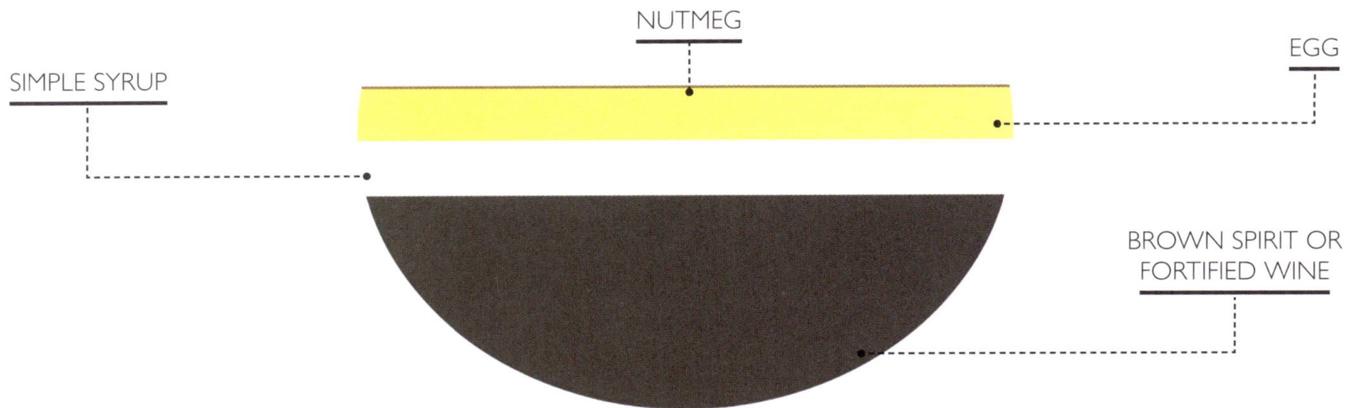

WHAT IS IT ?

A cocktail rich in flavour that works well with almost any brown spirit and fortified or mutated wine.

FAMILY

Flip

TYPE

Long drink

TYPE OF GLASS

Traditional: Martini glass
Alternative: coupette

EQUIPMENT

Jigger
Shaker
Single strainer
Fine-mesh strainer
Nutmeg grater

TECHNIQUES TO MASTER

Dry shake (see page 58)
Throwing (see page 59)
Shake (see page 58)
Double filtration (see page 53)

TIP

Break the yolk of the egg with a spoon before shaking.

SERVES 1

50ml (1⅔oz) brown spirit or fortified or sweet wine (such as port, cherry wine or madeira)
10ml (2 tsp) simple syrup
1 whole egg

TO DECORATE

freshly grated nutmeg

1 Pour the ingredients into the shaker.

2 Dry shake (see page 58) vigorously for 10 seconds without adding ice.

3 Throw (see page 59) the contents of the larger part of the shaker into the smaller part to incorporate air into the mixture.

4 Fill the larger part of the shaker to the brim with ice and shake (see page 58) vigorously for 10 seconds.

5 Double filter (see page 53) into the serving glass.

6 Finely grate nutmeg evenly over the top of the cocktail.

(SWEET) MANHATTAN

The Lowdown

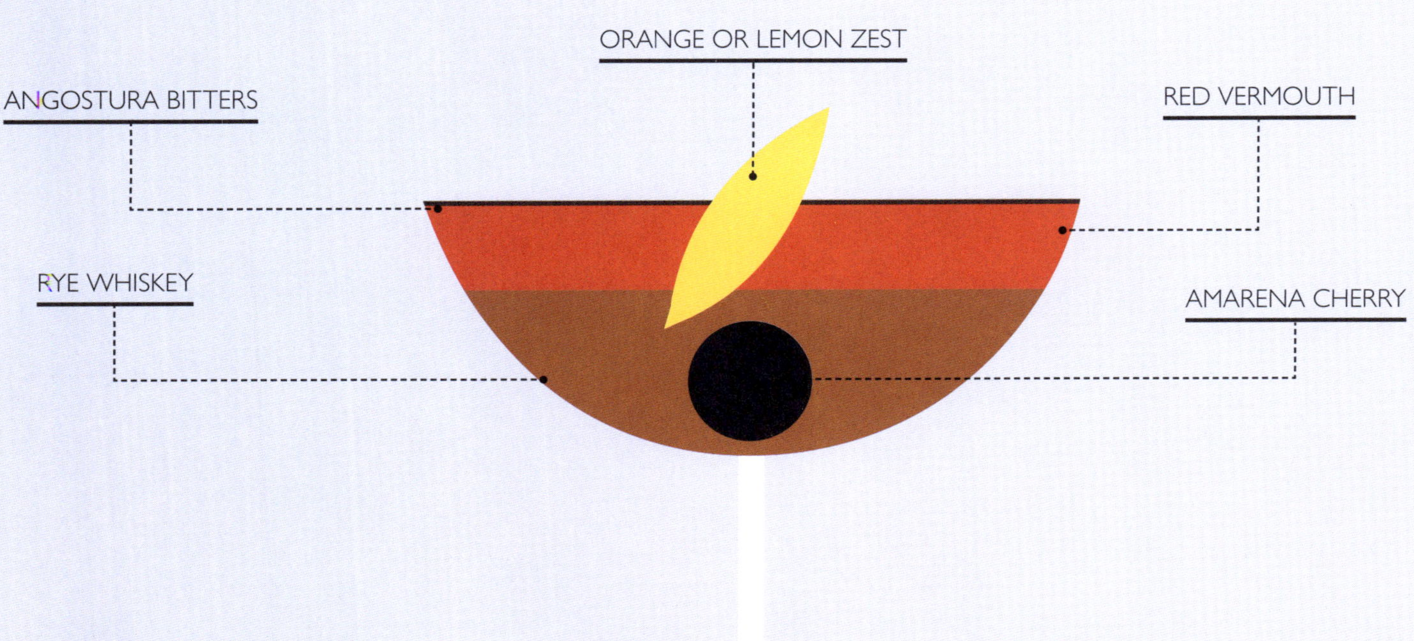

WHAT IS IT?

A skilful blend of vermouth and rye whiskey that owes its balance to the addition of Angostura bitters.

FAMILY

Spirit Forward

TYPE

Short drink

TYPE OF GLASS

Traditional: Martini glass

EQUIPMENT

Jigger
Mixing glass
Single strainer or Julep strainer
Knife
Cocktail tweezers
Bar spoon
Cocktail stick (pick)

TECHNIQUES TO MASTER

Making a cocktail in a mixing glass (see page 56)
Single filtration (see page 52)
Expressing zest (see page 46)
Cutting zest (see page 45)

VARIATIONS

Manhattan Perfect: make with 15ml (½oz) red vermouth and 15ml (½oz) extra-dry vermouth.
Manhattan Dry: make with 25ml (⅔oz plus 1 tsp) dry or extra-dry vermouth.
Harvard: replace the whiskey with Cognac.
Bobby Burns: see page 139.

TIP

Choose your decoration according to the particular ingredient you want to highlight when drinking the cocktail: orange zest will add smoothness, while lemon zest will bring out the spicy notes of the rye whiskey.

Discover

SERVES 1

50ml (1⅔oz) rye whiskey
25ml (⅔oz plus 1 tsp) red vermouth
2 dashes of Angostura bitters

TO DECORATE

zest of 1 unwaxed orange or lemon
1 amarena cherry

1 Pour all the ingredients into the mixing glass, which should be well chilled.

2 Add ice to come about two fingers above the liquid.

3 Mix (see page 56) for 40 seconds.

4 Taste to check the dilution is perfect, mixing a little more if necessary.

5 Single filter (see page 52) into the serving glass.

6 Express the zest (see page 46) in the centre of the glass and then rub it over the rim and stem of the glass.

7 Cut the zest (see page 45) and skewer on the cocktail stick (pick) with the cherry. Using the cocktail tweezers, place on the rim of the glass.

RED HOOK

The Lowdown

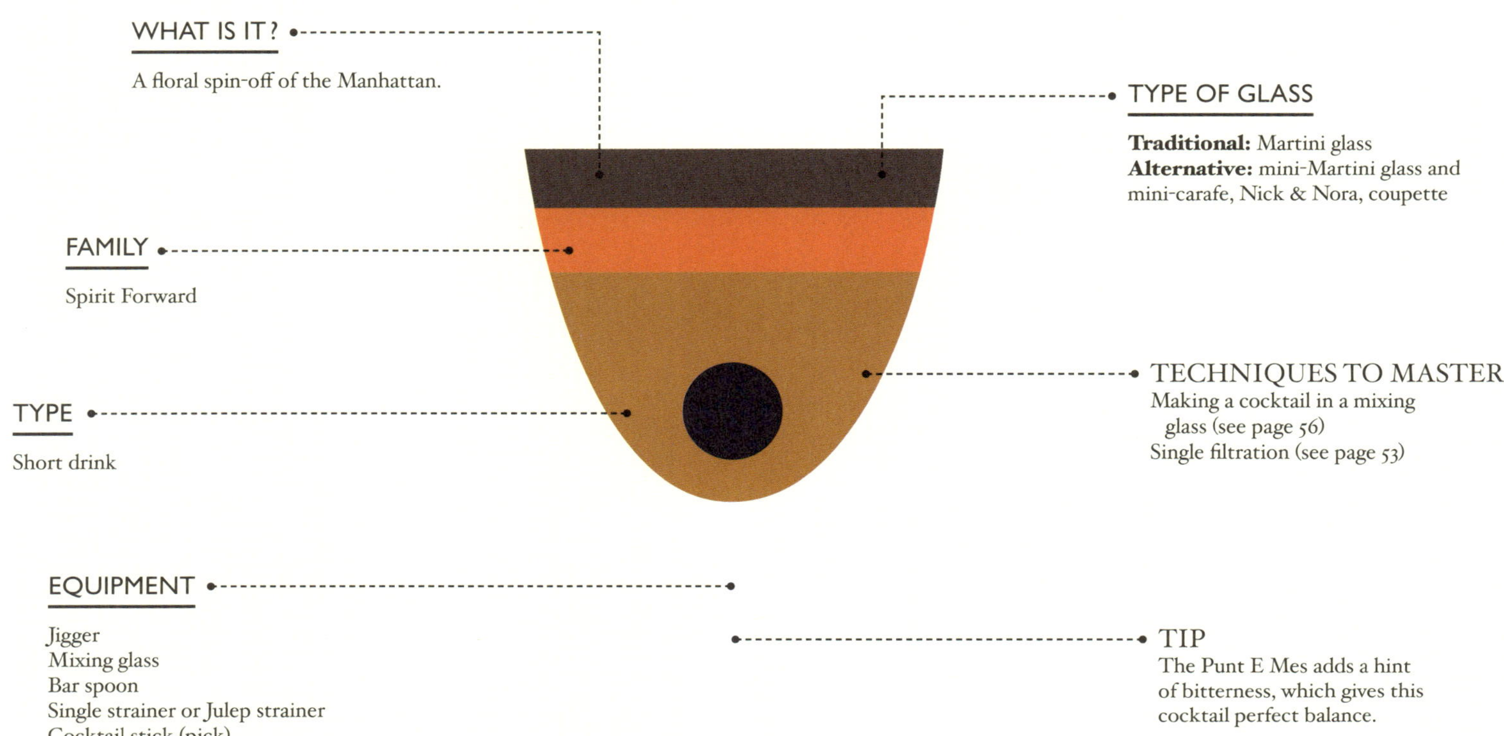

WHAT IS IT?

A floral spin-off of the Manhattan.

TYPE OF GLASS

Traditional: Martini glass
Alternative: mini-Martini glass and mini-carafe, Nick & Nora, coupette

FAMILY

Spirit Forward

TECHNIQUES TO MASTER

Making a cocktail in a mixing glass (see page 56)
Single filtration (see page 53)

TYPE

Short drink

EQUIPMENT

Jigger
Mixing glass
Bar spoon
Single strainer or Julep strainer
Cocktail stick (pick)

TIP

The Punt E Mes adds a hint of bitterness, which gives this cocktail perfect balance.

SERVES 1

50ml (1⅔oz) rye whiskey
15ml (½oz) Punt E Mes red vermouth
15ml (½oz) maraschino liqueur

TO DECORATE

1 amarena cherry

1. Pour all the ingredients into the mixing glass, which should be well chilled.
2. Add ice to come about two fingers above the liquid.
3. Mix (see page 56) for 40 seconds.
4. Taste to check the dilution is perfect, mixing a little more if necessary.
5. Single filter (see page 52) into the serving glass.
6. Skewer the cherry on the cocktail stick (pick) and place it in the cocktail with the stick (pick) resting against the side of the glass.

BOBBY BURNS

The Lowdown

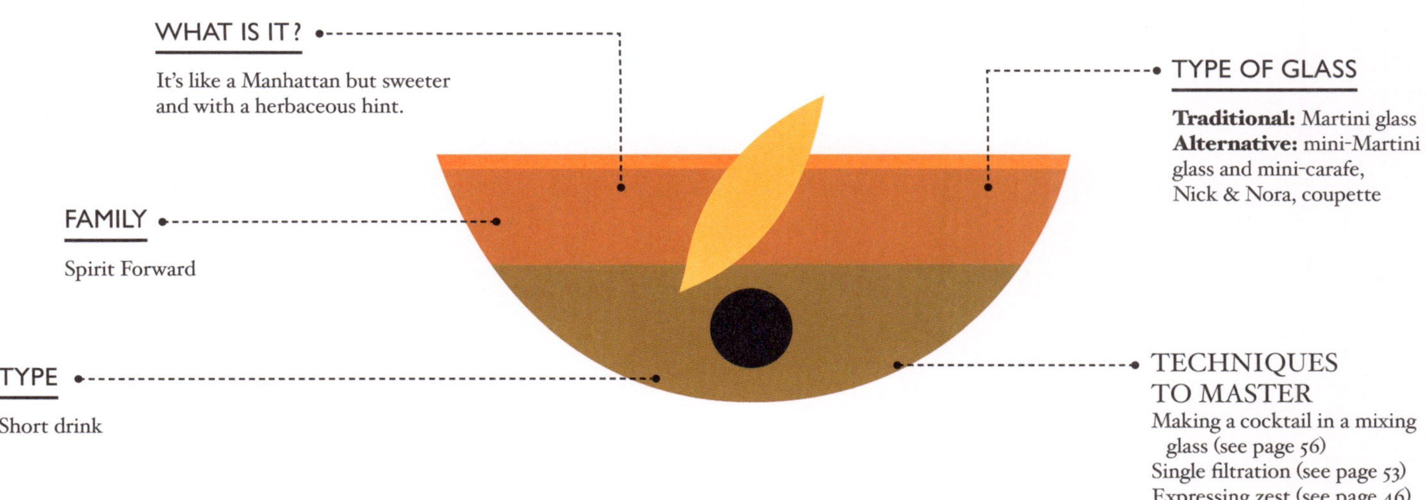

WHAT IS IT?

It's like a Manhattan but sweeter and with a herbaceous hint.

TYPE OF GLASS

Traditional: Martini glass
Alternative: mini-Martini glass and mini-carafe, Nick & Nora, coupette

FAMILY

Spirit Forward

TYPE

Short drink

TECHNIQUES TO MASTER

Making a cocktail in a mixing glass (see page 56)
Single filtration (see page 53)
Expressing zest (see page 46)

EQUIPMENT

Jigger
Mixing glass
Bar spoon
Single strainer or Julep strainer
Knife/peeler
Cocktail stick (pick)

TIP

A blended Scotch whisky rather than a single malt is preferable for making this cocktail, as it will integrate more smoothly into the drink's aromatic profile, which is already complex.

SERVES 1

45ml (1½oz) Scotch whisky
45ml (1½oz) red vermouth
7.5ml (1½ tsp) Bénédictine

TO DECORATE

zest of 1 unwaxed orange
1 amarena cherry

1. Pour all the ingredients into the mixing glass, which should be well chilled.
2. Add ice to come about two fingers above the liquid.
3. Mix (see page 56) for 40 seconds.
4. Taste to check the dilution is perfect, mixing a little more if necessary.
5. Single filter (see page 52) into the serving glass.
6. Express the zest (see page 46) in the centre of the glass and then rub it over the rim and stem of the glass.
7. Skewer the cherry on the cocktail stick (pick) and place it in the cocktail with the stick (pick) resting against the rim of the glass.

BIJOU

The Lowdown

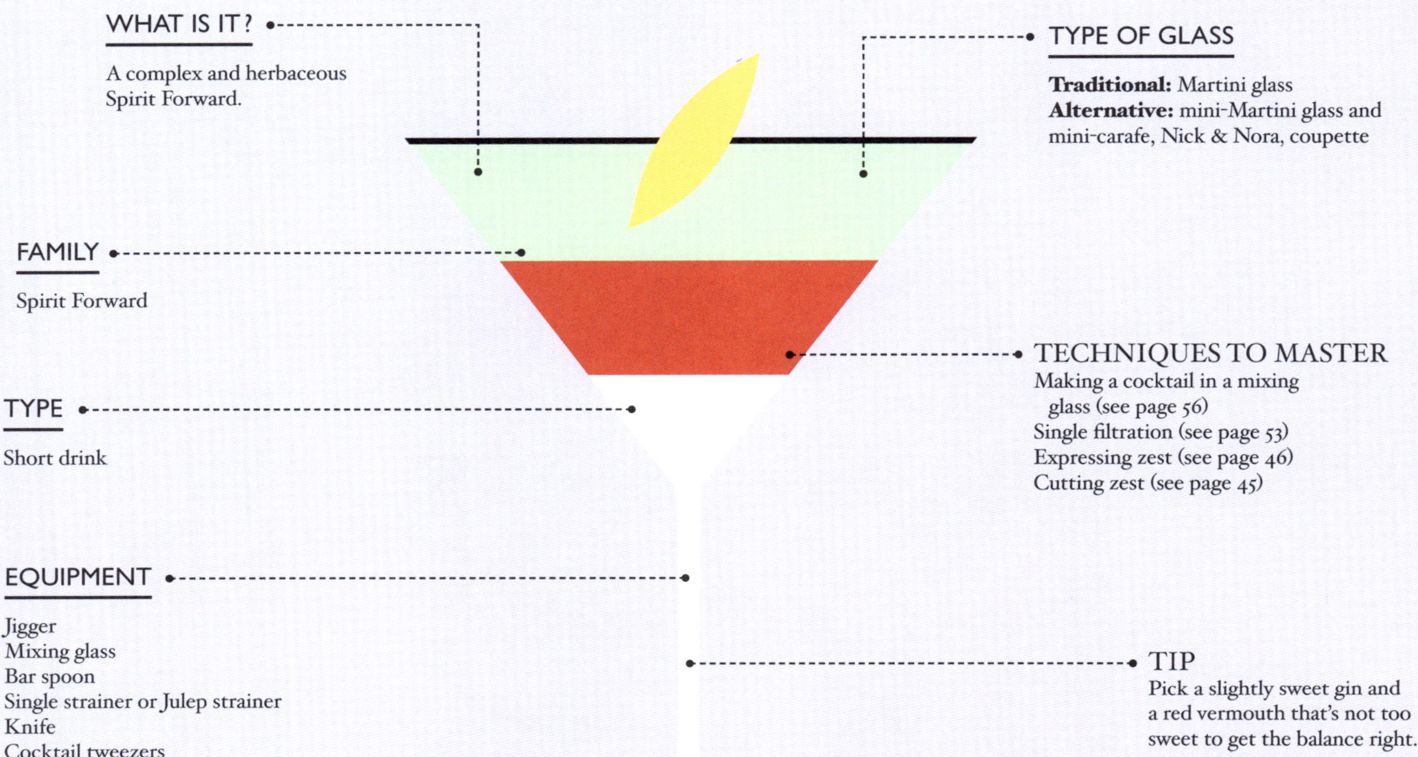

WHAT IS IT?

A complex and herbaceous Spirit Forward.

TYPE OF GLASS

Traditional: Martini glass
Alternative: mini-Martini glass and mini-carafe, Nick & Nora, coupette

FAMILY

Spirit Forward

TECHNIQUES TO MASTER

Making a cocktail in a mixing glass (see page 56)
Single filtration (see page 53)
Expressing zest (see page 46)
Cutting zest (see page 45)

TYPE

Short drink

EQUIPMENT

Jigger
Mixing glass
Bar spoon
Single strainer or Julep strainer
Knife
Cocktail tweezers

TIP

Pick a slightly sweet gin and a red vermouth that's not too sweet to get the balance right.

SERVES 1

25ml (⅔oz plus 1 tsp) gin
25ml (⅔oz plus 1 tsp) red vermouth
25ml (⅔oz plus 1 tsp) green Chartreuse
2 dashes of Angostura bitters

TO DECORATE

zest of 1 unwaxed lemon

1 Pour all the ingredients into the mixing glass, which should be well chilled.

2 Add ice to come about two fingers above the liquid.

3 Mix (see page 56) for 40 seconds.

4 Taste to check the dilution is perfect, mixing a little more if necessary.

5 Single filter (see page 52) into the serving glass.

6 Express the zest (see page 46) in the centre of the glass and then rub it over the rim and stem of the glass.

7 Cut the zest (see page 45) and, using the cocktail tweezers, sit it on the rim of the glass.

INCOME TAX

The Lowdown

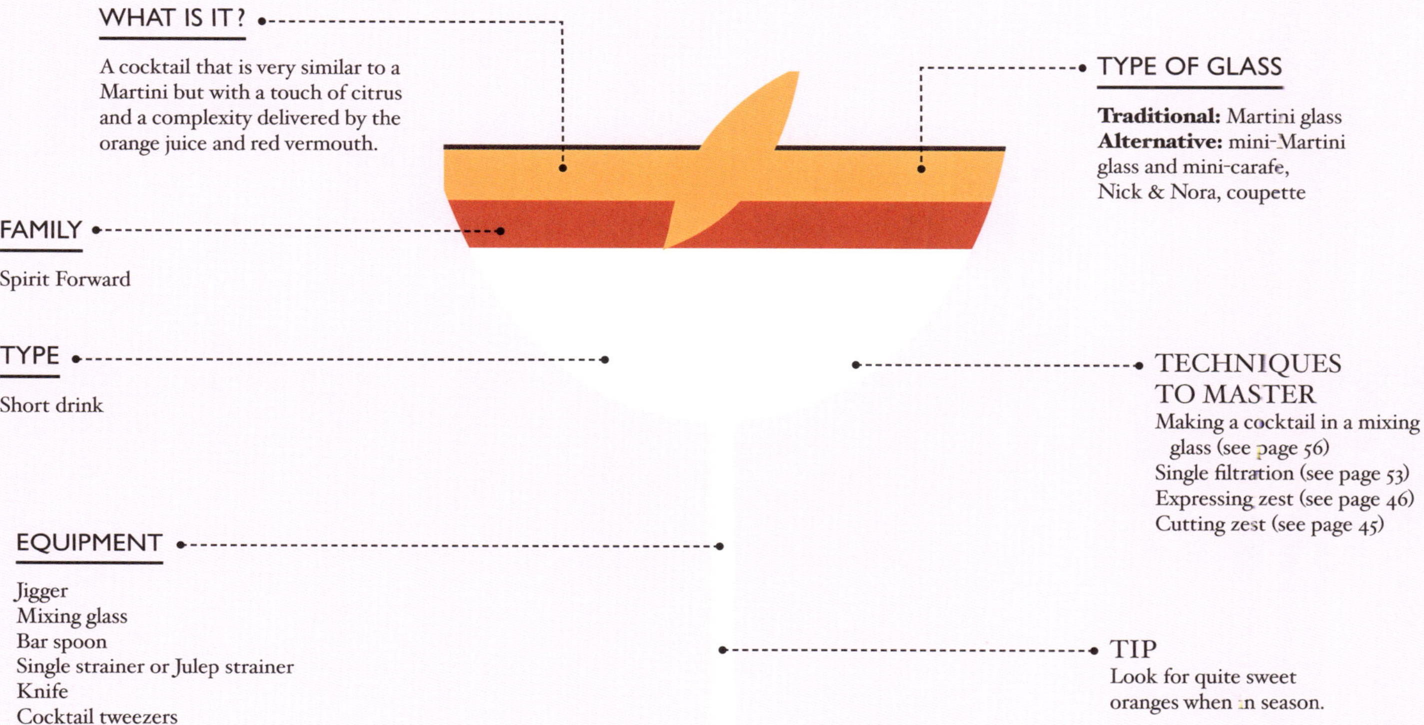

WHAT IS IT?

A cocktail that is very similar to a Martini but with a touch of citrus and a complexity delivered by the orange juice and red vermouth.

TYPE OF GLASS

Traditional: Martini glass
Alternative: mini-Martini glass and mini-carafe, Nick & Nora, coupette

FAMILY

Spirit Forward

TYPE

Short drink

TECHNIQUES TO MASTER

Making a cocktail in a mixing glass (see page 56)
Single filtration (see page 53)
Expressing zest (see page 46)
Cutting zest (see page 45)

EQUIPMENT

Jigger
Mixing glass
Bar spoon
Single strainer or Julep strainer
Knife
Cocktail tweezers

TIP

Look for quite sweet oranges when in season.

SERVES 1

40ml (1⅓oz) gin
20ml (⅔oz) dry or extra-dry vermouth
20ml (⅔oz) red vermouth
20ml (⅔oz) orange juice
2 dashes of orange bitters

TO DECORATE

zest of 1 unwaxed orange

1. Pour all the ingredients into the mixing glass, which should be well chilled.
2. Add ice to come about two fingers above the liquid.
3. Mix (see page 56) for 40 seconds.
4. Taste to check the dilution is perfect, mixing a little more if necessary.
5. Single filter (see page 52) into the serving glass.
6. Express the zest (see page 46) in the centre of the glass and then rub it over the rim and stem of the glass.
7. Cut the zest (see page 45) and, using the cocktail tweezers, sit it on the rim of the glass.

ALASKA

The Lowdown

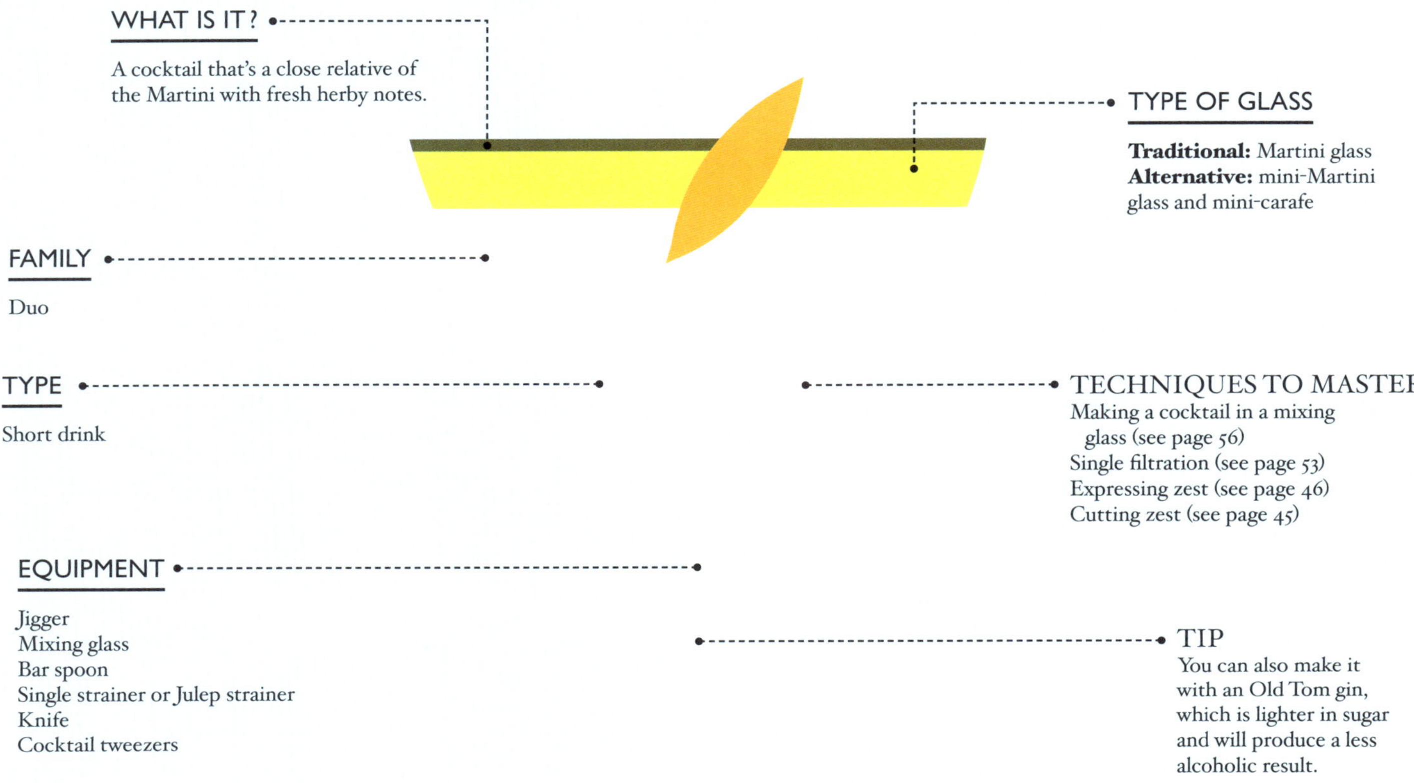

WHAT IS IT?

A cocktail that's a close relative of the Martini with fresh herby notes.

TYPE OF GLASS

Traditional: Martini glass
Alternative: mini-Martini glass and mini-carafe

FAMILY

Duo

TYPE

Short drink

TECHNIQUES TO MASTER

Making a cocktail in a mixing glass (see page 56)
Single filtration (see page 53)
Expressing zest (see page 46)
Cutting zest (see page 45)

EQUIPMENT

Jigger
Mixing glass
Bar spoon
Single strainer or Julep strainer
Knife
Cocktail tweezers

TIP

You can also make it with an Old Tom gin, which is lighter in sugar and will produce a less alcoholic result.

SERVES 1

60ml (2oz) gin
15ml (½oz) yellow Chartreuse
1 dash of orange bitters

TO DECORATE

zest of 1 unwaxed orange

1. Pour all the ingredients into the mixing glass, which should be well chilled.
2. Add ice to come about two fingers above the liquid.
3. Mix (see page 56) for 40 seconds.
4. Taste to check the dilution is perfect, mixing a little more if necessary.
5. Single filter (see page 52) into the serving glass.
6. Express the zest (see page 46) in the centre of the glass and then rub it over the rim and stem of the glass.
7. Cut the zest (see page 45), curl it, and, using the cocktail tweezers, place it over the rim of the glass.

EL PRESIDENTE

The Lowdown

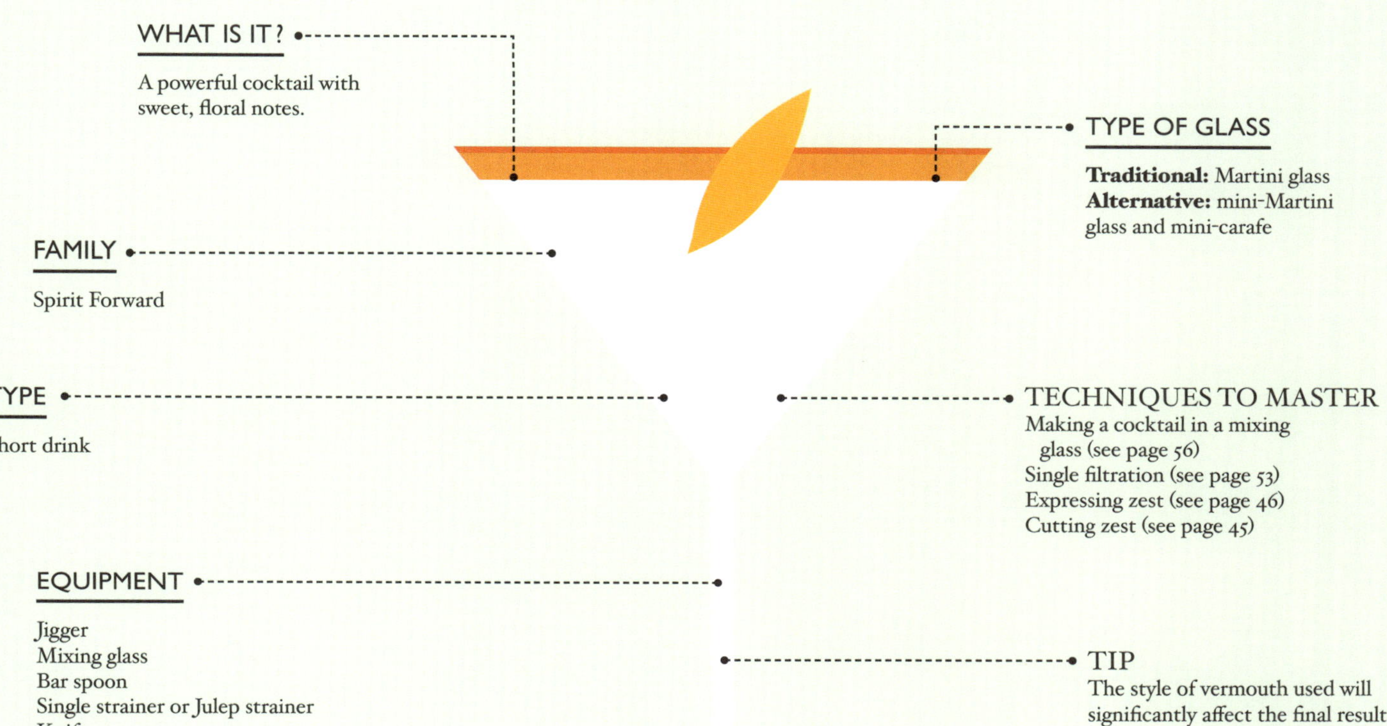

WHAT IS IT?

A powerful cocktail with sweet, floral notes.

TYPE OF GLASS

Traditional: Martini glass
Alternative: mini-Martini glass and mini-carafe

FAMILY

Spirit Forward

TYPE

Short drink

TECHNIQUES TO MASTER

Making a cocktail in a mixing glass (see page 56)
Single filtration (see page 53)
Expressing zest (see page 46)
Cutting zest (see page 45)

EQUIPMENT

Jigger
Mixing glass
Bar spoon
Single strainer or Julep strainer
Knife
Cocktail tweezers

TIP

The style of vermouth used will significantly affect the final result.

SERVES 1

45ml (1½oz) white Cuban rum
45ml (1½oz) white vermouth
7.5ml (1½ tsp) dry Curaçao
1 × 5ml bar spoon grenadine

TO DECORATE

zest of 1 unwaxed orange

1. Pour all the ingredients into the mixing glass, which should be well chilled.
2. Add ice to come about two fingers above the liquid.
3. Mix (see page 56) for 40 seconds.
4. Taste to check the dilution is perfect, mixing a little more if necessary.
5. Single filter (see page 52) into the serving glass.
6. Express the zest (see page 46) in the centre of the glass and then rub it over the rim and stem of the glass.
7. Cut the zest (see page 45) and, using the cocktail tweezers, sit it over the rim of the glass.

ROSITA

The Lowdown

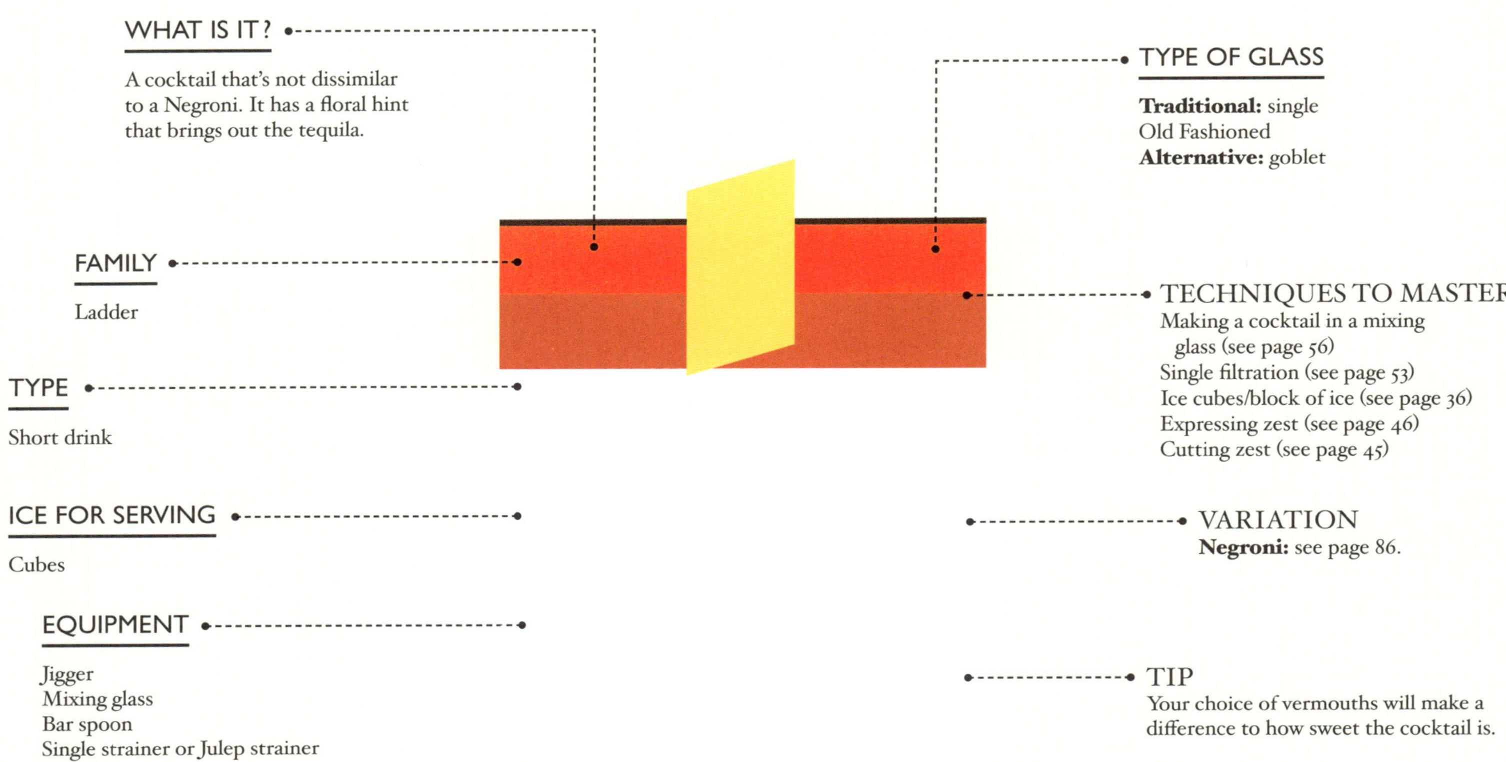

WHAT IS IT?

A cocktail that's not dissimilar to a Negroni. It has a floral hint that brings out the tequila.

FAMILY

Ladder

TYPE

Short drink

ICE FOR SERVING

Cubes

EQUIPMENT

Jigger
Mixing glass
Bar spoon
Single strainer or Julep strainer
Knife
Cocktail tweezers

TYPE OF GLASS

Traditional: single Old Fashioned
Alternative: goblet

TECHNIQUES TO MASTER

Making a cocktail in a mixing glass (see page 56)
Single filtration (see page 53)
Ice cubes/block of ice (see page 36)
Expressing zest (see page 46)
Cutting zest (see page 45)

VARIATION

Negroni: see page 86.

TIP

Your choice of vermouths will make a difference to how sweet the cocktail is.

SERVES 1

45ml (1½oz) silver or joven tequila
15ml (½oz) dry or extra-dry vermouth
15ml (½oz) red vermouth
15ml (½oz) Campari
1 dash of Angostura bitters

TO DECORATE

zest of 1 unwaxed lemon

1. Pour all the ingredients into the mixing glass, which should be well chilled.
2. Add ice to come about two fingers above the liquid.
3. Mix (see page 56) for 40 seconds.
4. Taste to check the dilution is perfect, mixing a little more if necessary.
5. Fill the serving glass with ice cubes or add a block of ice (see page 36) and single filter (see page 52) the mixture into it.
6. Express the zest (see page 46) in the centre of the glass and then rub it over the rim and stem of the glass.
7. Cut the zest (see page 45) and, using the cocktail tweezers, place it over the rim of the glass.

WIDOW'S KISS

The Lowdown

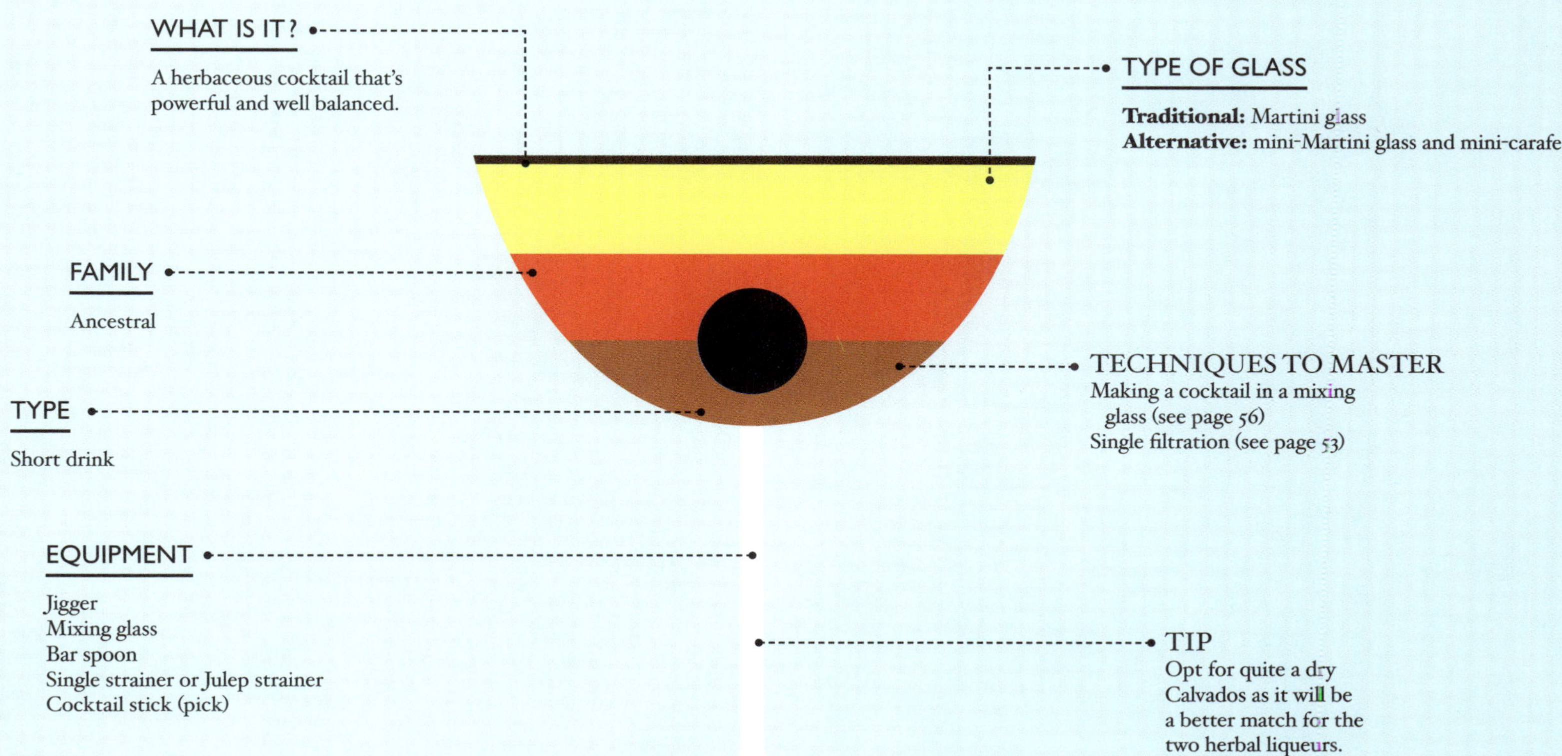

WHAT IS IT?

A herbaceous cocktail that's powerful and well balanced.

TYPE OF GLASS

Traditional: Martini glass
Alternative: mini-Martini glass and mini-carafe

FAMILY

Ancestral

TECHNIQUES TO MASTER

Making a cocktail in a mixing glass (see page 56)
Single filtration (see page 53)

TYPE

Short drink

EQUIPMENT

Jigger
Mixing glass
Bar spoon
Single strainer or Julep strainer
Cocktail stick (pick)

TIP

Opt for quite a dry Calvados as it will be a better match for the two herbal liqueurs.

SERVES 1

25ml (⅔oz plus 1 tsp) Calvados
25ml (⅔oz plus 1 tsp) Bénédictine
25ml (⅔oz plus 1 tsp) green Chartreuse
2 dashes of Angostura bitters

TO DECORATE

1 amarena cherry

1 Pour all the ingredients into the mixing glass, which should be well chilled.

2 Add ice to come about two fingers above the liquid.

3 Mix (see page 56) for 40 seconds.

4 Taste to check the dilution is perfect, mixing a little more if necessary.

5 Single filter (see page 52) into the serving glass.

6 Skewer the cherry onto the cocktail stick (pick) and place in the glass with the cocktail stick (pick) resting on the rim.

BOULEVARDIER

The Lowdown

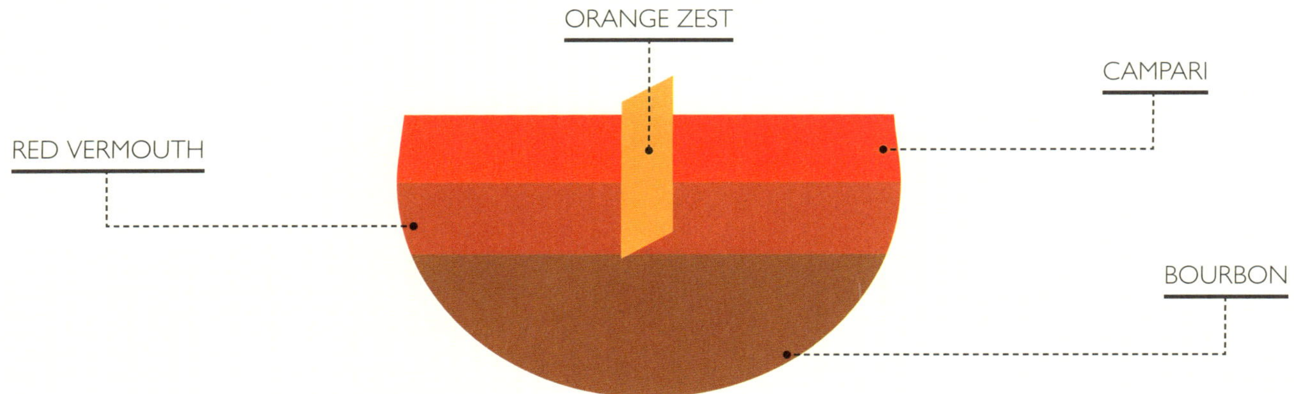

WHAT IS IT?

A twist on the Negroni but with more body thanks to the bourbon.

FAMILY

Ladder

TYPE

Short drink

TYPE OF GLASS

Traditional: Martini glass
Alternative: mini-Martini glass and mini-carafe

EQUIPMENT

Jigger
Mixing glass
Bar spoon
Single strainer or Julep strainer
Knife
Cocktail tweezers

TECHNIQUES TO MASTER

Making a cocktail in a mixing glass (see page 56)
Single filtration (see page 52)
Expressing zest (see page 46)
Cutting zest (see page 45)

VARIATIONS

Negroni: see page 86.

TIP

An equal measure of bourbon can also be used for a sweeter, less powerful cocktail.

Discover

SERVES 1

40ml (1⅓oz) bourbon
25ml (⅔oz plus 1 tsp) red vermouth
25ml (⅔oz plus 1 tsp) Campari

TO DECORATE

zest of 1 unwaxed orange or lemon

1. Pour all the ingredients into the mixing glass, which should be well chilled.
2. Add ice to come about two fingers above the liquid.
3. Mix (see page 56) for 40 seconds.
4. Taste to check the dilution is perfect, mixing a little more if necessary.
5. Single filter (see page 52) into the serving glass.
6. Express the zest (see page 46) in the centre of the glass and then rub it over the rim and stem of the glass.
7. Cut the zest (see page 45) and, using the cocktail tweezers, place it on the rim of the glass.

ROB ROY

The Lowdown

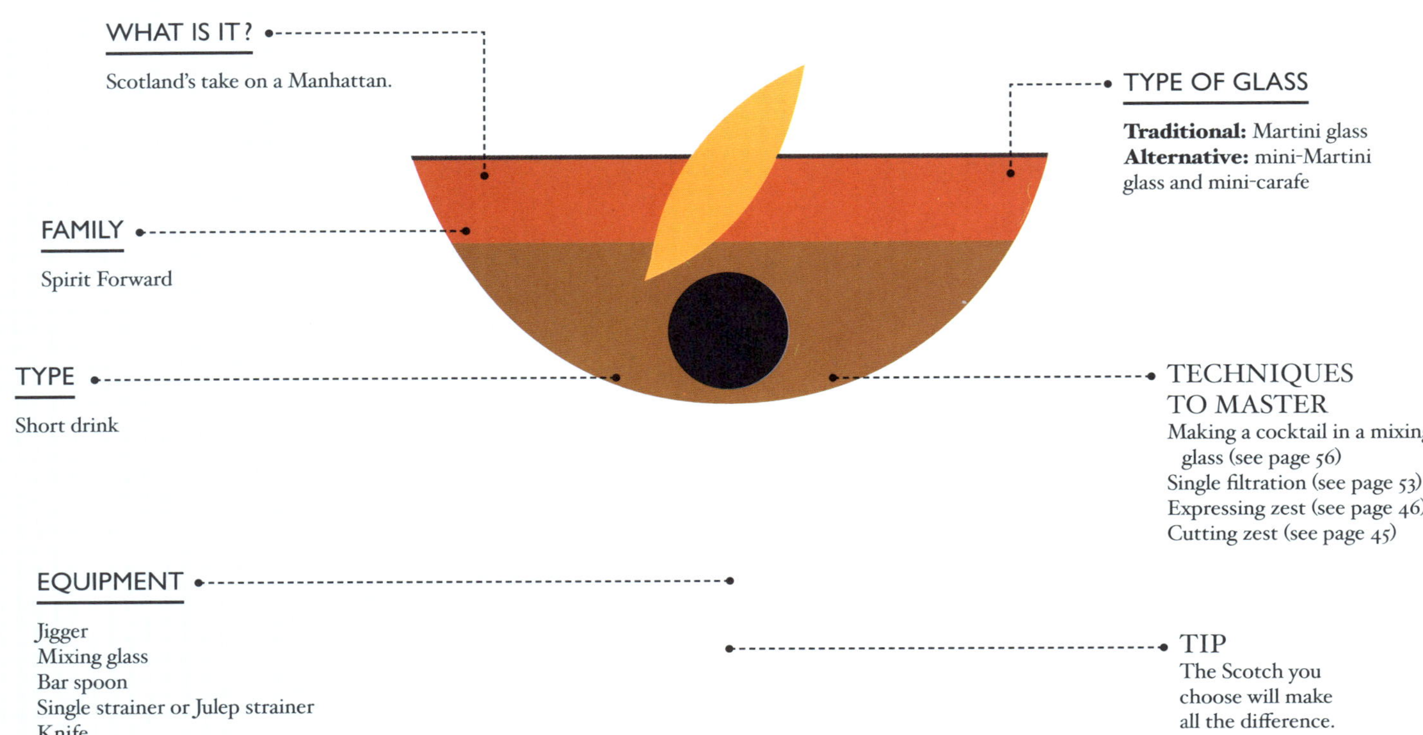

WHAT IS IT?
Scotland's take on a Manhattan.

TYPE OF GLASS
Traditional: Martini glass
Alternative: mini-Martini glass and mini-carafe

FAMILY
Spirit Forward

TYPE
Short drink

TECHNIQUES TO MASTER
Making a cocktail in a mixing glass (see page 56)
Single filtration (see page 53)
Expressing zest (see page 46)
Cutting zest (see page 45)

EQUIPMENT
Jigger
Mixing glass
Bar spoon
Single strainer or Julep strainer
Knife
Cocktail tweezers
Cocktail stick (pick)

TIP
The Scotch you choose will make all the difference.

SERVES 1

50ml (1⅔oz) Scotch whisky
25ml (⅔oz plus 1 tsp) red vermouth
2 dashes of Angostura bitters

TO DECORATE

zest of 1 unwaxed orange
1 amarena cherry

1 Pour all the ingredients into the mixing glass, which should be well chilled.

2 Add ice to come about two fingers above the liquid.

3 Mix (see page 56) for 40 seconds.

4 Taste to check the dilution is perfect, mixing a little more if necessary.

5 Single filter (see page 52) into the serving glass.

6 Express the zest (see page 46) in the centre of the glass and then rub it over the rim and stem of the glass.

7 Cut the zest (see page 45) and, using the cocktail tweezers, sit it on the rim of the glass. Skewer the cherry onto the cocktail stick (pick) and place in the glass with the cocktail stick (pick) resting against the rim.

MARTINEZ

The Lowdown

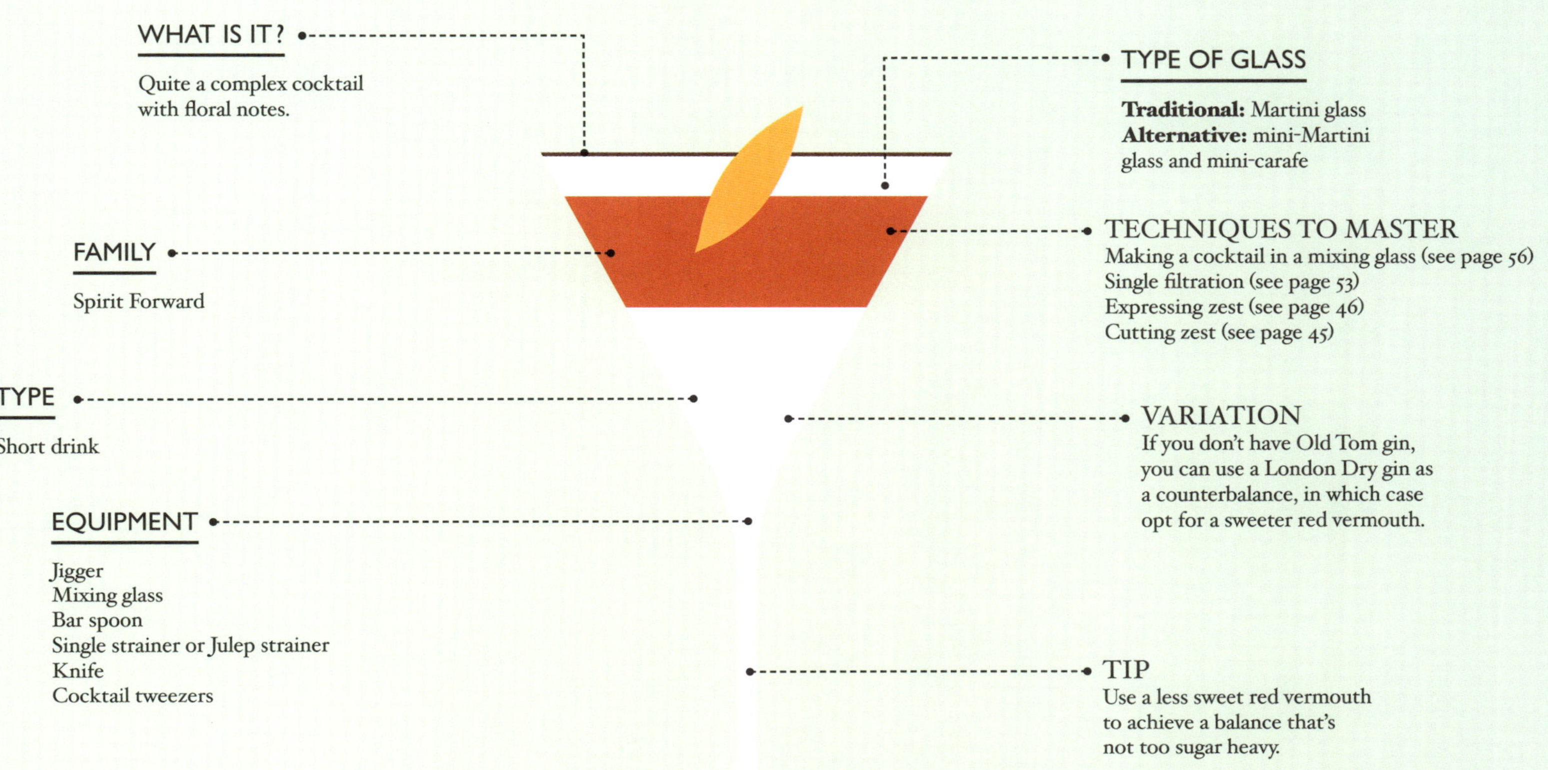

SERVES 1

50ml (1⅔oz) Old Tom gin
25ml (⅔oz plus 1 tsp) red vermouth
7.5ml (1½ tsp) maraschino liqueur
2 dashes of Angostura bitters

TO DECORATE

zest of 1 unwaxed orange

1. Pour all the ingredients into the mixing glass, which should be well chilled.
2. Add ice to come about two fingers above the liquid.
3. Mix (see page 56) for 40 seconds.
4. Taste to check the dilution is perfect, mixing a little more if necessary.
5. Single filter (see page 52) into the serving glass.
6. Express the zest (see page 46) in the centre of the glass and then rub it over the rim and stem of the glass.
7. Cut the zest (see page 45) and, using the cocktail tweezers, sit it on the rim of the glass.

WHISKEY SOUR

The Lowdown

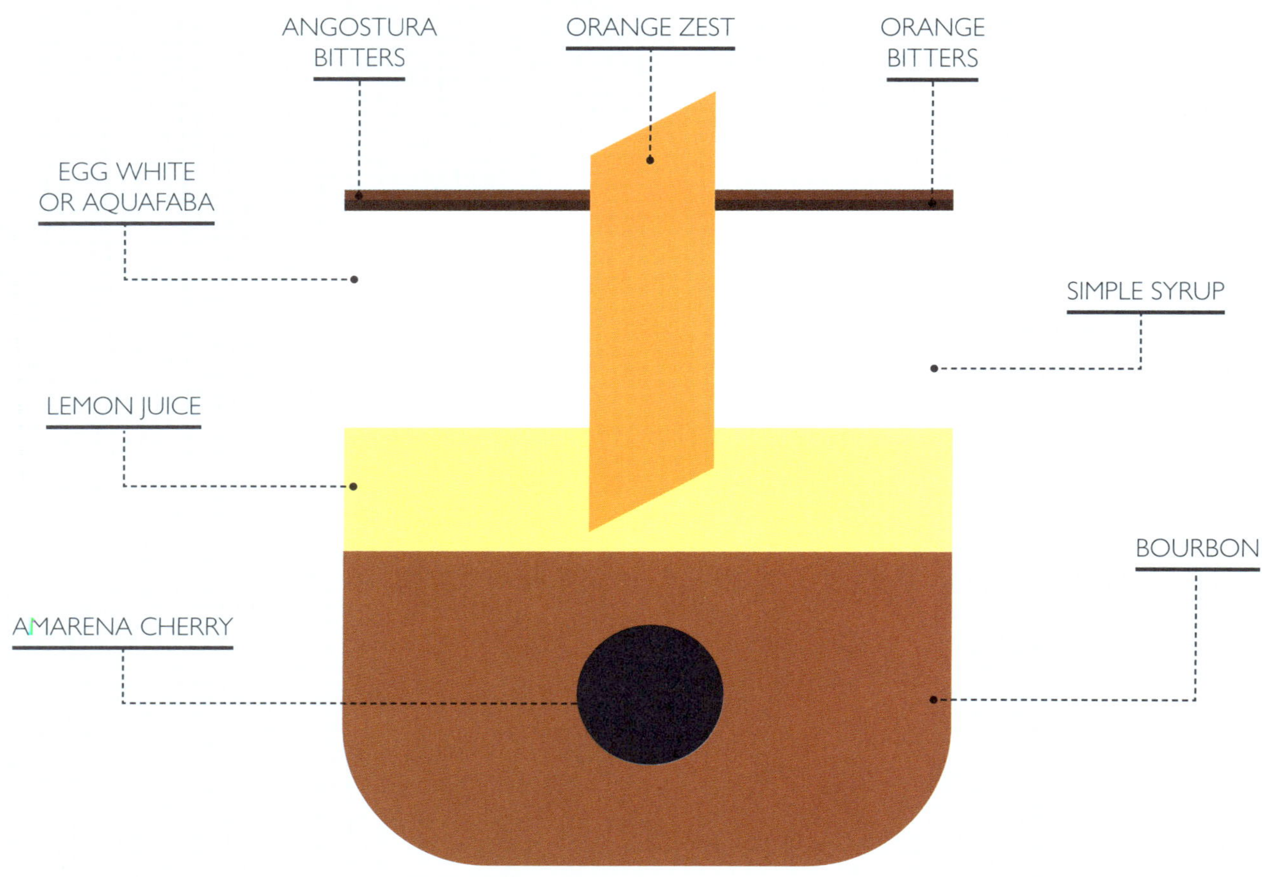

WHAT IS IT?

The benchmark for any Sour lover, it has perfect balance and is as smooth as velvet.

FAMILY

Sour

TYPE

Short drink

ICE FOR SERVING

Cubes

TYPE OF GLASS

Traditional: double Old Fashioned
Alternative: goblet

EQUIPMENT

Jigger
Shaker
Single strainer
Fine-mesh strainer
Cocktail tweezers
Knife
Cocktail stick (pick)

TECHNIQUES TO MASTER

Shake (see page 58)
Throwing (see page 59)
Dry shake (see page 58)
Ice cubes/block of ice (see page 36)
Expressing zest (see page 46)
Cutting zest (see page 45)

VARIATIONS

New York Sour: release a 'cloud' of red wine over the mousse by gently pouring it over the back of a bar spoon.
Continental Sour: the same recipe as a New York Sour but made with port.
Rattle Snake: use rye whiskey in place of the bourbon and a dash of absinthe.

ALTERNATIVE

Replace the egg white with aquafaba.

SERVES 1

50ml (1⅔oz) bourbon
25ml (⅔oz plus 1 tsp) lemon juice
25ml (⅔oz plus 1 tsp) simple syrup
1 dash of Angostura bitters
1 dash of orange bitters
1 egg white

TO DECORATE

zest of 1 unwaxed orange
1 amarena cherry

1 Pour all the ingredients into the shaker.

2 Dry shake (see page 58) vigorously for 5 seconds without ice.

3 Throw (see page 59) the cocktail from the larger part to the smaller part of the shaker to incorporate air into the mixture.

4 Fill the larger part of the shaker to the brim with ice and shake (see page 58) vigorously for 10 seconds.

5 Double filter (see page 53) into the serving glass.

6 Express the orange zest (see page 46) in the centre of the glass and then rub it over the rim and stem of the glass.

7 Cut the zest (see page 45) and, using the cocktail tweezers, place it in the glass resting against the rim.

8 Skewer the cherry onto the cocktail stick (pick) and stand it in the cocktail, balancing the cherry on the rim of the glass.

AMARETTO
SOUR

The Lowdown

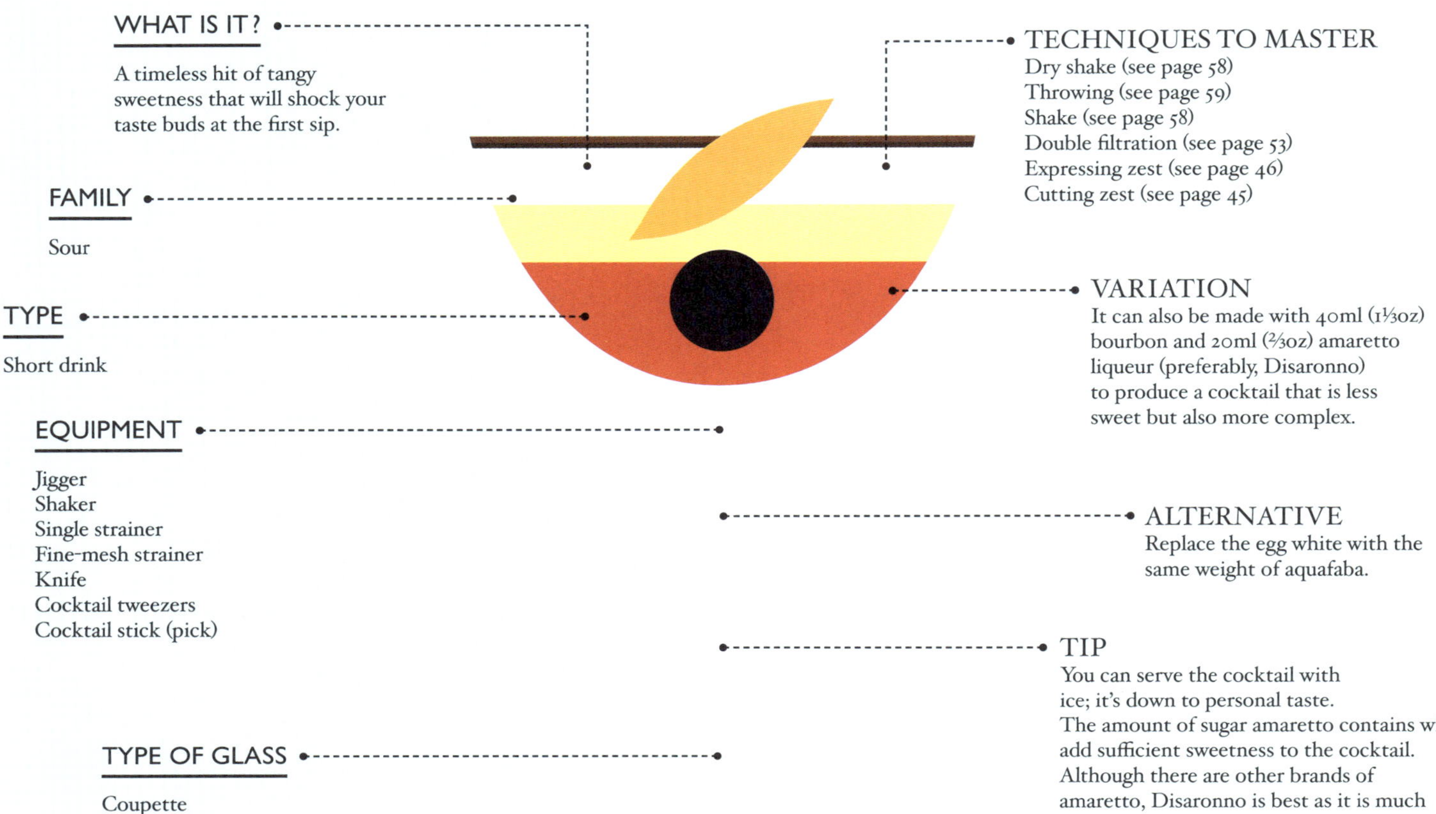

WHAT IS IT?

A timeless hit of tangy sweetness that will shock your taste buds at the first sip.

FAMILY

Sour

TYPE

Short drink

EQUIPMENT

Jigger
Shaker
Single strainer
Fine-mesh strainer
Knife
Cocktail tweezers
Cocktail stick (pick)

TYPE OF GLASS

Coupette

TECHNIQUES TO MASTER

Dry shake (see page 58)
Throwing (see page 59)
Shake (see page 58)
Double filtration (see page 53)
Expressing zest (see page 46)
Cutting zest (see page 45)

VARIATION

It can also be made with 40ml (1⅓oz) bourbon and 20ml (⅔oz) amaretto liqueur (preferably, Disaronno) to produce a cocktail that is less sweet but also more complex.

ALTERNATIVE

Replace the egg white with the same weight of aquafaba.

TIP

You can serve the cocktail with ice; it's down to personal taste.
The amount of sugar amaretto contains will add sufficient sweetness to the cocktail.
Although there are other brands of amaretto, Disaronno is best as it is much more complex than standard ones.

SERVES 1

45ml (1½oz) amaretto, such as Disaronno
25ml (⅔oz plus 1 tsp) lemon juice
1 dash of Angostura bitters
1 dash of orange bitters
1 egg white or 30ml (1oz) aquafaba

TO DECORATE

zest of 1 unwaxed orange
1 amareno cherry

1. Pour all the ingredients into the shaker.
2. Dry shake (see page 58) vigorously without ice for 5 seconds.
3. Throw (see page 59) the cocktail from the larger part to the smaller part of the shaker to incorporate air into the mixture.
4. Fill the larger part of the shaker to the brim with ice and shake (see page 58) vigorously for 10 seconds.
5. Double filter (see page 53) into the serving glass.
6. Express the orange zest (see page 46) in the centre of the glass and then rub it over the rim and stem of the glass.
7. Cut the zest (see page 45) and, using the cocktail tweezers, lay it over the rim of the glass.
8. Skewer the cherry onto the cocktail stick (pick) and place it in the cocktail, tucking it under the zest and resting the stick (pick) on the rim of the glass.

PISCO SOUR

The Lowdown

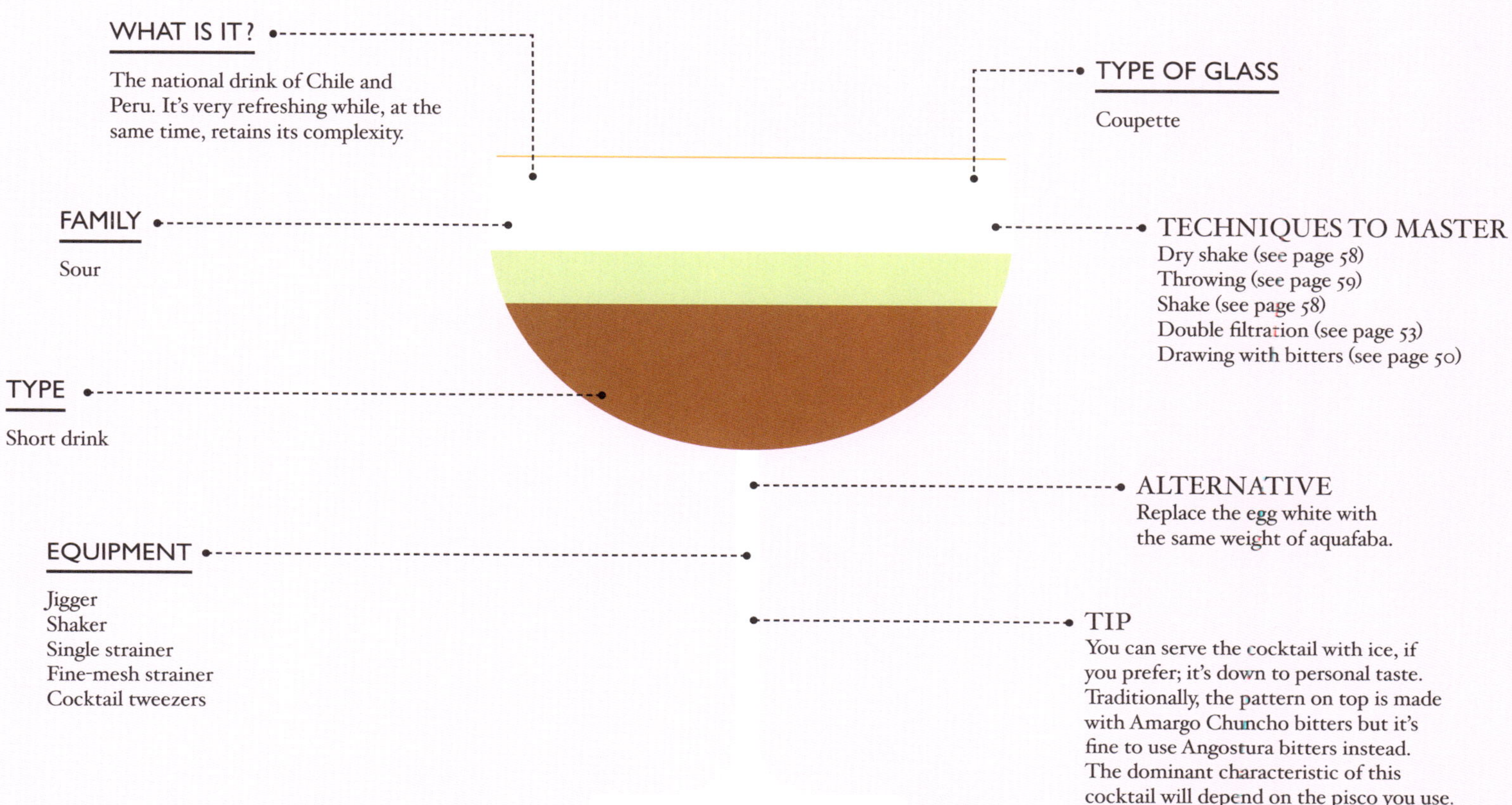

SERVES 1

50ml (1⅔oz) pisco (see 'Brandy', page 23)
25ml (⅔oz plus 1 tsp) lime juice
25ml (⅔oz plus 1 tsp) simple syrup
1 egg white or 30ml (1oz) aquafaba

TO DECORATE

Amargo Chuncho or Angostura bitters

1. Pour all the ingredients into the shaker.
2. Dry shake (see page 58) vigorously without ice for 5 seconds.
3. Throw (see page 59) the cocktail from the larger part to the smaller part of the shaker to incorporate air into the mixture.
4. Fill the larger part of the shaker to the brim with ice and shake (see page 58) vigorously for 10 seconds.
5. Double filter (see page 53) into the serving glass.
6. Draw a pattern in bitters on top (see page 50).

BACARDI

COCKTAIL

The Lowdown

WHAT IS IT?

A simple, balanced Sour.

TYPE OF GLASS

Traditional: Martini glass
Alternative: coupette

FAMILY

Sour

TYPE

Short drink

TECHNIQUES TO MASTER

Shake (see page 58)
Double filtration (see page 53)

EQUIPMENT

Jigger
Shaker
Single strainer
Fine-mesh strainer
Cocktail stick (pick)

SERVES 1

50ml (1⅔oz) white Cuban rum
20ml (⅔oz) lime juice
20ml (⅔oz) simple syrup

TO DECORATE

1 amarena cherry

1. Pour all the ingredients into the shaker.
2. Fill the larger part of the shaker to the brim with ice and shake (see page 58) vigorously for 10 seconds.
3. Double filter (see page 53) into the serving glass.
4. Skewer the cherry onto the cocktail stick (pick) and place in the cocktail, resting the stick (pick) against the side of the glass.

JACK ROSE

The Lowdown

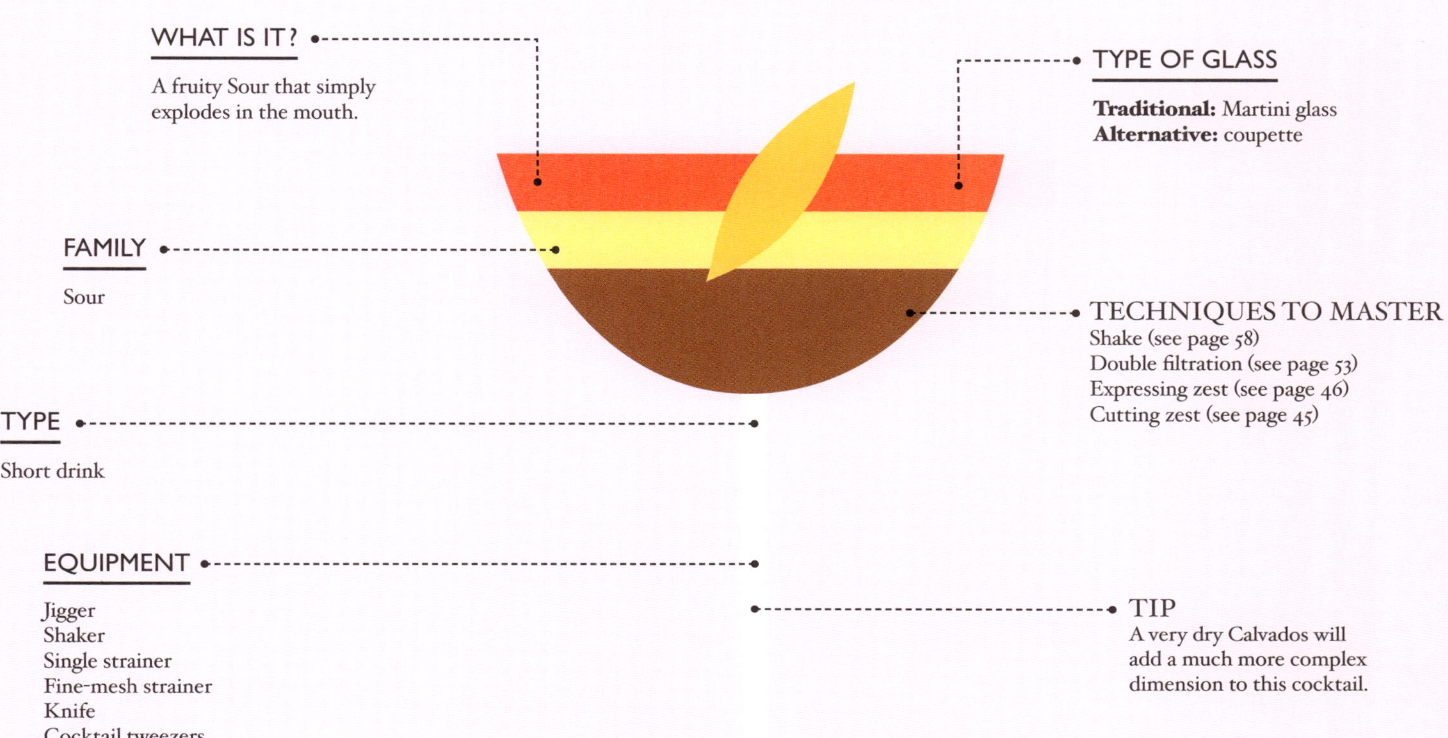

WHAT IS IT?

A fruity Sour that simply explodes in the mouth.

TYPE OF GLASS

Traditional: Martini glass
Alternative: coupette

FAMILY

Sour

TECHNIQUES TO MASTER

Shake (see page 58)
Double filtration (see page 53)
Expressing zest (see page 46)
Cutting zest (see page 45)

TYPE

Short drink

EQUIPMENT

Jigger
Shaker
Single strainer
Fine-mesh strainer
Knife
Cocktail tweezers

TIP

A very dry Calvados will add a much more complex dimension to this cocktail.

SERVES 1

50ml (1⅔oz) Calvados
25ml (⅔oz plus 1 tsp) lemon juice
25ml (⅔oz plus 1 tsp) grenadine

TO DECORATE

zest of 1 unwaxed lemon

1. Pour all the ingredients into the shaker.
2. Fill the larger part of the shaker to the brim with ice and shake (see page 58) vigorously for 10 seconds.
3. Double filter (see page 53) into the serving glass.
4. Express the lemon zest (see page 46) in the centre of the glass and then rub it over the rim and stem of the glass.
5. Cut the zest (see page 45) and, using the cocktail tweezers, stand it upright in the cocktail against the side of the glass.

DAIQUIRI

The Lowdown

WHAT IS IT?

One of the great classic cocktails which could be a family all on its own. It gives the rum plenty of opportunity to express itself.

FAMILY

Sour (subsidiary family: Daiquiri)

TYPE

Short drink

TYPE OF GLASS

Traditional: Martini glass
Alternative: coupette

EQUIPMENT

Jigger
Shaker
Single strainer
Fine-mesh strainer

TECHNIQUES TO MASTER

Shake (see page 58)
Double filtration (see page 53)

VARIATIONS

Frozen Daiquiri: see page 159.
Hemingway Daiquiri: see page 158.
Acapulco Daiquiri: use 45ml (1½oz) white rum, 15ml (½oz) triple sec, 25ml (⅔oz plus 1 tsp), lemon juice, 1 egg white or 30ml (1oz) aquafaba.

TIP

For a result that's even more mind-blowing, go for a rum with over 44% ABV (88 proof) and fill the shaker with one-third crushed ice and two-thirds ice cubes.

Discover

SERVES 1

60ml (2oz) Hispanic rum
30ml (1oz) lime juice
25ml (⅔oz plus 1 tsp) simple syrup

TO DECORATE

lime wedge (⅛ of a lime)

1. Pour all the ingredients into the shaker.
2. Fill the larger part of the shaker to the brim with ice and shake (see page 58) vigorously for 10 seconds.
3. Double filter (see page 53) into the serving glass.
4. Sit the lime wedge over the rim of the glass.

HEMINGWAY

DAIQUIRI

The Lowdown

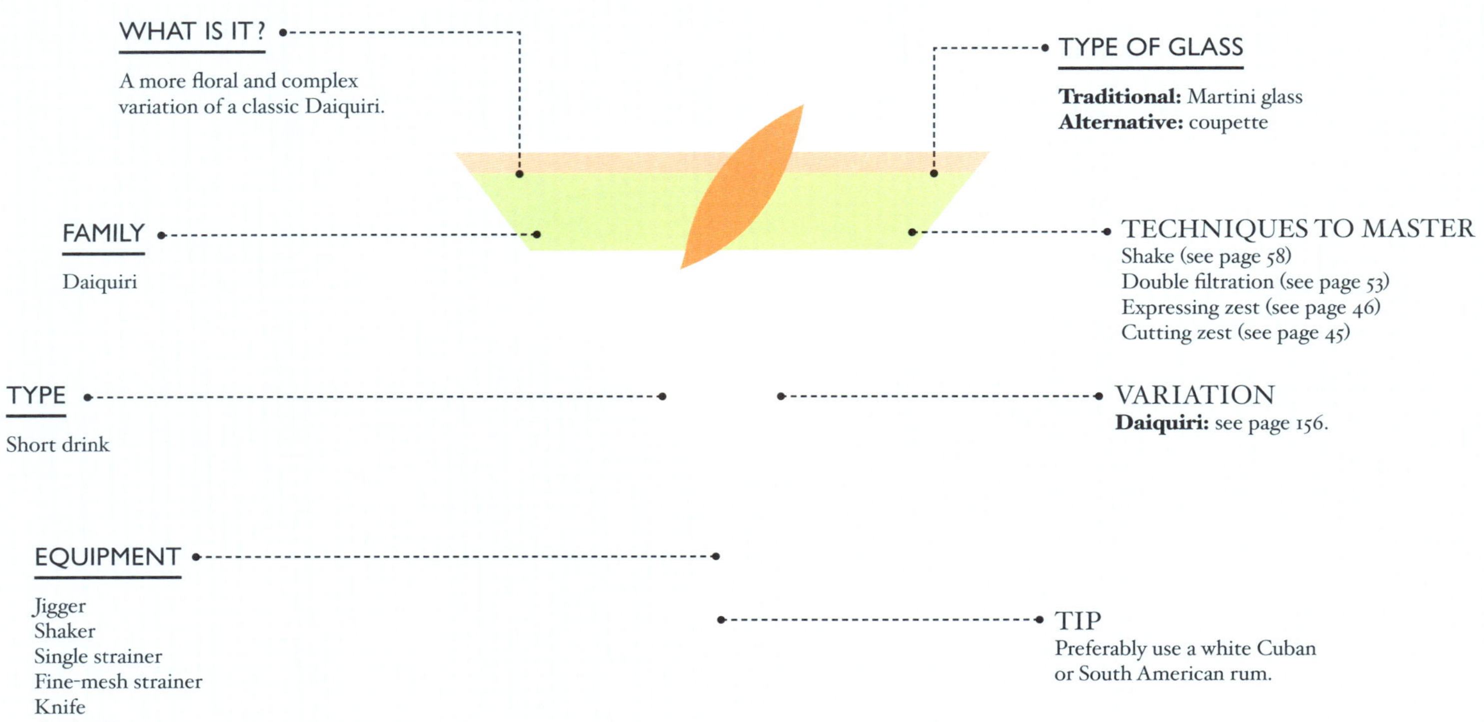

WHAT IS IT?

A more floral and complex variation of a classic Daiquiri.

TYPE OF GLASS

Traditional: Martini glass
Alternative: coupette

FAMILY

Daiquiri

TECHNIQUES TO MASTER

Shake (see page 58)
Double filtration (see page 53)
Expressing zest (see page 46)
Cutting zest (see page 45)

TYPE

Short drink

VARIATION

Daiquiri: see page 156.

EQUIPMENT

Jigger
Shaker
Single strainer
Fine-mesh strainer
Knife
Cocktail tweezers

TIP

Preferably use a white Cuban or South American rum.

SERVES 1

45ml (1½oz) white rum
7.5ml (1½ tsp) maraschino liqueur
25ml (⅔oz plus 1 tsp) lime juice
10ml (2 tsp) grapefruit juice

TO DECORATE

zest of 1 unwaxed grapefruit

1. Pour all the ingredients into the shaker.
2. Fill the larger part of the shaker to the brim with ice and shake (see page 58) vigorously for 10 seconds.
3. Double filter (see page 53) into the serving glass.
4. Express the grapefruit zest (see page 46) in the centre of the glass and then rub it over the rim and stem of the glass.
5. Cut the zest (see page 45) and, using the cocktail tweezers, sit it on the rim of the glass.

FROZEN

DAIQUIRI

The Lowdown

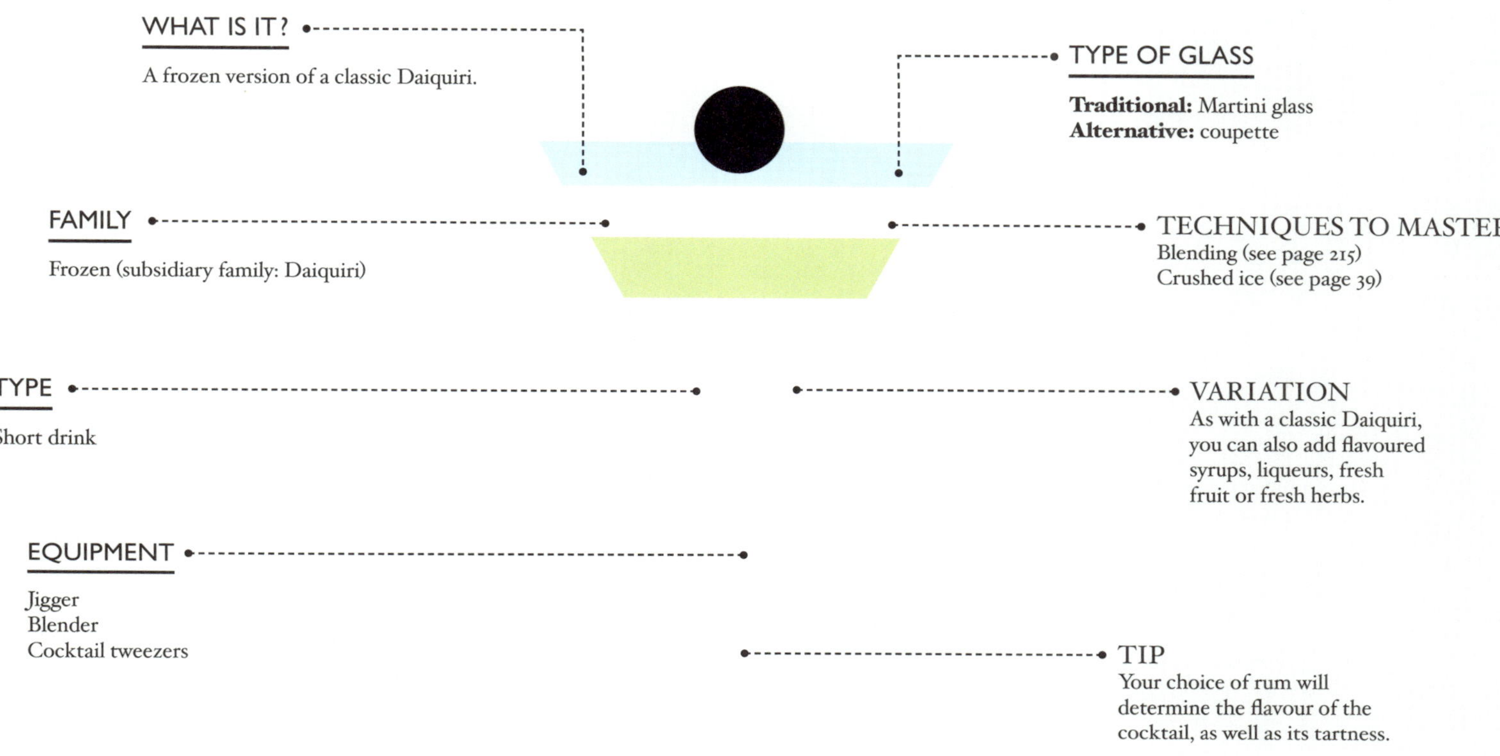

WHAT IS IT?

A frozen version of a classic Daiquiri.

TYPE OF GLASS

Traditional: Martini glass
Alternative: coupette

FAMILY

Frozen (subsidiary family: Daiquiri)

TECHNIQUES TO MASTER

Blending (see page 215)
Crushed ice (see page 39)

TYPE

Short drink

VARIATION

As with a classic Daiquiri, you can also add flavoured syrups, liqueurs, fresh fruit or fresh herbs.

EQUIPMENT

Jigger
Blender
Cocktail tweezers

TIP

Your choice of rum will determine the flavour of the cocktail, as well as its tartness.

SERVES 1

60ml (2oz) white Hispanic rum
25ml (⅔oz plus 1 tsp) lime juice
25ml (⅔oz plus 1 tsp) simple syrup
150ml (5oz) crushed ice

TO DECORATE

1 amarena cherry

1. Pour all the liquid ingredients into the blender.
2. Add the crushed ice (see page 39).
3. Blend (see page 215) on medium speed, then increase to full speed after 5 seconds.
4. Pour into the serving glass.
5. Use the cocktail tweezers to sit the cherry on top.

MARGARITA

The Lowdown

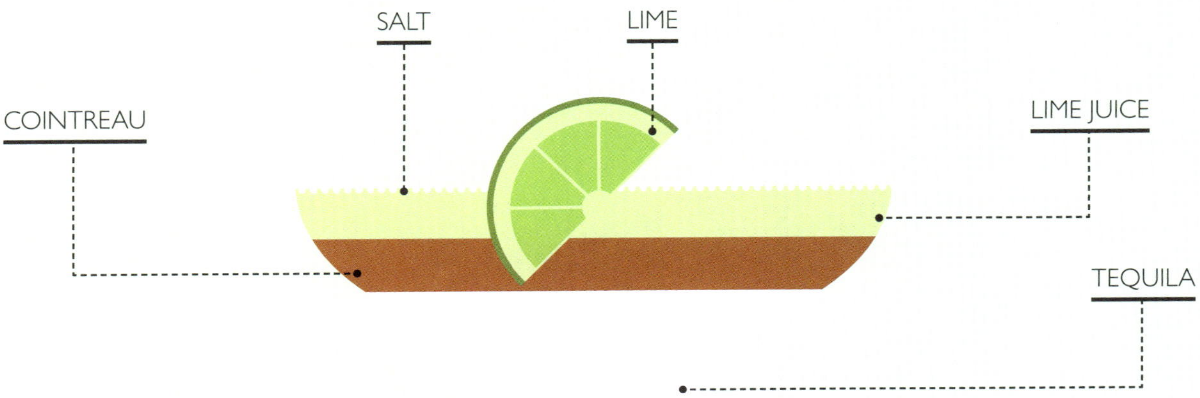

WHAT IS IT?

This iconic Daisy is a celebration of tequila.

FAMILY

Daisy (subsidiary family: Margarita)

TYPE

Short drink

TYPE OF GLASS

Traditional: Margarita glass
Alternative: coupette

EQUIPMENT

Jigger
Shaker
Single strainer
Fine-mesh strainer

TECHNIQUES TO MASTER

Shake (see page 58)
Rimming the glass (see page 48)
Double filtration (see page 53)

VARIATIONS

Frozen Margarita: see page 162.
Tommy's Margarita: see page 163.
Mezcal Margarita: with mezcal instead of tequila.

ALTERNATIVES

As with a classic Daiquiri, you can use flavoured syrups, liqueurs and fresh fruit or herbs. The style of this cocktail means you can add just about any flavour by selecting a sweetener with the taste you're looking for or by adding crushed fresh fruit.

TIP

Choose a silver or joven tequila if you're going down the classic route, while a reposado tequila (aged for between 2 months and 1 year in oak barrels) or añejo tequila (aged for between 1 and 3 years in small oak barrels) can bring plenty of body and complexity.

SERVES 1

50ml (1⅔oz) tequila
25ml (⅔oz plus 1 tsp) Cointreau
25ml (⅔oz plus 1 tsp) lime juice

TO DECORATE

salt
lime wedge (⅛ of a lime)

1. Pour all the ingredients into the shaker.
2. Fill the larger part of the shaker to the brim with ice and shake (see page 58) vigorously for 10 seconds.
3. Frost the rim of the serving glass with salt (see page 48).
4. Double filter (see page 53) the cocktail into the glass.
5. Tuck the lime wedge over the rim of the glass.

FROZEN
MARGARITA

The Lowdown

WHAT IS IT?

Another iconic Daisy that celebrates tequila.

FAMILY

Frozen (subsidiary family: Margarita)

TYPE

Short drink

EQUIPMENT

Jigger
Blender
Cocktail tweezers

TYPE OF GLASS

Traditional: Margarita glass
Alternative: coupette

TECHNIQUES TO MASTER

Blending (see page 215)
Crushed ice (see page 39)

VARIATION

As with a classic Margarita, you can use flavoured syrups, liqueurs, fresh fruit or fresh herbs.

TIP

See Margarita (page 160).

SERVES 1

50ml (1⅔oz) tequila
25ml (⅔oz plus 1 tsp) Cointreau
25ml (⅔oz plus 1 tsp) lime juice
120ml (4oz) crushed ice

TO DECORATE

1 amarena cherry

1. Pour all the liquid ingredients into the blender.
2. Add the crushed ice (see page 39).
3. Blend (see page 215) on medium speed, then increase to full speed after 5 seconds.
4. Pour into the serving glass.
5. Use the cocktail tweezers to sit the cherry on top.

TOMMY'S

MARGARITA

The Lowdown

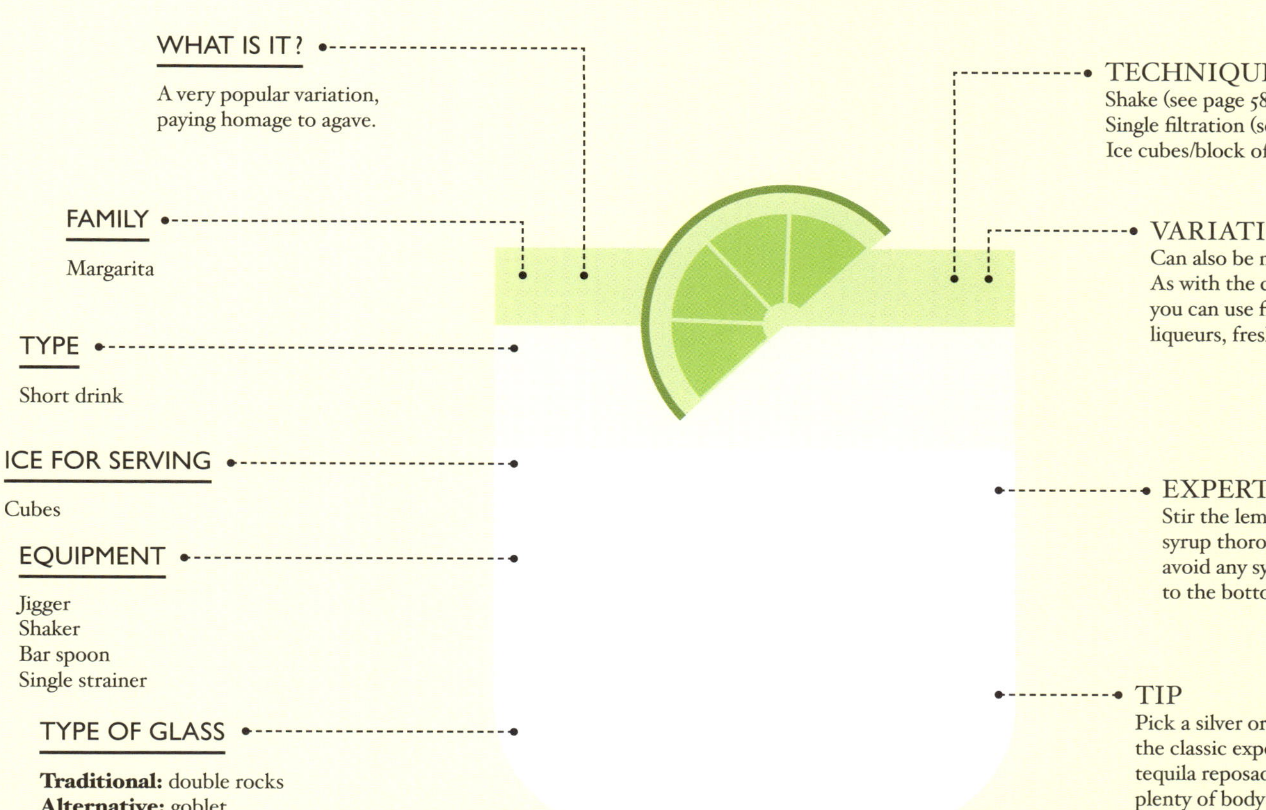

WHAT IS IT?

A very popular variation, paying homage to agave.

FAMILY

Margarita

TYPE

Short drink

ICE FOR SERVING

Cubes

EQUIPMENT

Jigger
Shaker
Bar spoon
Single strainer

TYPE OF GLASS

Traditional: double rocks
Alternative: goblet

TECHNIQUES TO MASTER

Shake (see page 58)
Single filtration (see page 52)
Ice cubes/block of ice (see page 36)

VARIATIONS

Can also be made with mezcal. As with the classic Margarita, you can use flavoured syrups, liqueurs, fresh fruit or fresh herbs.

EXPERT TRICK

Stir the lemon juice and agave syrup thoroughly together to avoid any syrup remaining stuck to the bottom of the shaker.

TIP

Pick a silver or joven tequila for the classic experience, while a tequila reposado or añejo can bring plenty of body and complexity.

SERVES 1

50ml (1⅔oz) tequila
15ml (½oz) agave syrup
25ml (⅔oz plus 1 tsp) lime juice

TO DECORATE

lime wedge (⅛ of an unwaxed lime)

1 Pour all the ingredients into the shaker. Mix with the bar spoon until the agave syrup is no longer sticking to the sides or bottom of the shaker.

2 Fill the larger part of the shaker to the brim with ice. Shake (see page 58) vigorously for 10 seconds.

3 Fill the serving glass with ice cubes or add a block of ice (see page 36) and single filter (see page 52) the cocktail into it.

4 Sit the lime wedge on top.

GIN FIZZ

The Lowdown

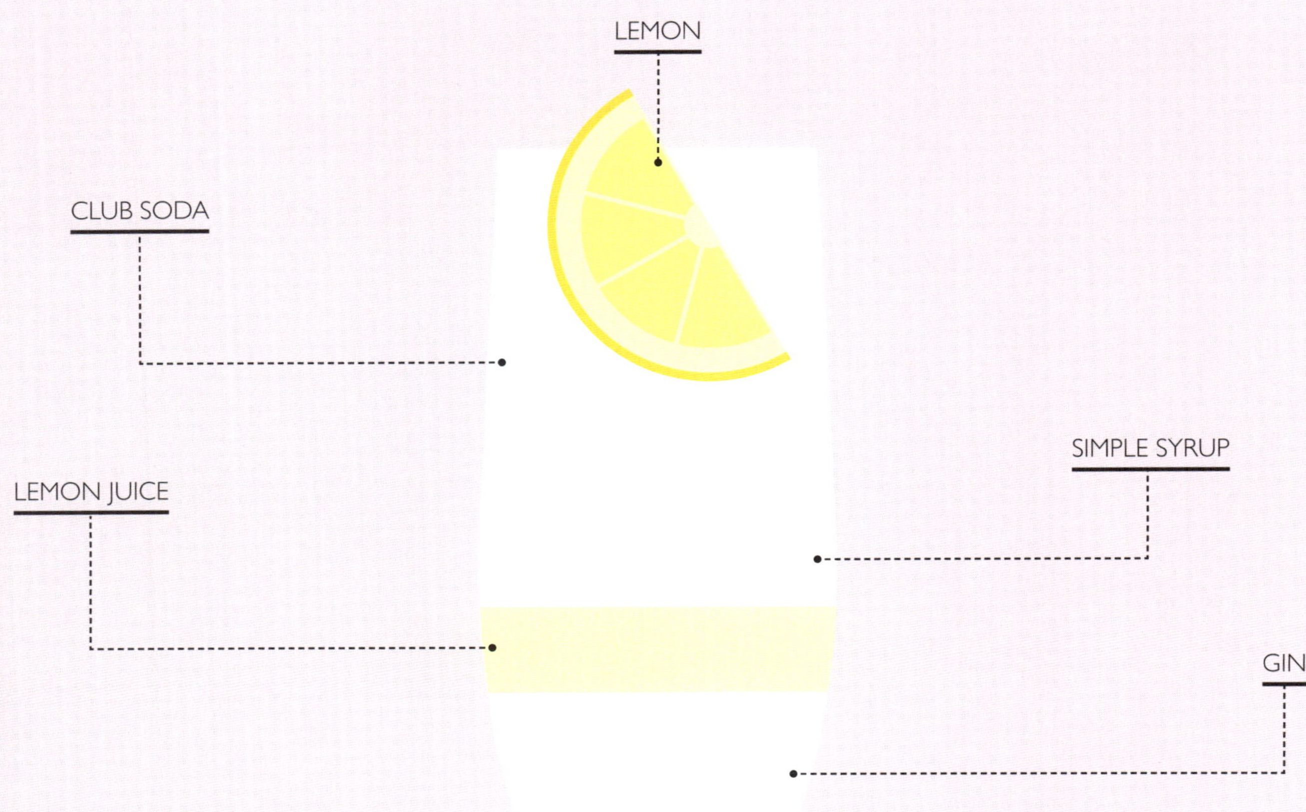

WHAT IS IT?

A fresh, well-balanced long drink and the godfather of many cocktails.

FAMILY

Fizz

TYPE

Long drink

TYPE OF GLASS

Traditional: highball
Alternative: goblet

EQUIPMENT

Jigger
Shaker
Single strainer

TECHNIQUES TO MASTER

Ice cubes/block of ice (see page 36)
Shake (see page 58)
Single filtration (see page 52)

VARIATIONS

Silver Fizz: see page 166.
Golden Fizz: with the addition of an egg yolk.
Ramos Gin Fizz: see page 167.
Morning Glory Fizz: replace gin with Scotch, 1 dash of absinthe and an egg white (or 30ml/1oz aquafaba).

ALTERNATIVES

An infinite number of Fizzes can be created by sticking to the rule of 2 measures of alcohol to 1 measure of sweetener, 1 measure of an acidifier and soda (sparkling water, ginger beer, ginger ale, depending on what you prefer).

TIP

Choose a club soda, such as Schweppes Premium Mixer or Fever Tree.

Discover

SERVES 1

50ml (1⅔oz) gin
25ml (⅔oz plus 1 tsp) lemon juice
25ml (⅔oz plus 1 tsp) simple syrup
100ml (3⅓oz) club soda

TO DECORATE

lemon wedge (⅛ of an unwaxed lemon)

1 Pour all the ingredients, except the sparkling water, into the shaker.

2 Fill the larger part of the shaker to the brim with ice and shake (see page 58) vigorously for 10 seconds.

3 Fill the serving glass with ice cubes or add a block of ice (see page 36) and single filter (see page 52) the cocktail into it.

4 Stand the lemon wedge upright in the cocktail against the side of the glass.

SILVER FIZZ

The Lowdown

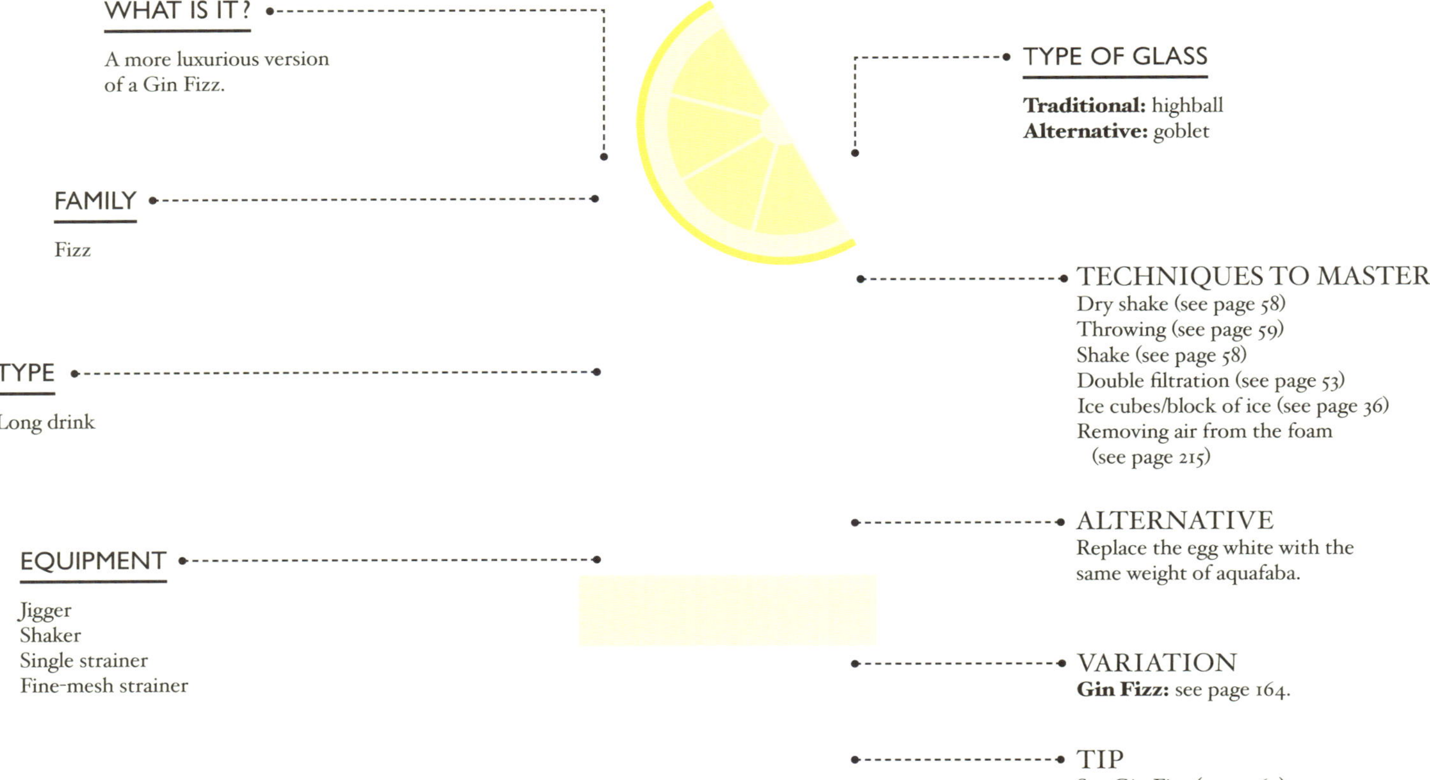

WHAT IS IT?

A more luxurious version of a Gin Fizz.

FAMILY

Fizz

TYPE

Long drink

EQUIPMENT

Jigger
Shaker
Single strainer
Fine-mesh strainer

TYPE OF GLASS

Traditional: highball
Alternative: goblet

TECHNIQUES TO MASTER

Dry shake (see page 58)
Throwing (see page 59)
Shake (see page 58)
Double filtration (see page 53)
Ice cubes/block of ice (see page 36)
Removing air from the foam (see page 215)

ALTERNATIVE

Replace the egg white with the same weight of aquafaba.

VARIATION

Gin Fizz: see page 164.

TIP

See Gin Fizz (page 164).

SERVES 1

50ml (1⅔oz) gin
25ml (⅔oz plus 1 tsp) lemon juice
25ml (⅔oz plus 1 tsp) simple syrup
1 egg white
100ml (3⅓oz) sparkling water

TO DECORATE

lemon wedge (⅛ of an unwaxed lemon)

1. Pour all the ingredients, except the sparkling water, into the shaker.
2. Dry shake (see page 58) vigorously for 5 seconds without ice.
3. Throw (see page 59) the cocktail from the larger part to the smaller part of the shaker to incorporate air into the mixture.
4. Fill the larger part of the shaker to the brim with ice and shake (see page 58) vigorously for 10 seconds.
5. Add 50ml (1⅔oz) of the sparkling water to the shaker and immediately double filter (see page 53) into the serving glass.
6. Remove air from the foam (see page 215) and add the rest of the sparkling water.
7. Tuck the lemon wedge over the rim of the glass.

RAMOS GIN FIZZ

The Lowdown

WHAT IS IT?

An extremely creamy Fizz that you have to earn – due to the length of shaking time needed!

FAMILY

Fizz

TYPE

Long drink

EQUIPMENT

Jigger
Shaker
Single strainer
Reuseable or biodegradable straw

TYPE OF GLASS

Traditional: highball

TECHNIQUES TO MASTER

Dry shake (see page 58)
Throwing (see page 59)
Shake (see page 58)
Single filtration (see page 52)
Removing air from the foam (see page 215)

VARIATION

To add extra flavour to the cocktail, replace the simple syrup with a flavoured syrup or add a dash of bitters.

ALTERNATIVE

Replace the egg white with the same weight of aquafaba.

TIP

The shaking time can exhaust even the fittest bartender, but it is necessary as it ensures the cocktail reaches the right consistency. It can also be made in a siphon by putting all the ingredients, except the sparkling water, into the siphon, charging with a cartridge and shaking. Leave to sit in the refrigerator for 45 minutes before serving.

SERVES 1

50ml (1⅔oz) Old Tom gin
15ml (½oz) lemon juice
15ml (½oz) lime juice
15ml (½oz) simple syrup
15ml (½oz) full-fat (whole) milk
15ml (½oz) double (heavy) cream
2.5ml (½ tsp) orange flower water
3 drops of vanilla extract (optional)
1 egg white
10ml (2 tsp) sparkling water

1. Pour all the ingredients, except the sparkling water, into the shaker.
2. Dry shake (see page 58) vigorously for 30 seconds without ice.
3. Throw (see page 59) the cocktail from the larger part to the smaller part of the shaker to incorporate air into the mixture.
4. Fill the larger part of the shaker to the brim with ice and shake (see page 58) vigorously for 2 minutes.
5. Single filter (see page 52) into the smaller part of the shaker.
6. Add the sparkling water.
7. Shake without ice for 10 seconds.
8. Pour half the mixture into the serving glass.
9. Remove the air from the foam (see page 215) and leave to stand for at least 30 seconds.
10. Gently pour the rest of the cocktail into the centre of the glass so that the foam rises as high as possible. A hole will form in the centre of the foam so place the straw into this.

SLOE GIN FIZZ

The Lowdown

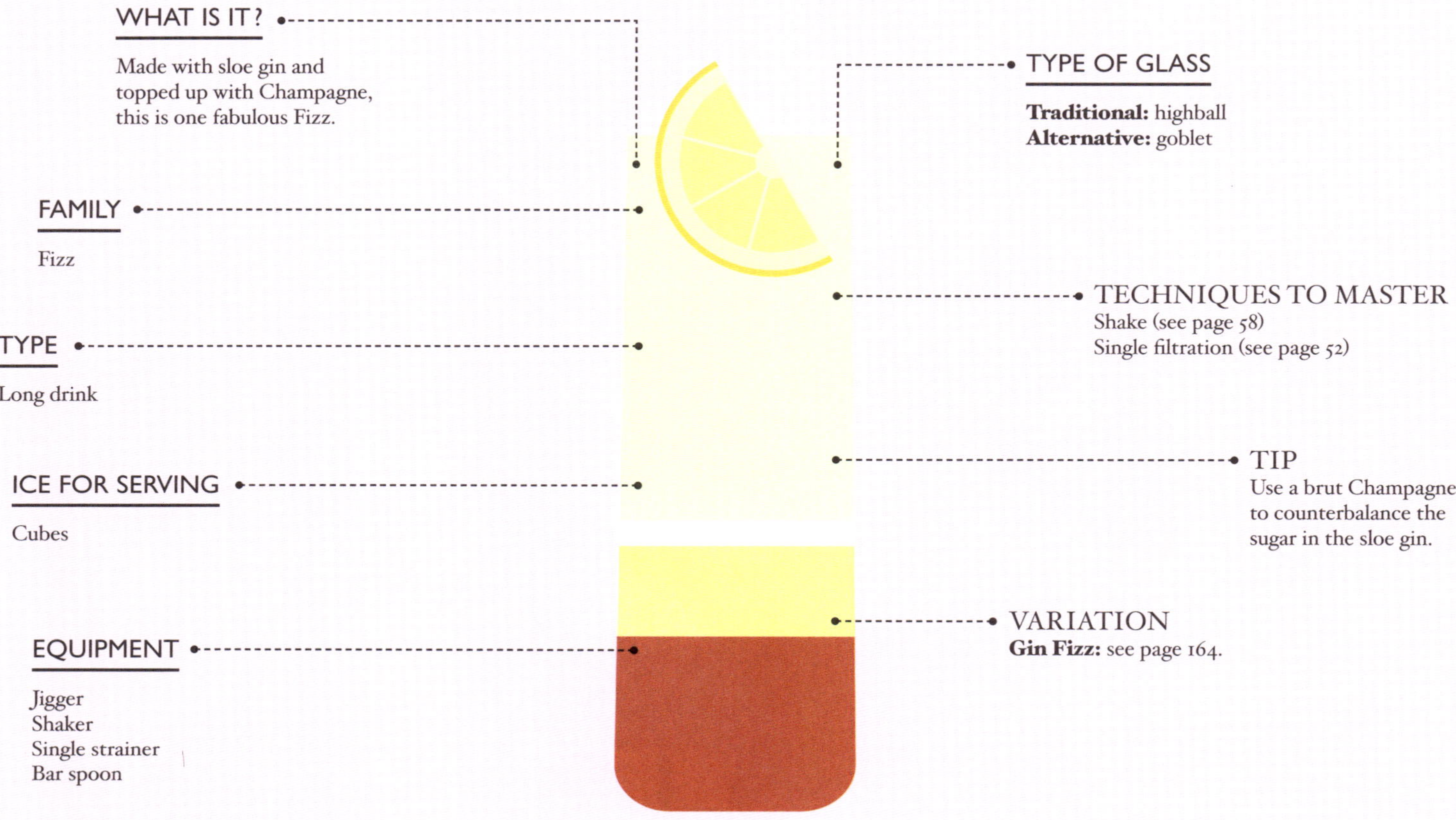

SERVES 1

45ml (1½oz) sloe gin
25ml (⅔oz plus 1 tsp) lemon juice
1 × 5ml bar spoon simple syrup
100ml (3⅓oz) Champagne

TO DECORATE

lemon wedge (⅛ of an unwaxed lemon)

1. Pour all the ingredients, except the Champagne, into the shaker.
2. Fill the larger part of the shaker to the brim with ice and shake (see page 58) vigorously for 10 seconds.
3. Single filter (see page 52) into the serving glass.
4. Top up with the Champagne.
5. Tuck the lemon wedge over the rim of the glass.

CHICAGO FIZZ

The Lowdown

WHAT IS IT?

A complex Fizz.

FAMILY

Fizz

TYPE

Long drink

EQUIPMENT

Jigger
Shaker
Single strainer
Fine-mesh strainer

TYPE OF GLASS

Traditional: highball
Alternative: goblet

TECHNIQUES TO MASTER

Dry shake (see page 58)
Throwing (see page 59)
Shake (see page 58)
Double filtration (see page 53)
Removing air from the foam (see page 215)

ALTERNATIVE

Replace the egg white with the same quantity of aquafaba.

VARIATION

Gin Fizz: see page 164.

TIP

See Gin Fizz (page 164).

SERVES 1

45ml (1½oz) amber rum
20ml (⅔oz) port
20ml (⅔oz) lime juice
10ml (2 tsp) simple syrup
1 egg white or 30ml (1oz) aquafaba
100ml (3⅓oz) sparkling water

TO DECORATE

lime wedge (⅛ of an unwaxed lime)

1. Pour all the ingredients, except the sparkling water, into the shaker.
2. Dry shake (see page 58) vigorously for 5 seconds without ice.
3. Throw (see page 59) the cocktail from the larger part to the smaller part of the shaker to incorporate air into the mixture.
4. Fill the larger part of the shaker to the brim with ice and shake (see page 58) vigorously for 10 seconds.
5. Add 50ml (1 ⅔oz) sparkling water to the shaker and double filter (see page 53) into the serving glass.
6. Remove the air from the foam (see page 215) and add the rest of the sparkling water.
7. Tuck the lime wedge over the rim of the glass.

TOM COLLINS

The Lowdown

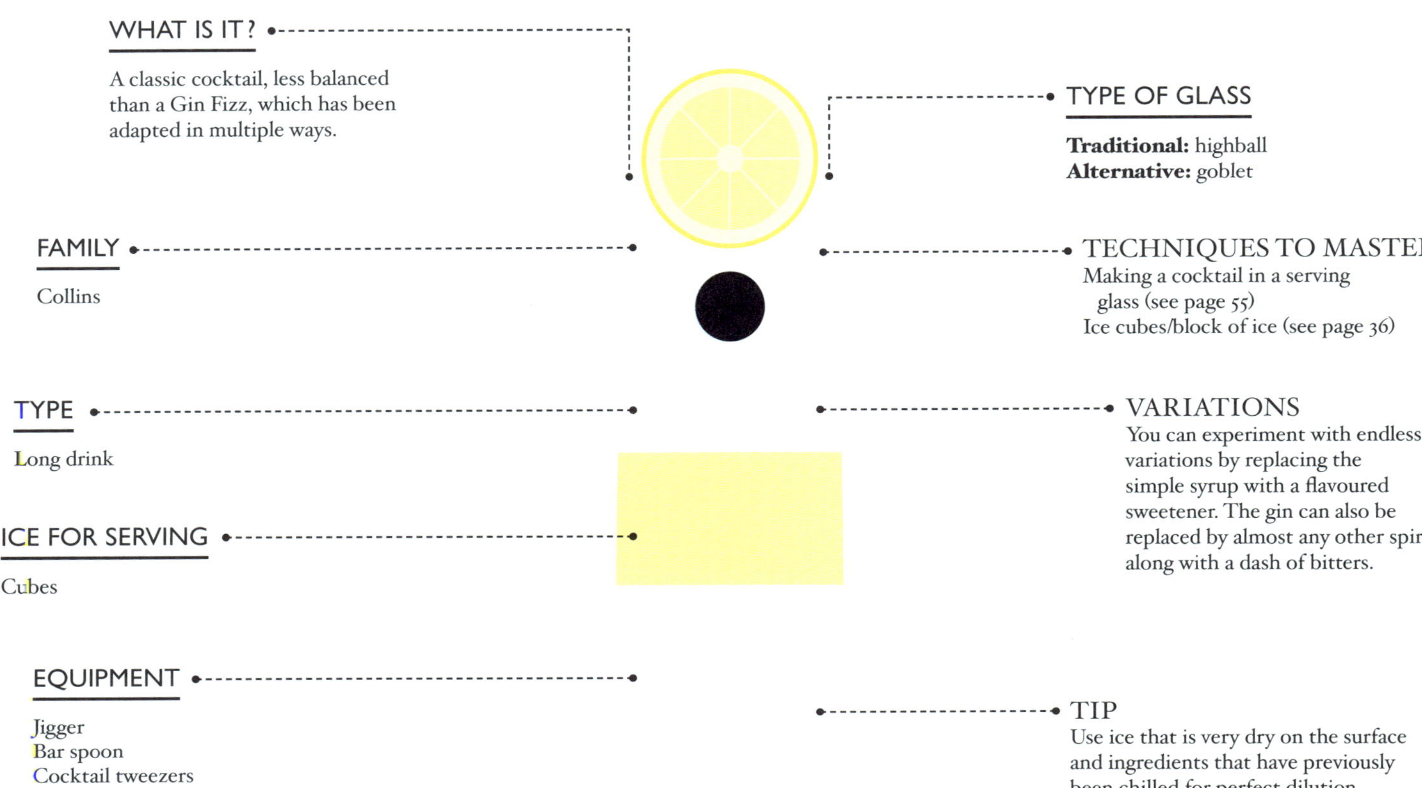

WHAT IS IT?

A classic cocktail, less balanced than a Gin Fizz, which has been adapted in multiple ways.

TYPE OF GLASS

Traditional: highball
Alternative: goblet

FAMILY

Collins

TECHNIQUES TO MASTER

Making a cocktail in a serving glass (see page 55)
Ice cubes/block of ice (see page 36)

TYPE

Long drink

VARIATIONS

You can experiment with endless variations by replacing the simple syrup with a flavoured sweetener. The gin can also be replaced by almost any other spirit along with a dash of bitters.

ICE FOR SERVING

Cubes

EQUIPMENT

Jigger
Bar spoon
Cocktail tweezers
Cocktail stick (pick)

TIP

Use ice that is very dry on the surface and ingredients that have previously been chilled for perfect dilution.

SERVES 1

50ml (1⅔oz) gin
25ml (⅔oz plus 1 tsp) lemon juice
15ml (½oz) simple syrup
50ml (1⅔oz) sparkling water

TO DECORATE

1 lemon slice
1 maraschino or amarena cherry

1 Fill the serving glass with ice cubes or a block of ice (see page 36) and pour all the ingredients, except the sparkling water, into it.

2 Mix for 10 seconds with the bar spoon.

3 Top up with the sparkling water.

4 Mix for 5 seconds.

5 Using the cocktail tweezers, place the lemon slice in the glass close to the rim and gently swirl it around the glass a few times.

6 Skewer the cherry on the cocktail stick (pick) and stand it in the glass close to the lemon slice.

VIEUX CARRÉ

The Lowdown

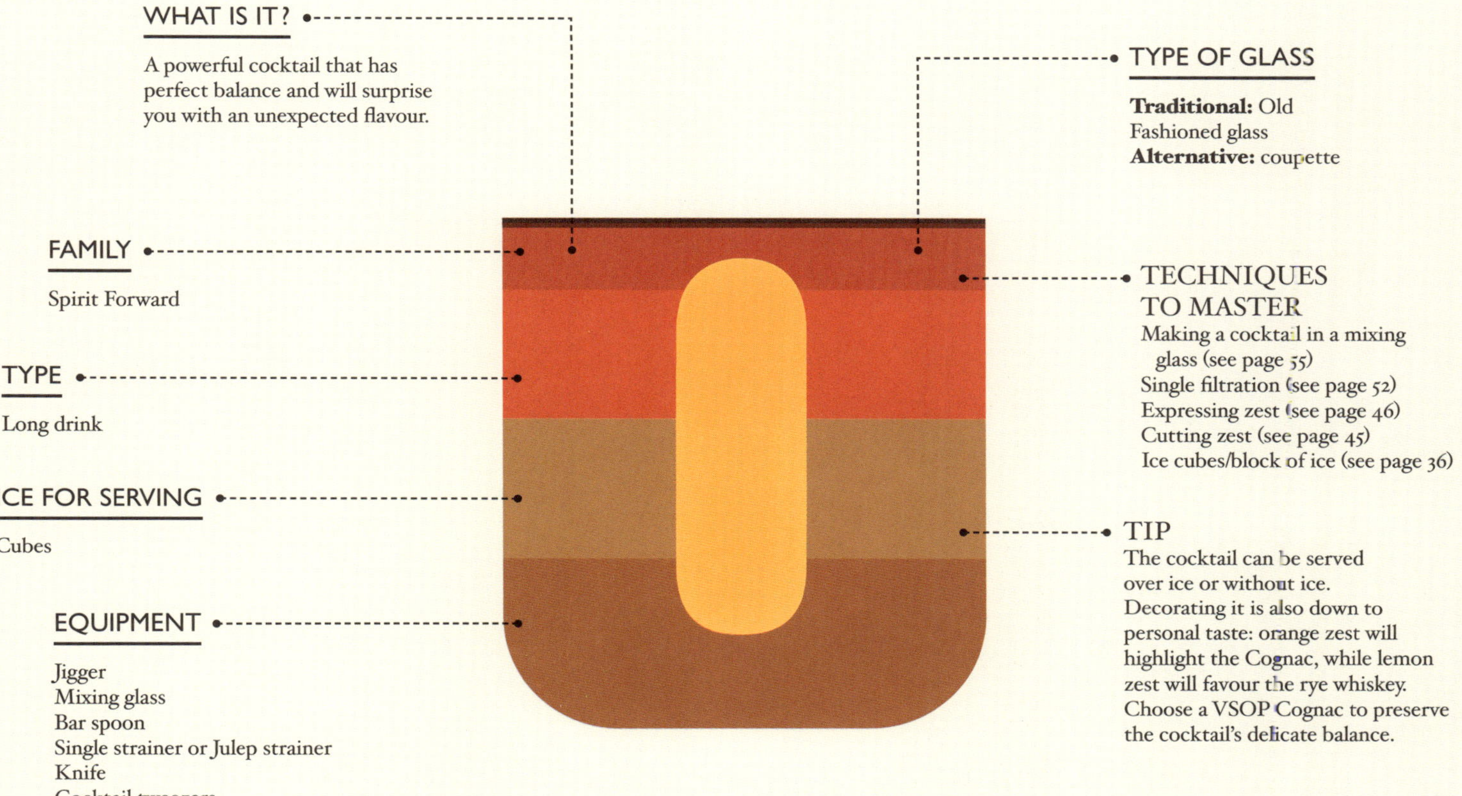

WHAT IS IT?

A powerful cocktail that has perfect balance and will surprise you with an unexpected flavour.

FAMILY

Spirit Forward

TYPE

Long drink

ICE FOR SERVING

Cubes

EQUIPMENT

Jigger
Mixing glass
Bar spoon
Single strainer or Julep strainer
Knife
Cocktail tweezers

TYPE OF GLASS

Traditional: Old Fashioned glass
Alternative: coupette

TECHNIQUES TO MASTER

Making a cocktail in a mixing glass (see page 55)
Single filtration (see page 52)
Expressing zest (see page 46)
Cutting zest (see page 45)
Ice cubes/block of ice (see page 36)

TIP

The cocktail can be served over ice or without ice. Decorating it is also down to personal taste: orange zest will highlight the Cognac, while lemon zest will favour the rye whiskey. Choose a VSOP Cognac to preserve the cocktail's delicate balance.

SERVES 1

30ml (1oz) Cognac
30ml (1oz) rye whiskey
30ml (1oz) red vermouth
7.5ml (1½ tsp) Bénédictine
2 dashes of Angostura bitters
2 dashes of Peychaud's bitters

TO DECORATE

zest of 1 unwaxed orange or 1 lemon

1. Pour all the ingredients into a well-chilled mixing glass.
2. Add ice cubes to come to about 2 fingers above the liquid.
3. Mix (see page 56) for 40 seconds.
4. Taste to check the dilution is perfect, mixing a little more if necessary.
5. Single filter (see page 52) into the serving glass.
6. Add ice cubes or a block of ice (see page 36) to reach the brim of the glass.
7. Express the zest (see page 46) in the centre of the glass and then rub it over the rim of the glass.
8. Cut the zest (see page 45) and, using the cocktail tweezers, curl it into the glass.

BOURBON

OLD FASHIONED

The Lowdown

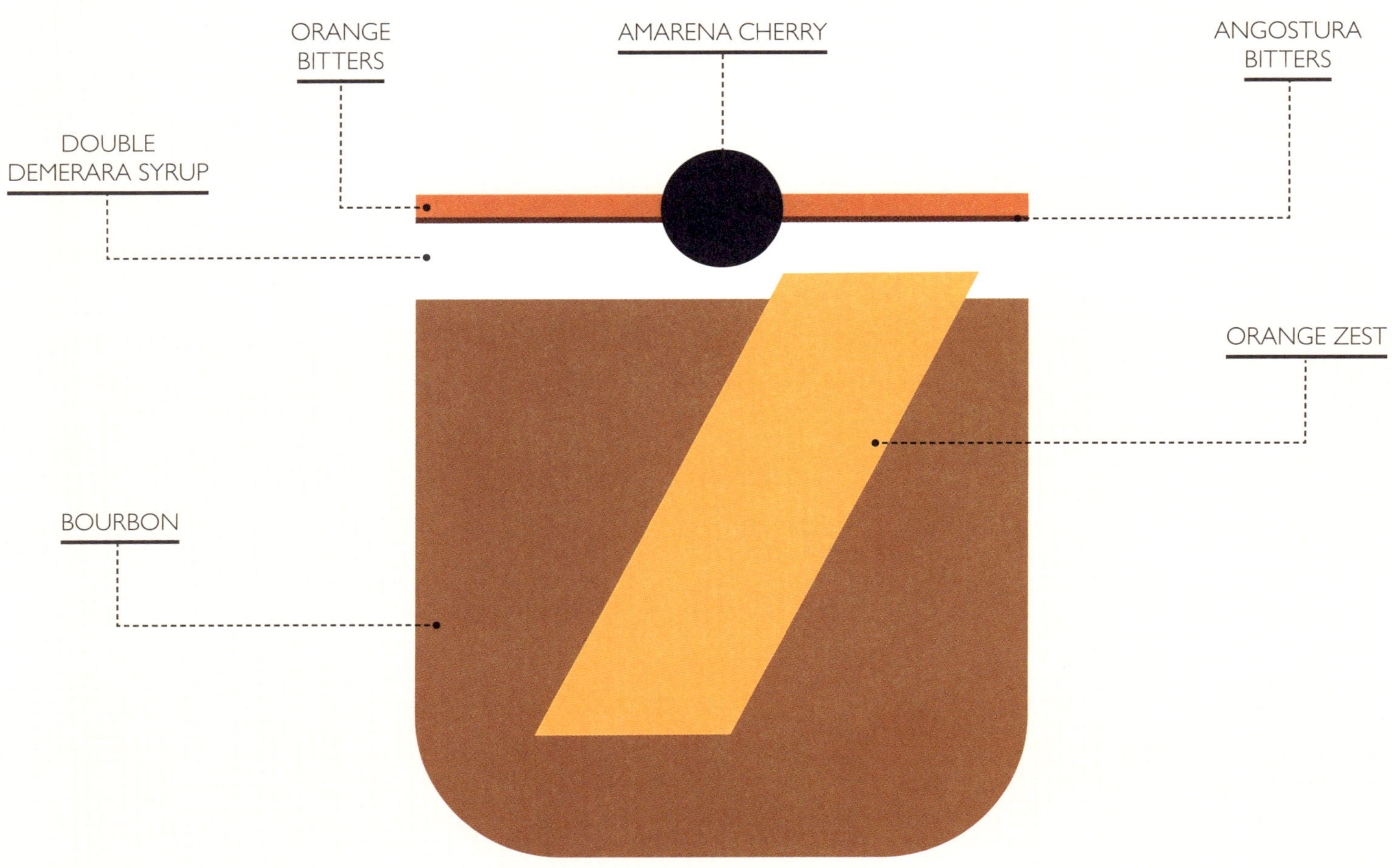

WHAT IS IT?

A giant of the cocktail world but one that can be tricky to execute successfully.

FAMILY

Ancestral (subsidiary family: Old Fashioned)

TYPE

Short drink

ICE FOR SERVING

Cubes

TYPE OF GLASS

Traditional: highball
Alternative: goblet

EQUIPMENT

Jigger
Serving glass or mixing glass
Bar spoon
Ice cube tongs
Single strainer or Julep strainer
Knife
Cocktail tweezers
Cocktail stick (pick)

TECHNIQUES TO MASTER

Making a cocktail in a serving glass (see page 55) or mixing glass (see page 56)
Single filtration (see page 52)
Expressing zest (see page 46)
Cutting zest (see page 45)
Ice cubes/block of ice (see page 36)

TIP

Use ice that is very dry on the surface and previously chilled ingredients for perfect dilution. If making in a mixing glass, taste to check the dilution is perfect, mixing a little more if necessary.

SERVES 1

10ml (2 tsp) double demerara or brown simple syrup
2 dashes of Angostura bitters
6 dashes of orange bitters
60ml (2oz) bourbon

TO DECORATE

2 pieces of zest from an unwaxed orange
2 pieces of zest from an unwaxed lemon
1 amarena cherry

MAKING IN A SERVING GLASS

1 Pour the syrup into the serving glass. Add the bitters and mix until the ingredients are evenly combined.

2 Add three good-sized ice cubes and pour in 30ml (1oz) of the bourbon. Mix for 30 seconds with the bar spoon.

3 Remove the ice cubes with the ice cube tongs and add three more. Pour in the rest of the bourbon and mix for 30 seconds with the bar spoon. Remove these ice cubes using the tongs.

4 Express (see page 46) the orange and lemon zests in the centre of the glass.

5 Fill the glass with ice cubes or add a block of ice (see page 36).

6 Cut (see page 45) one of the orange zests and place it in the glass, using the cocktail tweezers. Skewer the cherry onto the cocktail stick (pick) and place it in the cocktail next to the zest, resting the cherry on the rim of the glass.

MAKING IN A MIXING GLASS

1 Pour all the ingredients into a chilled mixing glass.

2 Add ice to come two fingers above the liquid. Mix (see page 56) for 40 seconds.

3 Single filter into the serving glass.

4 Express (see page 46) the lemon and orange zests in the centre of the glass.

5 Fill the glass with ice cubes or add a block of ice (see page 36).

6 Cut (see page 45) one of the orange zests and place it in the glass, using the cocktail tweezers. Skewer the cherry on the cocktail stick (pick) and place it in the cocktail next to the zest, resting the cherry on the rim of the glass.

SAZERAC

The Lowdown

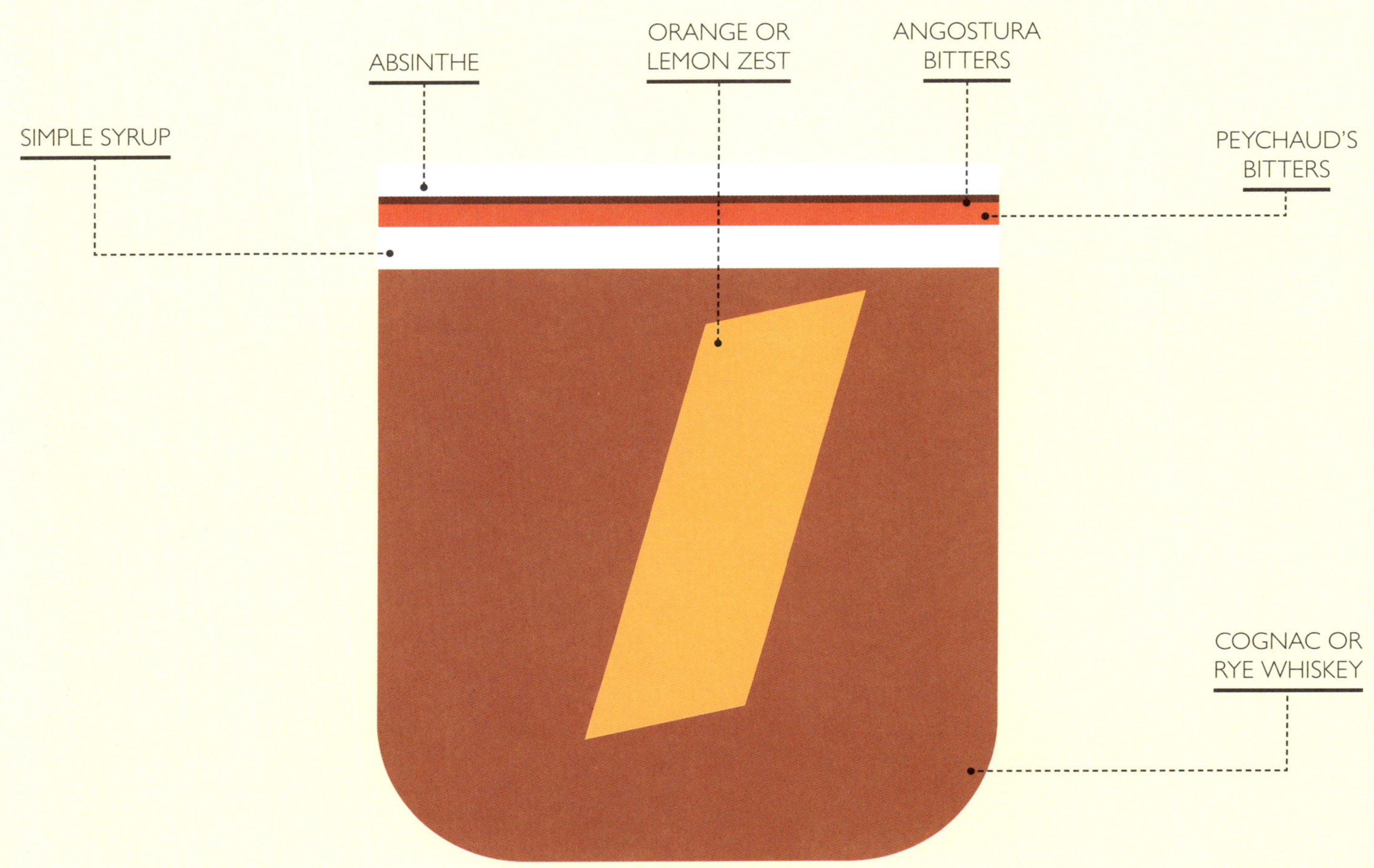

WHAT IS IT?

A colossus of a cocktail that has spanned centuries despite its alcoholic strength.

FAMILY

Ancestral

TYPE

Short drink

TYPE OF GLASS

Old Fashioned

EQUIPMENT

Jigger
Mixing glass
Bar spoon
Single strainer or Julep strainer

TECHNIQUES TO MASTER

Making a cocktail in a mixing glass (see page 56)
Single filtration (see page 52)
Expressing zest (see page 46)

VARIATIONS

New York Sazerac: use equal parts of Cognac and rye whiskey.
Tequila Sazerac: use tequila and agave syrup in place of simple syrup.

TIPS

It is always served without ice.
The spirit you choose will determine the aromatic palette of this cocktail.
For the same result – but a more economical one – you can spray absinthe into the glass instead of using 10ml (2 tsp) to rinse it.
The choice of zest is down to personal taste (see Manhattan, page 136).

Discover

SERVES 1

10ml (2 tsp) absinthe (to rinse the glass)
mineral or filtered water
60ml (2oz) Cognac or rye whiskey
10ml (2 tsp) simple syrup
7 dashes of Peychaud's bitters
2 dashes of Angostura bitters

TO DECORATE

zest of 1 unwaxed orange or lemon

1 Fill the serving glass with ice cubes, pour in the absinthe and then top up with mineral or filtered water.

2 Pour all the other ingredients into a well-chilled mixing glass.

3 Add ice to the mixing glass to come to about two fingers above the liquid.

4 Taste to check that the dilution is perfect, mixing a little more if necessary.

5 Discard the contents of the serving glass and single filter the contents of the mixing glass into it.

6 Express the zest (see page 46) in the centre of the glass, then rub it over the rim.

MINT JULEP

The Lowdown

WHAT IS IT?

A cocktail that never goes out of fashion but is actually quite complicated and therefore tricky to make.

FAMILY

Julep

TYPE

Short drink

ICE FOR SERVING

Crushed

TYPE OF GLASS

Traditional: Julep cup
Alternative: Old Fashioned

EQUIPMENT

Jigger
Muddler or pestle
Bar spoon
2 reuseable or biodegradable straws

TECHNIQUES TO MASTER

Muddling (see page 214)
Expressing mint (see page 47)
Making a cocktail in a serving glass (see page 55)
Crushed iced (see page 39)

VARIATIONS

Prescription Julep: make with honey instead of the sugar, 15ml (½oz) rye whiskey and 45ml (1½oz) Cognac.
Georgia Mint Julep: make with 40ml (1⅓oz) Cognac or bourbon and 20ml (⅔oz) peach liqueur instead of the sugar.
Champagne Julep: make with 15ml (½oz) Cognac, 90ml (3oz) Champagne, 1 × 5ml bar spoon sugar, 10 fresh mint leaves and 1 dash of Angostura bitters.

TIPS

Bourbon or Cognac... it's up to you.

Discover

SERVES 1

10 fresh mint leaves
10ml (2 tsp) simple syrup
60ml (2oz) Cognac or bourbon

TO DECORATE

2 mint sprigs

1 Fill the serving glass one-quarter full with crushed ice (see page 39).

2 Add the mint leaves and cover with crushed ice so the glass is half full.

3 Pour in the simple syrup and press the crushed ice with the muddler or pestle (see page 214) until it is compacted.

4 Pour in 30ml (1oz) of the spirit and mix vigorously with the bar spoon for 5 seconds (at this stage, you should be able to smell the strong combined aroma of mint and spirit).

5 Top up the serving glass by three-quarters with crushed ice and add the remaining 30ml (1oz) spirit.

6 Mix vigorously with the bar spoon for 5 seconds.

7 Add more crushed ice, piling it up in the centre in a dome shape (see page 214).

8 Place the straws in the glass, express the mint sprigs (see step 2, page 47) into it and place them close to the straws.

MOJITO

The Lowdown

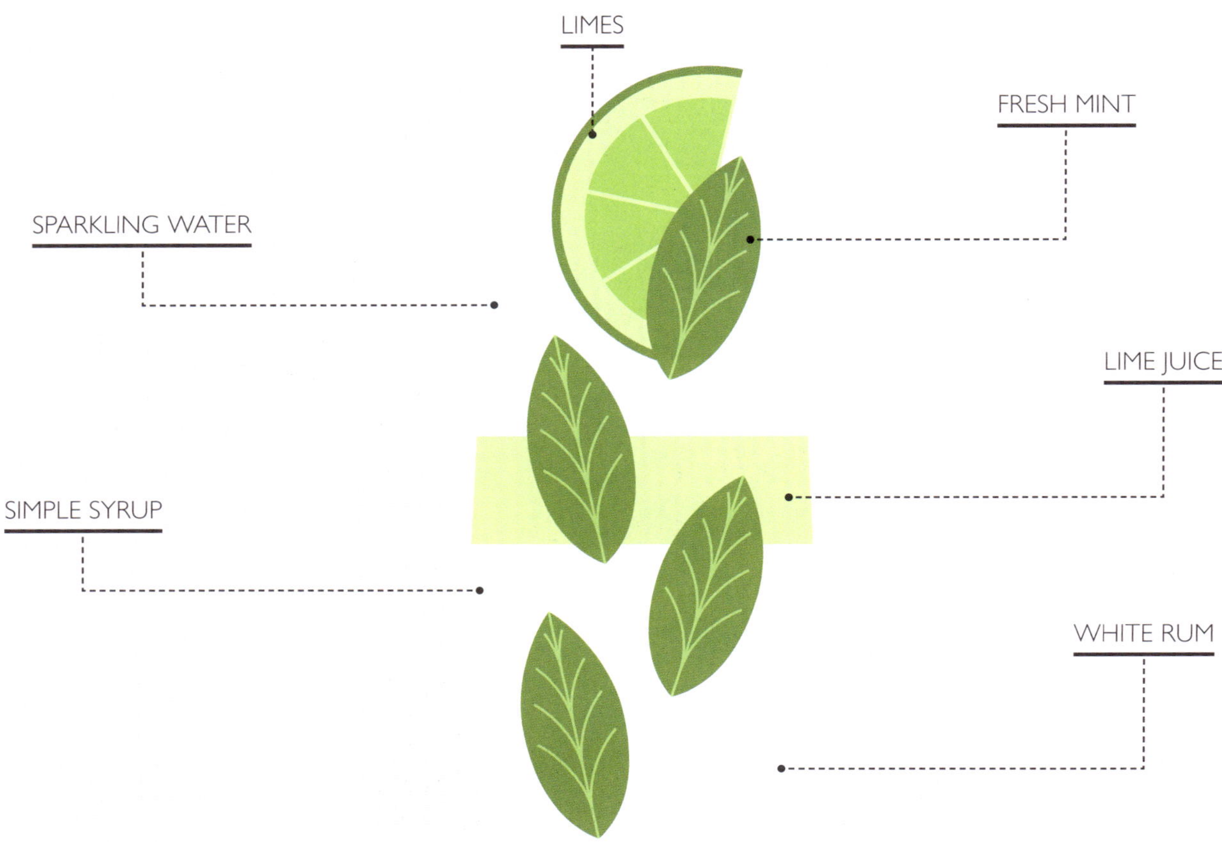

WHAT IS IT?

The classic cocktail for sunny days.

FAMILY

Mojito

TYPE

Long drink

ICE FOR SERVING

Cubes or crushed

TYPE OF GLASS

Tumbler

EQUIPMENT

Jigger
Muddler or pestle
Bar spoon
Reuseable or biodegradable straw

TECHNIQUES TO MASTER

Making a cocktail in a serving glass (see page 55)
Muddling (see page 214)
Expressing mint (see page 47)
Ice cubes and crushed iced (see page 39)

VARIATIONS

Fruit Mojito: add fresh fruits or fruit purées with the lemon (step 2).
Deluxe Mojito: add fresh fruits or fruit purées with the lemon (step 2) and replace the sparkling water with Champagne.
Mocktail: replace the rum with apple juice or sparkling water.

TIP

Crushed ice, ice cubes, herb sprigs, leaves, whole lemon or just juice, once again it is all a matter of taste. It's up to you to experiment to discover what best suits your palate.

SERVES 1

12 fresh mint leaves or 2 mint sprigs with leaves
25ml (2/3oz plus 1 tsp) simple syrup or 2 tsp white sugar
25ml (2/3oz plus 1 tsp) lime juice or 1/8 of a lime, cut into small pieces
50ml (1 2/3oz) white Cuban or South American rum
sparkling water

TO DECORATE

2 mint sprigs
1 lime wedge (1/8 of a lime)

MAKING WITH ICE CUBES

1 Put the mint in the bottom of the serving glass.

2 Add the syrup (or the sugar) and the lime juice (or pieces of lime).

3 Muddle or crush (see page 214) until the mint smells strongly.

4 Add ice cubes to fill the glass to the brim. Finish by adding the rum and sparkling water.

5 Mix briskly with the bar spoon for 5 seconds.

6 Add the straw. Express the mint sprigs (see step 2, page 47) and place them in the glass close to the straw, with the lime wedge alongside.

MAKING WITH CRUSHED ICE

1 Fill the serving glass one-quarter full with crushed ice and add the mint. Cover with crushed ice.

2 Add the syrup (or sugar) and the lime juice (or pieces of lime).

3 Muddle or crush (see page 214) until the mint smells strongly.

4 Pour in the rum and mix briskly for 5 seconds. Fill the glass with crushed ice and top up with sparkling water.

5 Mix again and add more crushed ice, piling it up to form a dome shape (see page 214). Finish as for the method using ice cubes (step 6).

MOSCOW MULE

The Lowdown

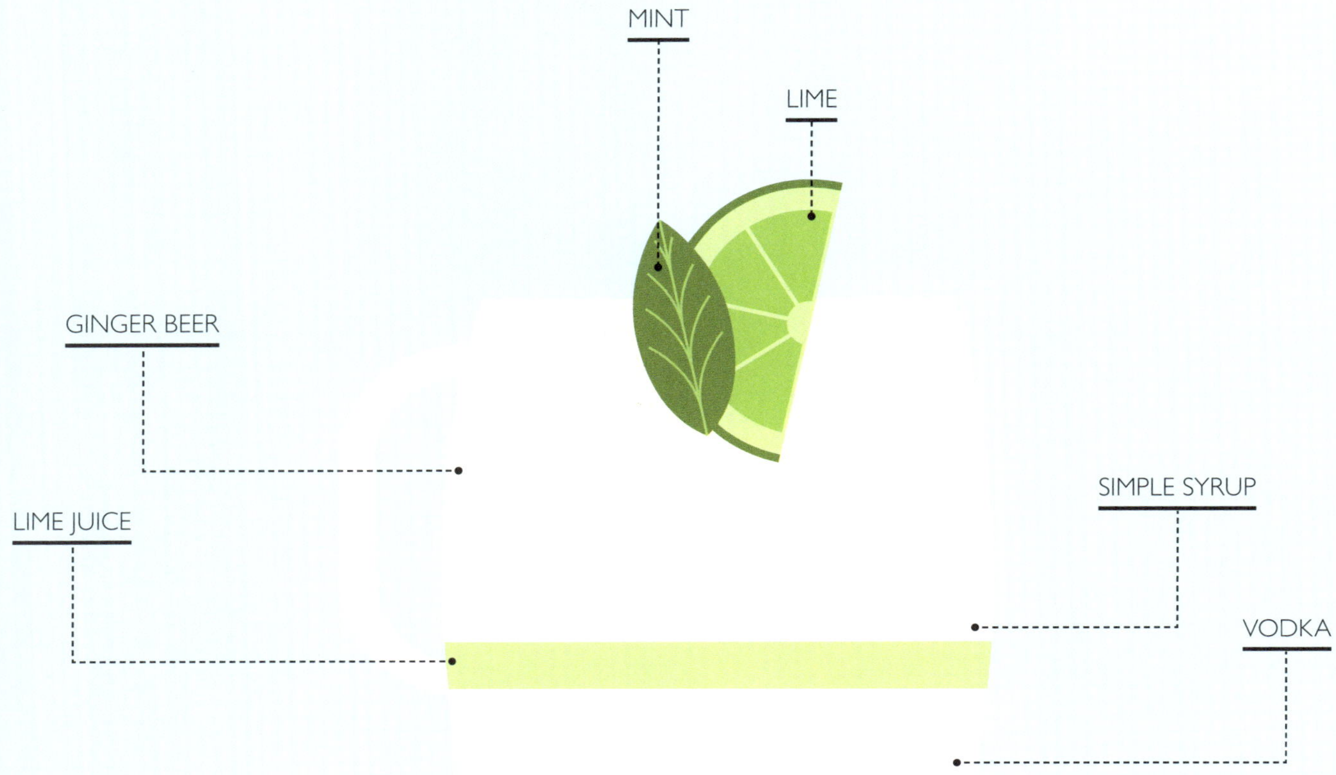

WHAT IS IT?

A modern classic that's spicy, tangy and can be endlessly adapted.

FAMILY

Mule

TYPE

Long drink

ICE FOR SERVING

Cubes

TYPE OF GLASS

Traditional: Mule cup
Alternative: tumbler

EQUIPMENT

Jigger
Bar spoon
Reuseable or biodegradable straw

TECHNIQUES TO MASTER

Making a cocktail in a serving glass (see page 55)
Expressing mint (see page 47)
Ice cubes (see page 39)

VARIATIONS

Ginger Mule: shake 50ml (1⅔oz) gin, 20ml (⅔oz) lime juice and 15ml (½oz) simple syrup with cucumber and mint, then top up with the ginger beer.
Bohemian Mule: use 40ml (1⅓oz) absinthe instead of vodka and omit the syrup.
Mocktail: omit the spirit.

TIP

The type of ginger beer you use will make all the difference in this cocktail. Preferably choose one made from fermented ginger rather than from a flavouring.

SERVES 1

50ml (1⅔oz) vodka
20ml (⅔oz) lime juice
10ml (2 tsp) simple syrup (depending on how sweet the ginger beer is)
100ml (3⅓oz) ginger beer

TO DECORATE

2 mint sprigs
1 lime wedge (⅛ of a lime)

1. Pour all the ingredients, except the ginger beer, into the serving glass.
2. Fill the glass to the brim with ice cubes and top up with the ginger beer.
3. Mix quickly (see page 56) with the bar spoon.
4. Place the reuseable or biodegradable straw in the glass.
5. Express the mint sprigs (see step 2, page 47) and place them and the lime wedge close to the straw.

DARK &

STORMY

The Lowdown

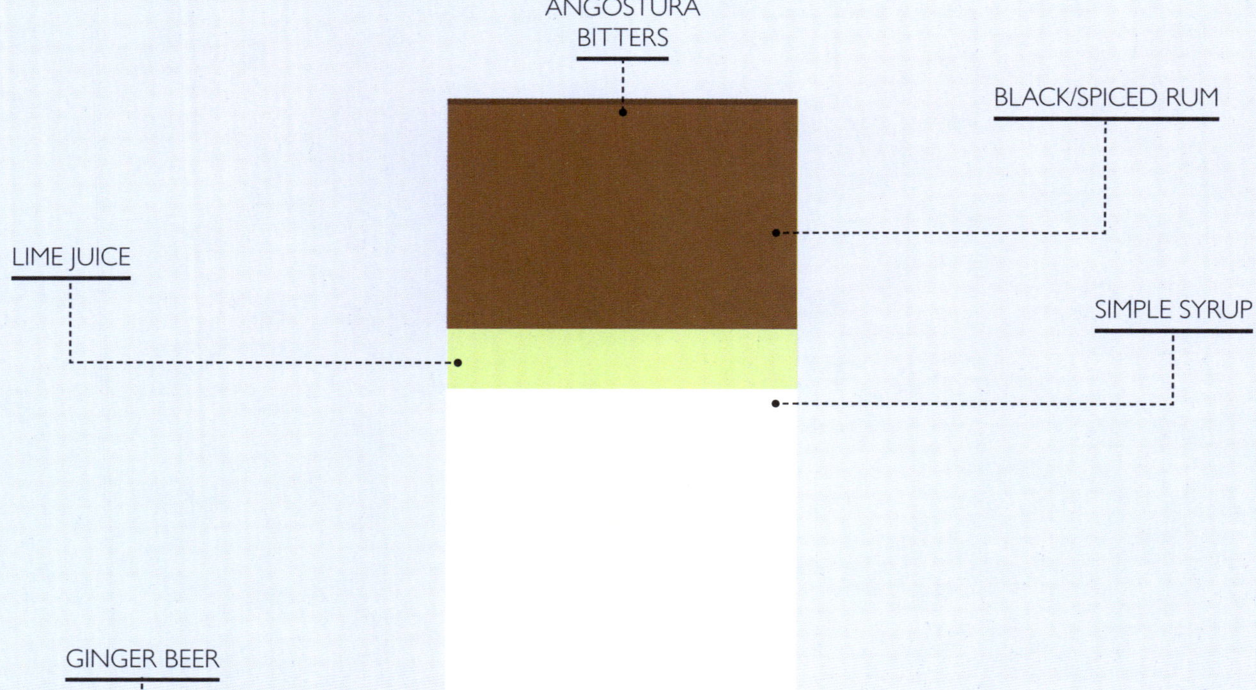

WHAT IS IT?

A spicier twist on the Moscow Mule.

FAMILY

Mule

TYPE

Long drink

ICE FOR SERVING

Cubes

TYPE OF GLASS

Tumbler

EQUIPMENT

Jigger
Bar spoon

TECHNIQUES TO MASTER

Making a cocktail in a serving glass (see page 55)
Layering (see page 57)

VARIATION

Moscow Mule: see page 180.

TIP

Always drunk without a straw.
Your chosen rum will define the cocktail's individual character.

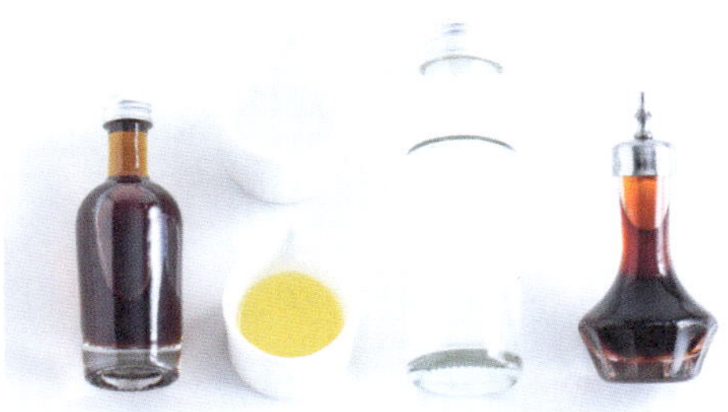

SERVES 1

20ml (⅔oz) lime juice
10ml (2 tsp) simple syrup (depending on how sweet the ginger beer is)
100ml (3⅓oz) ginger beer
50ml (1⅔oz) black/spiced rum
3 dashes Angostura bitters

1. Pour all the ingredients, except the rum and Angostura bitters, into the serving glass.
2. Mix quickly (see page 56) with the bar spoon.
3. Fill the glass to the brim with ice cubes.
4. Layer (see page 57) the rum on top, then add the Angostura bitters.

MAI TAI

The Lowdown

WHAT IS IT?

Powerful and complex, this is the most classic of the Tikis.

FAMILY

Tiki

TYPE

Short drink

ICE FOR SERVING

Cubes, crushed

TYPE OF GLASS

Old Fashioned or Tiki

EQUIPMENT

Jigger
Shaker
Single strainer
Reuseable or biodegradable straw
Cocktail tweezers

TECHNIQUES TO MASTER

Shake (see page 58)
Single filtration (see page 52)
Expressing mint (see page 47)
Ice cubes/crushed ice (see page 39)

VARIATION

If you wish, use a triple sec in place of the dry orange Curaçao and a different mix of rums. However, if you want to truly experience the original cocktail, stick to the exact ingredients.

Discover

SERVES 1

30ml (1oz) overproof white rum (more than 50% ABV/100 proof)
30ml (1oz) black/spiced rum
15ml (½oz) dry orange Curaçao
15ml (½oz) lime juice
15ml (½oz) orgeat syrup

TO DECORATE

1 pineapple leaf
1 amarena cherry
1 mint sprig
1 lime wedge (⅛ of a lime)

1. Pour all the ingredients into the shaker.
2. Fill the larger part of the shaker to the brim with ice and shake (see page 58) vigorously for 10 seconds.
3. Fill the serving glass with ice cubes to the brim and single filter (see page 52) the mixture into it.
4. Add crushed ice (see page 39), piling it up in a dome shape (see page 214).
5. Place the reuseable or biodegradable straw in the glass.
6. Express the mint (see step 2, page 47) and, using the cocktail tweezers, arrange all the decorations around the straw.

ZOMBIE

The Lowdown

WHAT IS IT?

One of the best-known Tikis, it contains a number of ingredients which make it exceptionally complex but accessible.

FAMILY

Tiki

TYPE

Long drink

ICE FOR SERVING

Cubes

EQUIPMENT

Jigger
Shaker
Single strainer
Cocktail tweezers

TYPE OF GLASS

Traditional: Tiki
Alternative: double Old Fashioned

TECHNIQUES TO MASTER

Shake (see page 58)
Single filtration (see page 52)
Expressing mint (see page 47)

SERVES 1

25ml (⅔oz plus 1 tsp) Jamaican rum
25ml (⅔oz plus 1 tsp) white rum
15ml (½oz) Don's Mix (the cinnamon-grapefruit syrup central to the cocktail: mix 1 part cinnamon syrup with 2 parts grapefruit juice)
15ml (½oz) Velvet Falernum liqueur
25ml (⅔oz plus 1 tsp) lime juice
10ml (2 tsp) grenadine
2 dashes of absinthe
1 dash of Angostura bitters

TO DECORATE

1 pineapple leaf
1 mint sprig
1 amarena cherry

1 Pour all the ingredients into the shaker.

2 Fill the larger part of the shaker to the brim with ice and shake (see page 58) vigorously for 10 seconds.

3 Fill the serving glass to the brim with ice cubes and single filter (see page 52) the mixture into it.

4 Stand a pineapple leaf in the glass. Express and roll the mint sprig (see page 47) and, using the cocktail tweezers, place it and the cherry next to the pineapple leaf.

PAINKILLER

The Lowdown

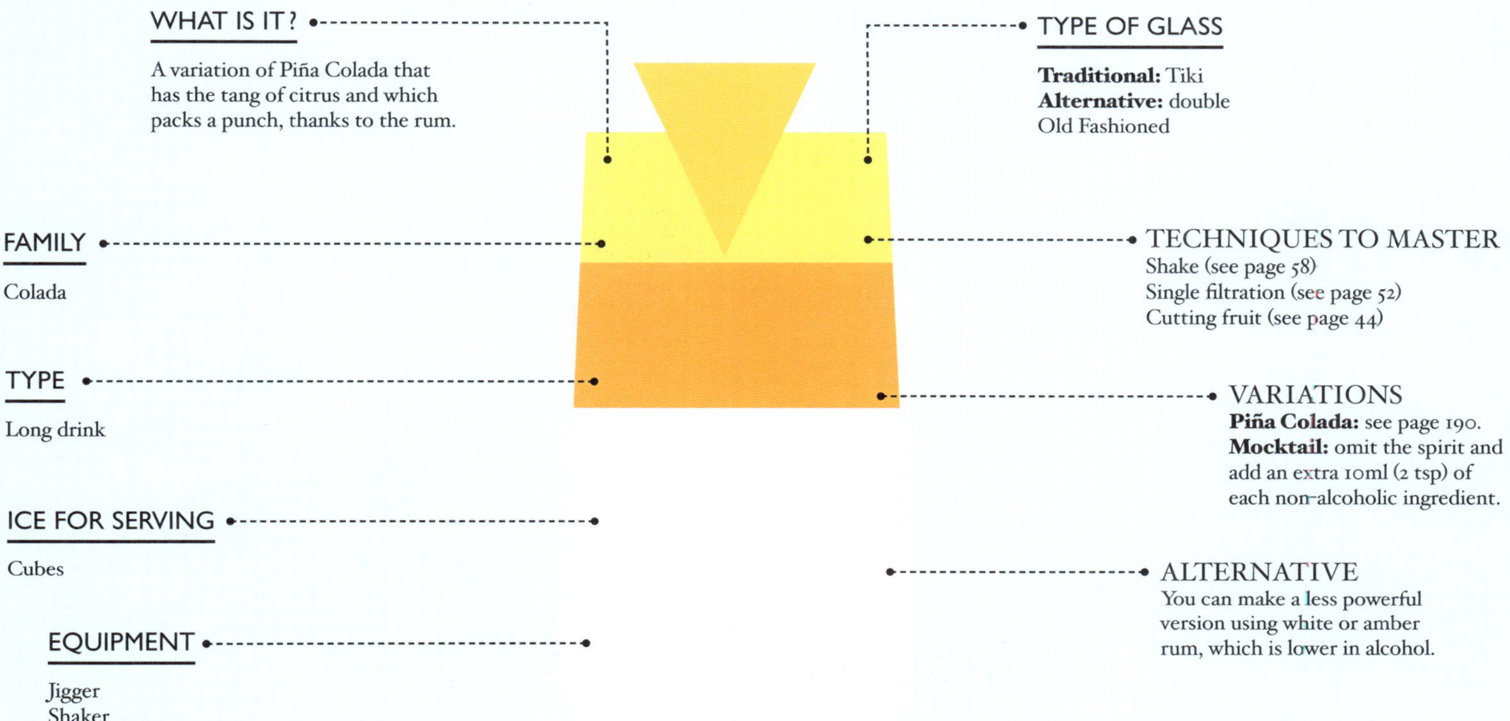

WHAT IS IT?

A variation of Piña Colada that has the tang of citrus and which packs a punch, thanks to the rum.

TYPE OF GLASS

Traditional: Tiki
Alternative: double Old Fashioned

FAMILY

Colada

TECHNIQUES TO MASTER

Shake (see page 58)
Single filtration (see page 52)
Cutting fruit (see page 44)

TYPE

Long drink

VARIATIONS

Piña Colada: see page 190.
Mocktail: omit the spirit and add an extra 10ml (2 tsp) of each non-alcoholic ingredient.

ICE FOR SERVING

Cubes

ALTERNATIVE

You can make a less powerful version using white or amber rum, which is lower in alcohol.

EQUIPMENT

Jigger
Shaker
Single strainer

SERVES 1

60ml (2oz) navy rum (50% ABV/100 proof)
20ml (⅔oz) coconut cream
30ml (1oz) orange juice
30ml (1oz) pineapple

TO DECORATE

1 pineapple wedge

1. Pour all the ingredients into the shaker.
2. Fill the larger part of the shaker to the brim with ice and shake (see page 58) vigorously for 10 seconds.
3. Fill the serving glass to the brim with ice cubes and single filter (see page 52) the mixture into it.
4. Sit the pineapple wedge (see page 44) on the rim of the glass.

JUNGLE BIRD

The Lowdown

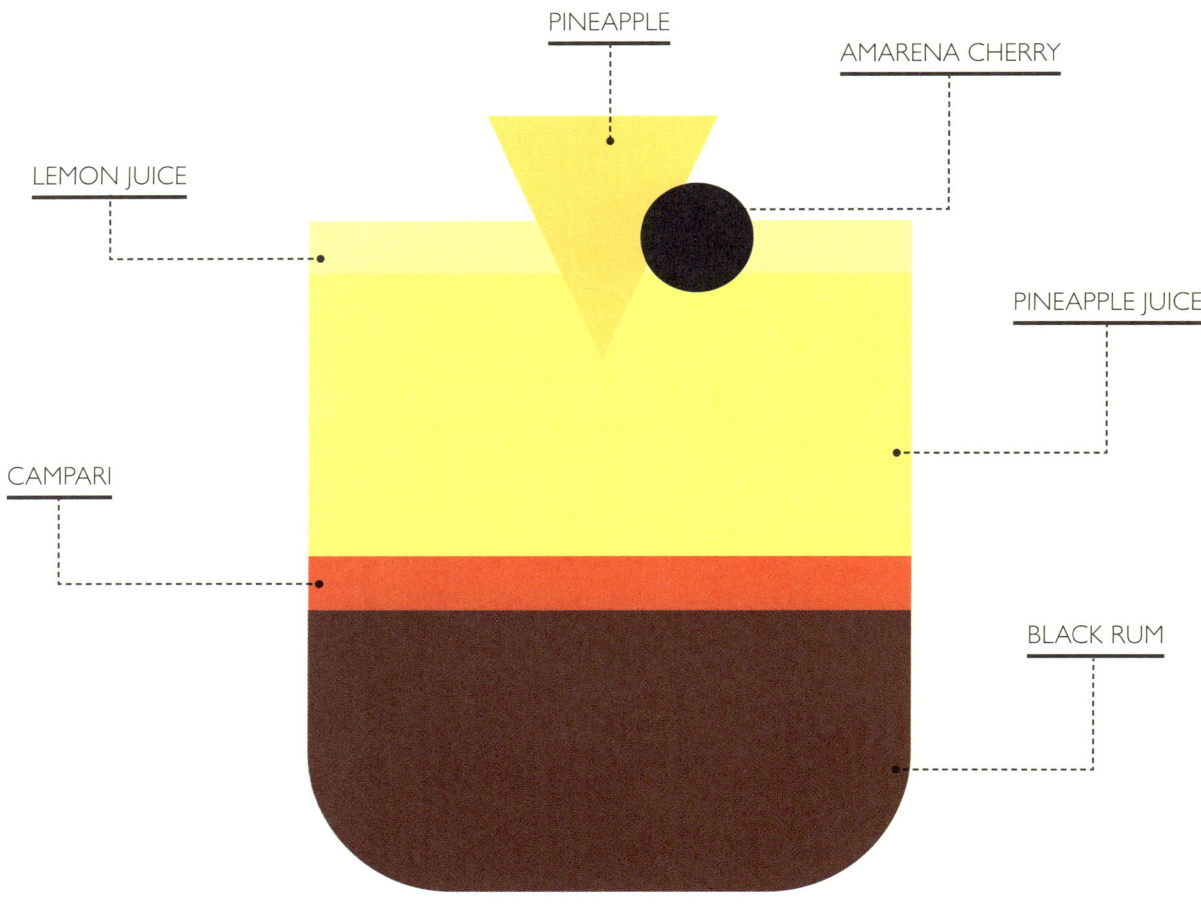

WHAT IS IT?

An interesting Tiki that blends the sweetness of fruit with a lovely touch of bitterness.

FAMILY

Tiki

TYPE

Long drink

ICE FOR SERVING

Cubes or block

TYPE OF GLASS

Old Fashioned or Tiki

EQUIPMENT

Jigger
Shaker
Single strainer
Cocktail stick (pick)

TECHNIQUES TO MASTER

Shake (see page 58)
Single filtration (see page 52)
Cutting fruit (see page 44)

TIP

Use fresh pineapple juice, or one that has been squeezed using a juice extractor just before making the cocktail, for a really refreshing result.

Discover

SERVES 1

45ml (1½oz) black rum
15ml (½oz) Campari
40ml (1⅓oz) pineapple juice
15ml (½oz) lemon juice

TO DECORATE

1 pineapple wedge
1 amarena cherry

1 Pour all the ingredients into the shaker.

2 Fill the larger part of the shaker to the brim with ice and shake (see page 58) vigorously for 10 seconds.

3 Fill the serving glass with ice cubes to the brim and single filter (see page 52) the mixture into it.

4 Skewer both the pineapple wedge (see page 44) and the cherry on the cocktail stick (pick) and place on the rim of the glass.

PIÑA COLADA

The Lowdown

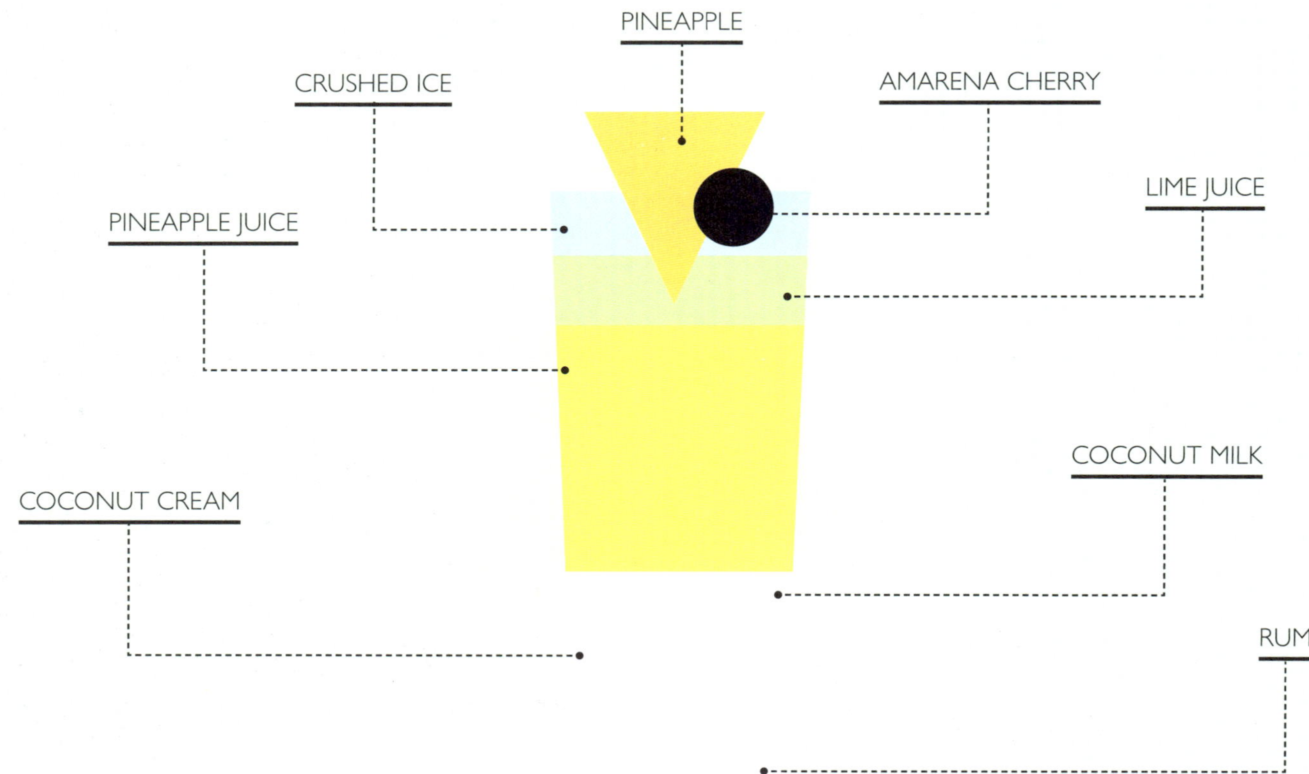

WHAT IS IT?

A long, smooth, feel-good, timeless drink.

FAMILY

Colada

TYPE

Long drink

ICE FOR SERVING

Cubes

TYPE OF GLASS

Highball

EQUIPMENT

Jigger
Shaker or blender
Single strainer

TECHNIQUES TO MASTER

Shake (see page 58)
Blending (see page 215)
Single filtration (see page 52)
Crushed ice (see page 39)
Cutting fruit (see page 44)

VARIATIONS

Painkiller: see page 187.
Mocktail: omit the rum.

ALTERNATIVE

Traditionally, this cocktail is made with Cuban or South American white rum, but you can also use aged rum or rhum agricole to give the drink more body.

Discover

SERVES 1

50ml (1⅔oz) rum
25ml (⅔oz plus 1 tsp) coconut cream
10ml (2 tsp) coconut milk
75ml (2⅓oz plus 1 tsp) pineapple juice or 200g (7oz) fresh pineapple if made in the blender
15ml (½oz) lime juice
150ml (5oz) crushed ice (if made in the blender)

TO DECORATE

1 amarena cherry
1 pineapple wedge

MAKING IN THE SHAKER

1 Pour all the ingredients into the shaker.

2 Fill the larger part of the shaker to the brim with crushed ice (see page 39) and shake (see page 58) vigorously for 10 seconds.

3 Fill the serving glass with ice cubes to the brim and single filter (see page 52) the mixture into it.

4 Skewer the cherry on the cocktail stick (pick) and balance it on the rim of the glass. Place the pineapple wedge (see page 44) on the other side of the glass.

MAKING IN THE BLENDER

1 Pour all the ingredients into the blender. Cut the pineapple into pieces and add as well.

2 Add the crushed ice (see page 39).

3 Blend (see page 215) on medium speed increasing to maximum speed after 5 seconds.

4 Pour into the serving glass.

5 Skewer the cherry on the cocktail stick (pick) and balance it on the rim of the glass. Place the pineapple wedge (see page 44) on the other side of the glass.

CUBA LIBRE

The Lowdown

WHAT IS IT?

A rum cola with a touch of lime.

FAMILY

Highball

TYPE

Long drink

ICE FOR SERVING

Cubes

TYPE OF GLASS

Highball

EQUIPMENT

Jigger
Bar spoon

TECHNIQUES TO MASTER

Making a cocktail in a serving glass (see page 55)

TIP

The characteristics of your chosen rum will be reflected in this simple cocktail. Avoid colas with added sweeteners as they often react badly with acid and produce a metallic taste.

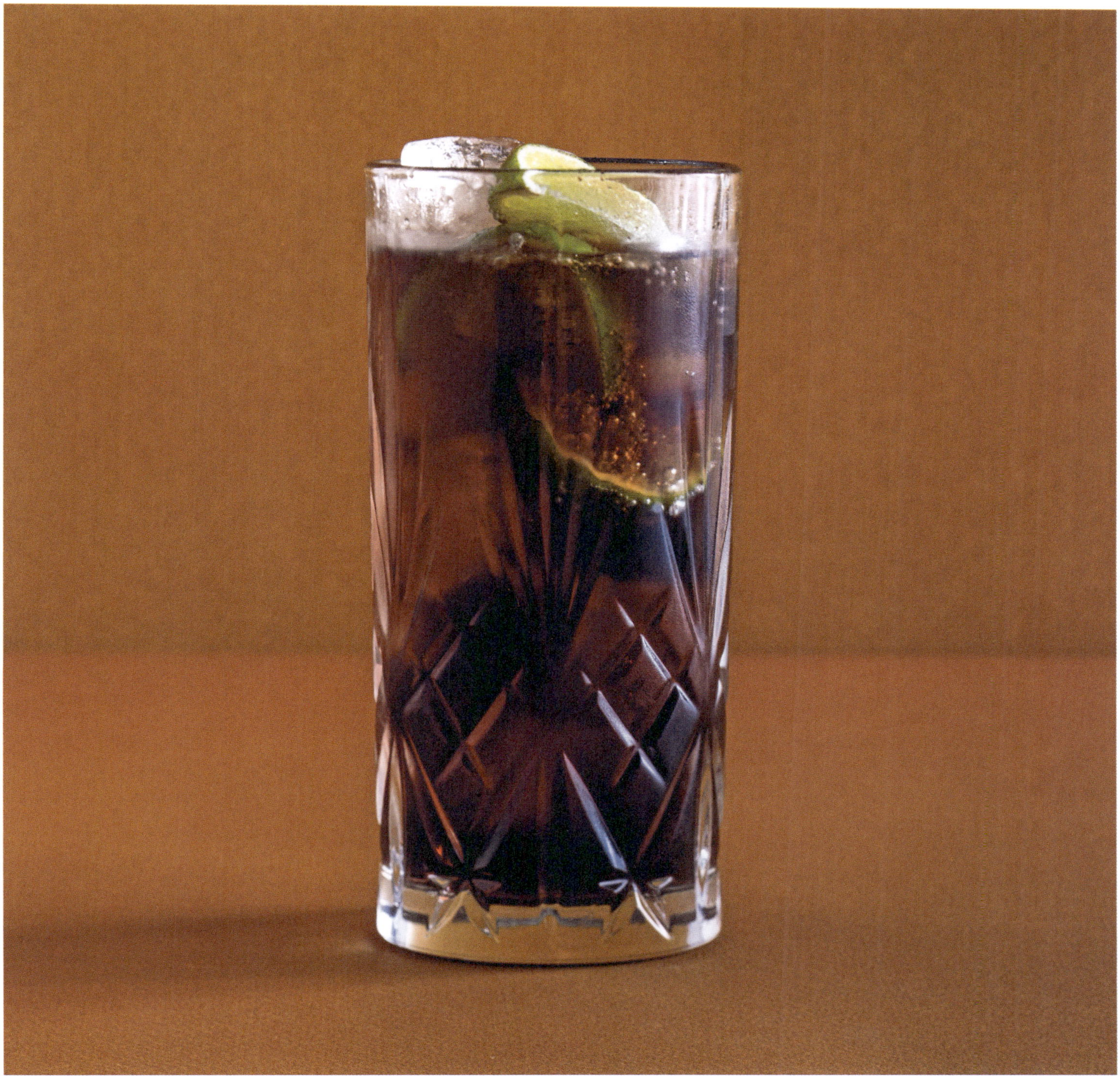

SERVES 1

2 lime wedges (each 1/8 of a lime)
50ml (1⅔oz) Cuban or South American rum
150ml (5oz) cola

TO DECORATE

1 lime wedge (1/8 of a lime)

1. Squeeze the 2 lime wedges into the serving glass and then drop them into the glass.
2. Fill the glass with ice cubes.
3. Pour in the rum, followed by the cola.
4. Stir briskly with the bar spoon.
5. Sit the remaining lime wedge on top of the cocktail.

PALOMA

The Lowdown

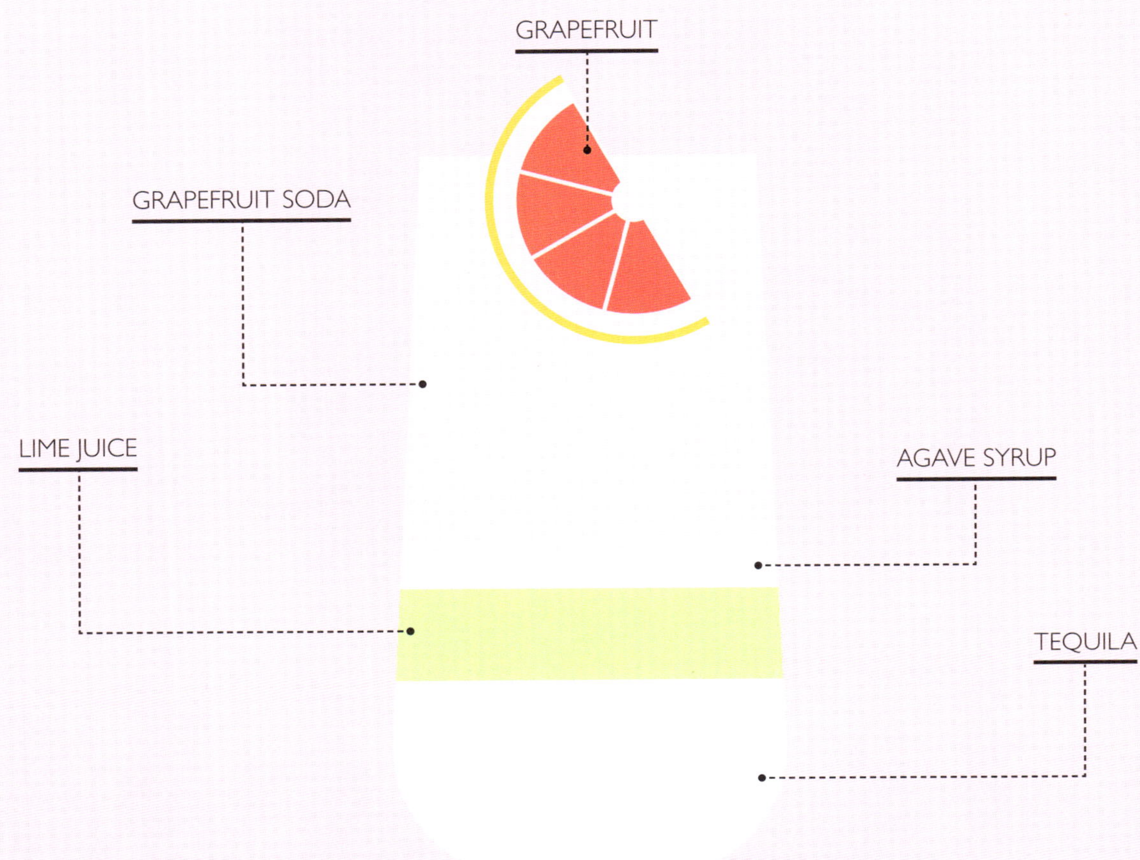

WHAT IS IT?

A classic cocktail that's very refreshing and currently enjoying a revival.

FAMILY

Rickey

TYPE

Long drink

ICE FOR SERVING

Cubes

TYPE OF GLASS

Highball

EQUIPMENT

Jigger
Shaker
Single strainer
Bar spoon
Cocktail tweezers

TECHNIQUES TO MASTER

Shake (see page 58)
Single filtration (see page 52)

ALTERNATIVES

It can also be made with gin.
You can replace the soda with 40ml (1⅓oz) grapefruit juice and 60ml (2oz) sparkling water.

Discover

SERVES 1

50ml (1⅔oz) silver or joven tequila
25ml (⅔oz) lime juice
10ml (2 tsp) agave syrup
100ml (3⅓oz) grapefruit soda

TO DECORATE

½ slice of ruby grapefruit

1. Pour all the ingredients, except the soda, into the shaker.
2. Fill the larger part of the shaker to the brim with ice and shake (see page 58) vigorously for 10 seconds.
3. Fill the serving glass with ice cubes to the brim and single filter (see page 52) the mixture into it.
4. Mix with the bar spoon.
5. Using the cocktail tweezers, sit the half grapefruit slice upright in the glass by the rim, stirring the slice a few times around the glass.

HARVARD

COOLER

The Lowdown

WHAT IS IT?

A very fresh Rickey with the gorgeous aromas and flavour of apple.

EQUIPMENT

Jigger
Shaker
Single strainer
Bar spoon

FAMILY

Rickey

TYPE OF GLASS

Highball

TYPE

Long drink

TECHNIQUES TO MASTER

Shake (see page 58)
Single filtration (see page 52)
Ice cubes/block of ice (see page 36)

VARIATIONS

Mocktail: replace the Calvados with apple juice.

ICE FOR SERVING

Cubes

TIP

Opt for a young Calvados so you don't reduce the cocktail's freshness.

SERVES 1

50ml (1⅔oz) Calvados
25ml (⅔oz plus 1 tsp) lime juice
25ml (⅔oz plus 1 tsp) simple syrup
120ml (4oz) sparkling water

TO DECORATE

1 lime wedge (⅛ of a lime)

1. Pour all the ingredients, except the sparkling water, into the shaker.
2. Fill the larger part of the shaker to the brim with ice and shake (see page 58) vigorously for 10 seconds.
3. Fill the serving glass to the brim with ice cubes or add a block of ice (see page 36) and single filter (see page 52) the mixture into it.
4. Pour in the sparkling water to come about two fingers from the rim of the glass.
5. Mix with the bar spoon.
6. Place the lime wedge on top of the cocktail against the side of the glass.

HORSE'S NECK

The Lowdown

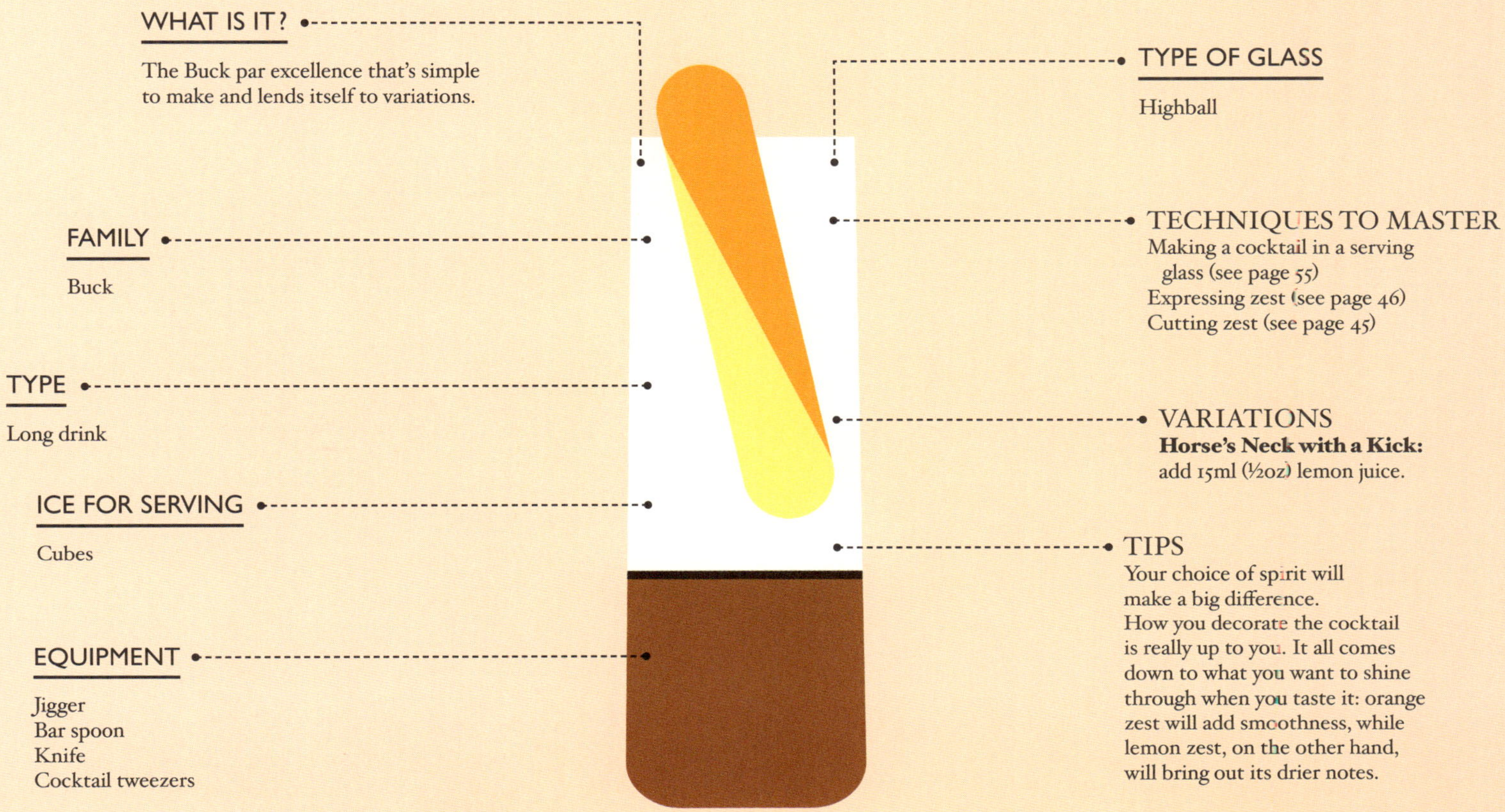

WHAT IS IT?

The Buck par excellence that's simple to make and lends itself to variations.

FAMILY

Buck

TYPE

Long drink

ICE FOR SERVING

Cubes

EQUIPMENT

Jigger
Bar spoon
Knife
Cocktail tweezers

TYPE OF GLASS

Highball

TECHNIQUES TO MASTER

Making a cocktail in a serving glass (see page 55)
Expressing zest (see page 46)
Cutting zest (see page 45)

VARIATIONS

Horse's Neck with a Kick: add 15ml (½oz) lemon juice.

TIPS

Your choice of spirit will make a big difference.
How you decorate the cocktail is really up to you. It all comes down to what you want to shine through when you taste it: orange zest will add smoothness, while lemon zest, on the other hand, will bring out its drier notes.

SERVES 1

50ml (1⅔oz) Cognac or bourbon
120ml (4oz) ginger ale
2 dashes of Angostura bitters

TO DECORATE

1 long strip of unwaxed orange or lemon zest

1 Fill the serving glass with ice cubes and pour the spirit into it.

2 Pour in the ginger ale.

3 Express the citrus zest (see page 46) in the centre of the glass. Use the cocktail tweezers to place the zest at the bottom of the glass and then twist it in a spiral all the way up the sides of the glass to the top.

4 Add the 2 dashes of bitters.

CHAMPAGNE

COCKTAIL

The Lowdown

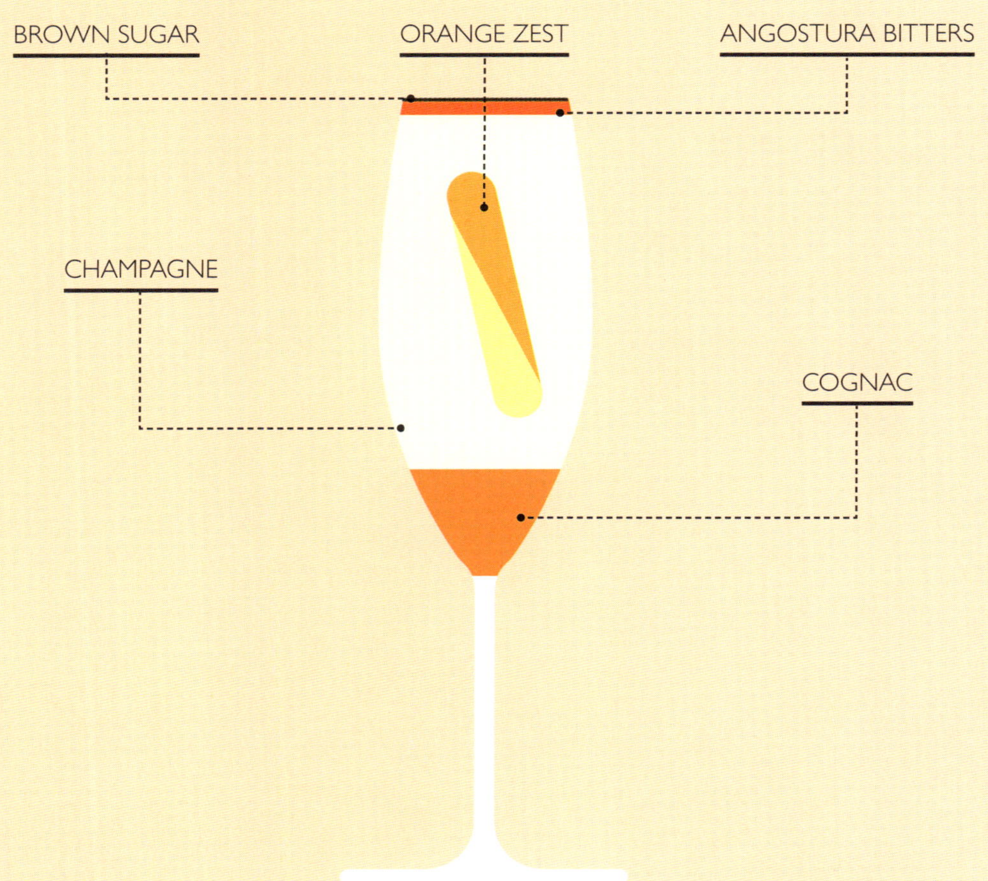

WHAT IS IT?

The first and most famous of the Champagne cocktails; it's complex and evocative.

FAMILY

Champagne cocktail

TYPE

Long drink

TYPE OF GLASS

Flute

EQUIPMENT

Jigger
Bar spoon
Knife/peeler
Cocktail tweezers

TECHNIQUES TO MASTER

Making a cocktail in a serving glass (see page 55)
Expressing zest (see page 46)

ALTERNATIVES

Depending on your choice of Cognac and Champagne, the finished cocktail can turn out completely differently. To ensure it is well balanced, opt for a well-rounded VSOP Cognac and a brut Champagne.

Discover

SERVES 1

1 brown sugar cube
4 dashes of Angostura bitters
1 dash of orange bitters
30ml (1oz) Cognac
100ml (3⅓oz) Champagne

TO DECORATE

1 long strip of unwaxed orange zest

1. Put the sugar cube in the serving glass.
2. Add the dashes of bitters.
3. Crush together with the bar spoon to make a smooth paste.
4. Pour in the Cognac and stir lightly with the bar spoon.
5. Pour in the Champagne.
6. Express the zest (see page 46) in the centre of the glass and then rub it over the rim of the glass.
7. Use the cocktail tweezers to place the zest at the bottom of the glass and then twist it in a spiral all the way up the sides of the glass to the top.

AIR MAIL

The Lowdown

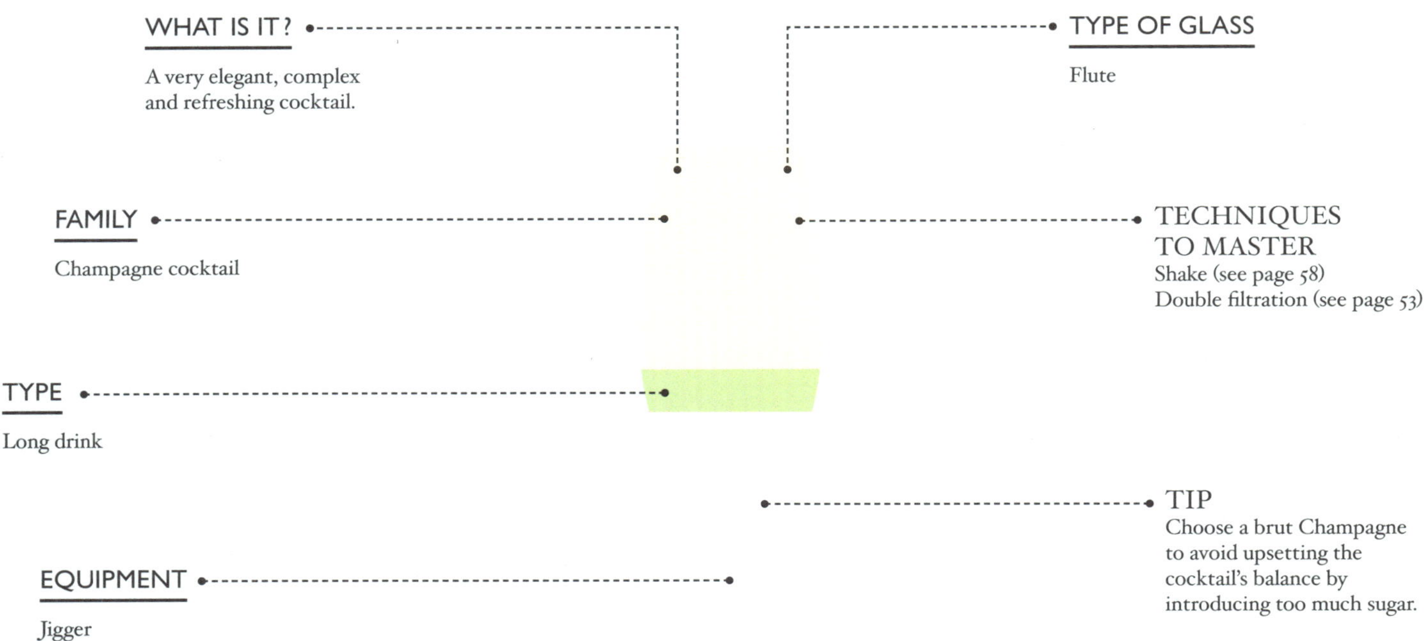

WHAT IS IT?

A very elegant, complex and refreshing cocktail.

TYPE OF GLASS

Flute

FAMILY

Champagne cocktail

TECHNIQUES TO MASTER

Shake (see page 58)
Double filtration (see page 53)

TYPE

Long drink

TIP

Choose a brut Champagne to avoid upsetting the cocktail's balance by introducing too much sugar.

EQUIPMENT

Jigger
Shaker
Bar spoon
Single strainer
Fine-mesh strainer

SERVES 1

35ml (1oz plus 1 tsp) Cuban or South American rum
20ml (⅔oz) triple honey syrup (see page 30)
20ml (⅔oz) lime juice
100ml (3⅓oz) Champagne

1. Pour all the ingredients, except the Champagne, into the shaker.
2. Mix with the bar spoon to prevent the syrup remaining on the sides of the shaker.
3. Fill the larger part of the shaker to the brim with ice and shake (see page 58) vigorously for 10 seconds.
4. Double filter (see page 53) into the serving glass.
5. Top up with the Champagne.
6. Stir quickly with the bar spoon.

OLD CUBAN

The Lowdown

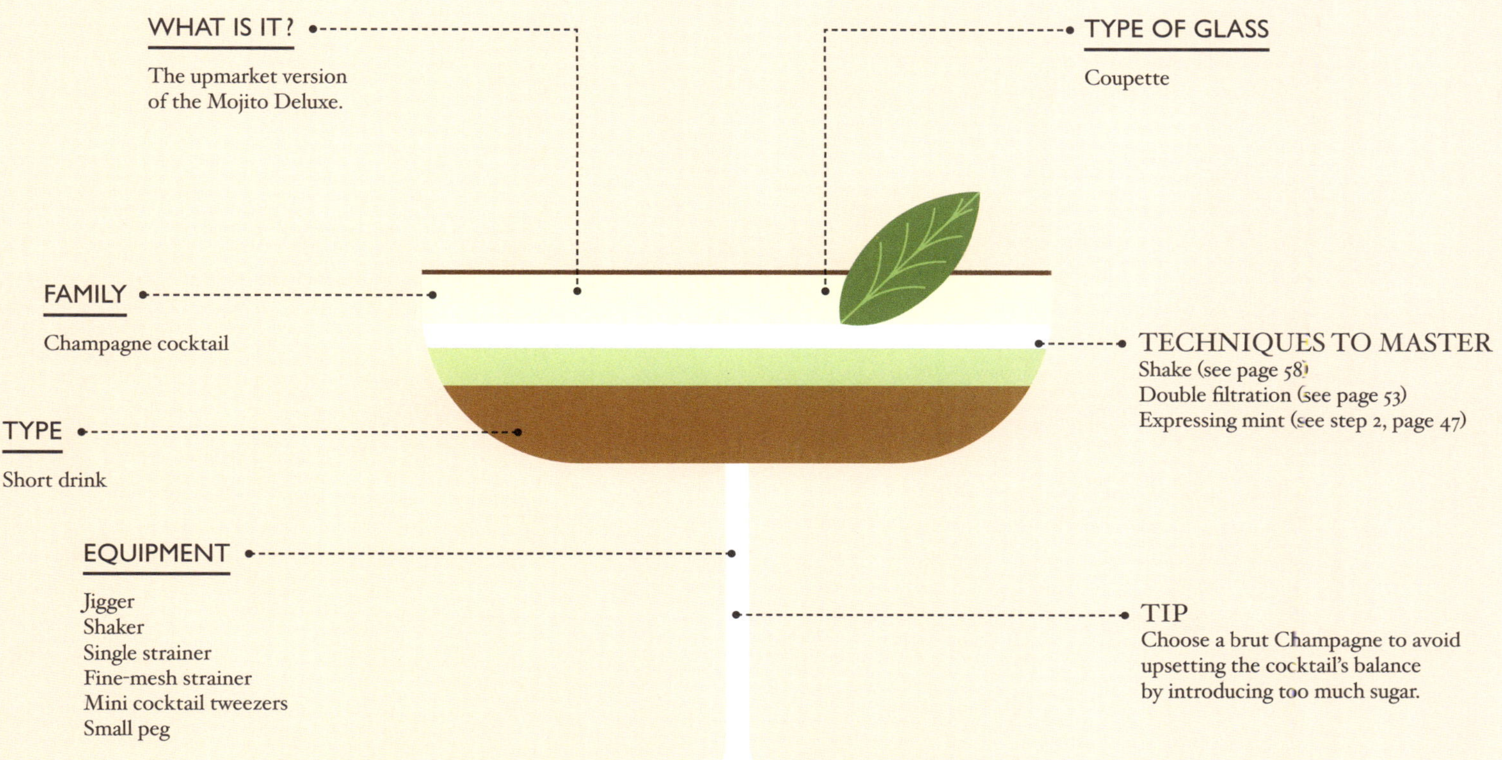

SERVES 1

45ml (1½oz) Cuban or South American brown rum
20ml (⅔oz) lime juice
15ml (½oz) simple syrup
2 dashes of Angostura bitters
30ml (1oz) Champagne
1 mint leaf

1. Pour all the ingredients, except the Champagne and the mint, into the shaker.
2. Fill the larger part of the shaker to the brim with ice and shake (see page 58) vigorously for 10 seconds.
3. Double filter (see page 53) into the serving glass.
4. Pour in the Champagne.
5. Express the mint (see step 2, page 47). Using the mini cocktail tweezers, position the leaf on the outside of the glass, fixing it into place with a small peg.

FRENCH 75

The Lowdown

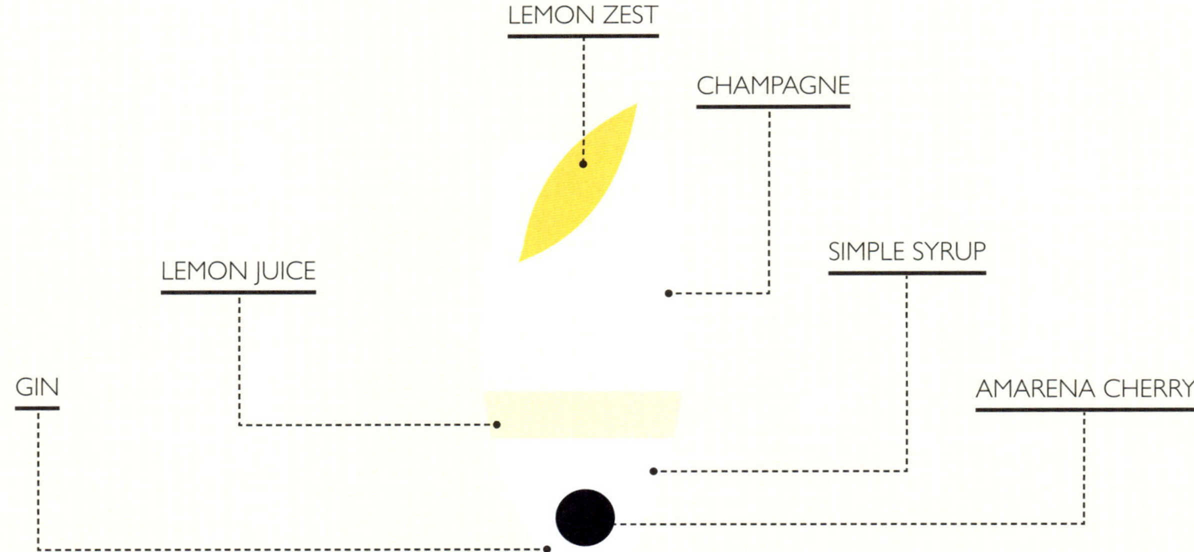

WHAT IS IT?

An explosion of freshness.

FAMILY

Champagne cocktail

TYPE

Long drink

TYPE OF GLASS

Flute

EQUIPMENT

Jigger
Shaker
Single strainer
Fine-mesh strainer
Cocktail tweezers

TECHNIQUES TO MASTER

Shake (see page 58)
Double filtration (see page 53)
Expressing zest (see page 46)

VARIATIONS

French 95: use bourbon in place of the gin.
French 125: use Cognac in place of the gin.

ALTERNATIVE

It's very easy to add a twist to this cocktail by using a flavoured syrup instead of simple syrup.

TIP

Choose a gin with a strong citrus flavour so the cocktail's freshness explodes in your mouth.

Discover

SERVES 1

40ml (1⅓oz) gin
20ml (⅔oz) simple syrup
20ml (⅔oz) lemon juice
100ml (3⅓oz) Champagne

TO DECORATE

zest of 1 unwaxed lemon
1 amarena cherry

1. Pour all the ingredients, except the Champagne, into the shaker.
2. Fill the larger part of the shaker to the brim with ice and shake (see page 58) vigorously for 10 seconds.
3. Double filter (see page 53) into the serving glass.
4. Pour in the Champagne.
5. Express the zest (see page 46) in the centre of the glass, then rub it over the rim and stem of the glass.
6. Gently drop the cherry into the glass, using the cocktail tweezers.

BELLINI

The Lowdown

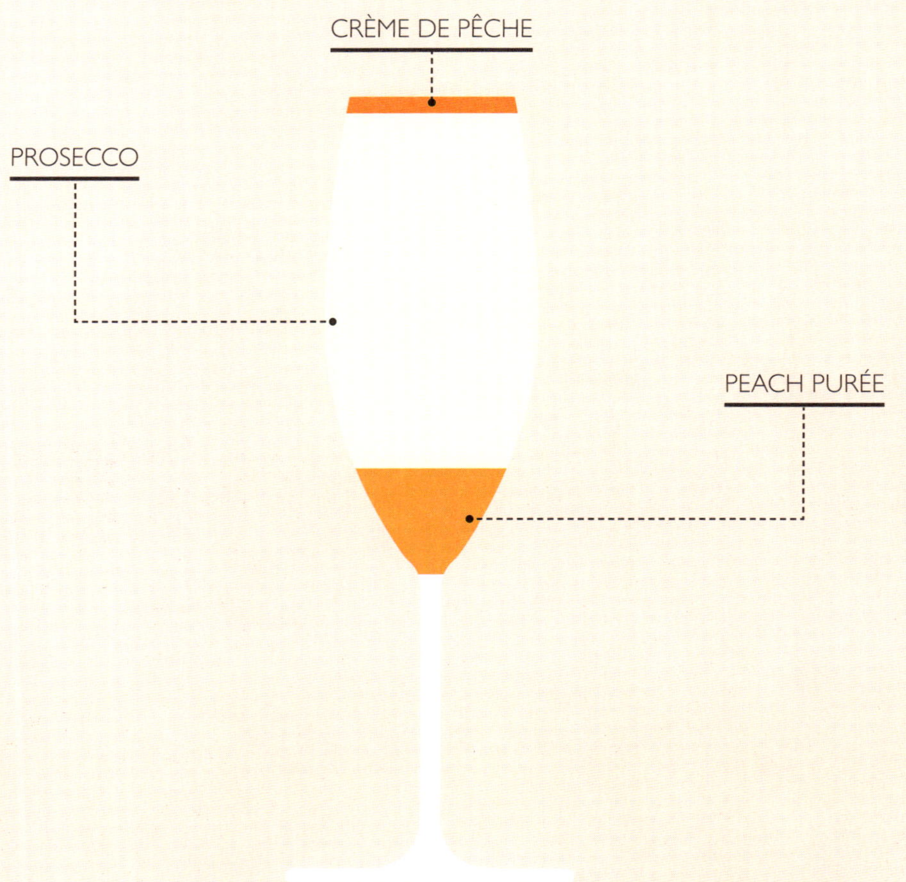

WHAT IS IT?

Of all the cocktails made with sparkling wine, this is the most classic and easy to adapt.

FAMILY

Champagne cocktail

TYPE

Long drink

TYPE OF GLASS

Highball or flute

EQUIPMENT

Jigger
Shaker
Bar spoon
Single strainer or Julep strainer

TECHNIQUES TO MASTER

Throwing (see page 59)

VARIATIONS

Rossini: add puréed red fruits and a liqueur or crème of red fruits, such as Chambord.
Mocktail: add a sparkling non-alcoholic wine and peach syrup in place of the crème de pêche.

ALTERNATIVES

You can also make this with Champagne. Endless variations of this cocktail can be created by adding different fruit purées and liqueurs.

Discover

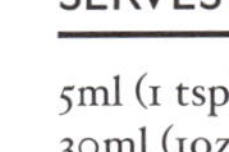

SERVES 1

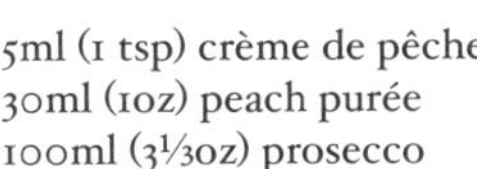

5ml (1 tsp) crème de pêche
30ml (1oz) peach purée
100ml ($3\frac{1}{3}$oz) prosecco

1. Pour all the ingredients into the smaller part of the shaker and mix rapidly with the bar spoon.
2. Fill the larger part of the shaker two-thirds full with ice cubes, pour in the cocktail and place the strainer on top.
3. Throw (see page 59) the cocktail twice from the larger part of the shaker to the smaller part.
4. Pour into the serving glass.

PISCO PUNCH

The Lowdown

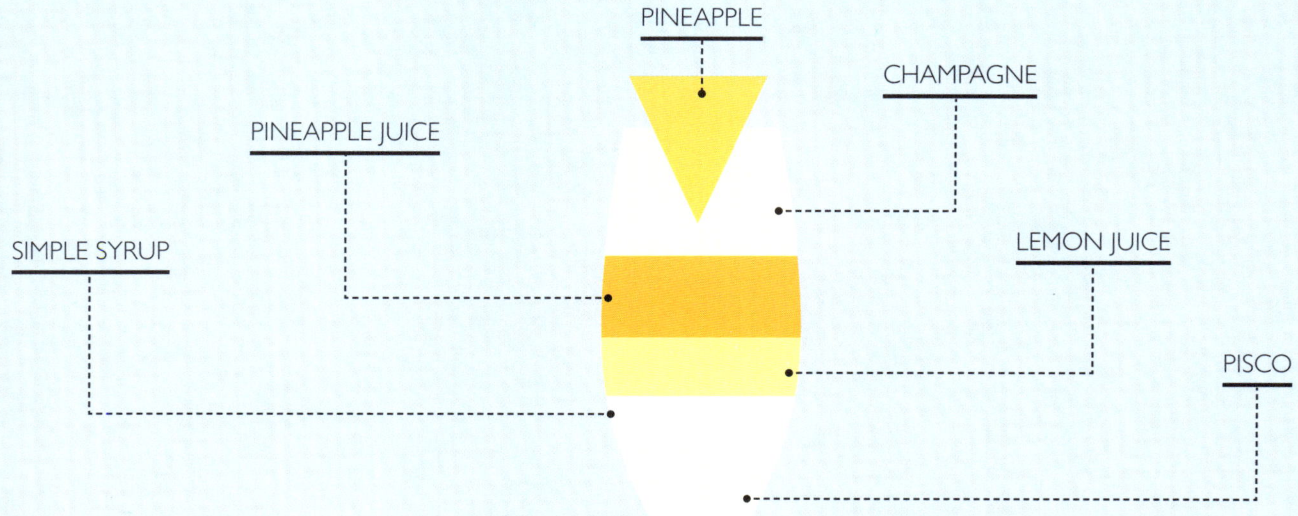

WHAT IS IT?

A Champagne cocktail with fruity and floral notes.

FAMILY

Champagne cocktail

TYPE

Long drink

TYPE OF GLASS

Flute

EQUIPMENT

Jigger
Shaker
Single strainer
Fine-mesh strainer
Bar spoon

TECHNIQUES TO MASTER

Shake (see page 58)
Double filtration (see page 53)
Cutting fruits (see page 44)

TIP

Depending on which pisco and pineapple juice you use, you may need to adjust the quantity of simple syrup.

SERVES 1

50ml (1⅔oz) pisco
10ml (2 tsp) simple syrup
25ml (⅔oz plus 1 tsp) lemon juice
30ml (1oz) pineapple juice
35ml (1oz plus 1 tsp) Champagne

TO DECORATE

1 pineapple wedge

1 Pour all the ingredients, except the Champagne, into the shaker.

2 Fill the upper part of the shaker to the brim with ice and shake (see page 58) vigorously for 10 seconds.

3 Fill the serving glass with ice cubes and double filter (see page 53) the mixture into it.

4 Pour in the Champagne.

5 Stir rapidly with the bar spoon.

6 Tuck the pineapple wedge (see page 44) upright on the rim of the glass.

CHAPTER 3

ILLUSTRATED GLOSSARY

UTENSILS

GLASSES

BASIC TERMS/TECHNIQUES

TASTING GUIDE

UTENSILS

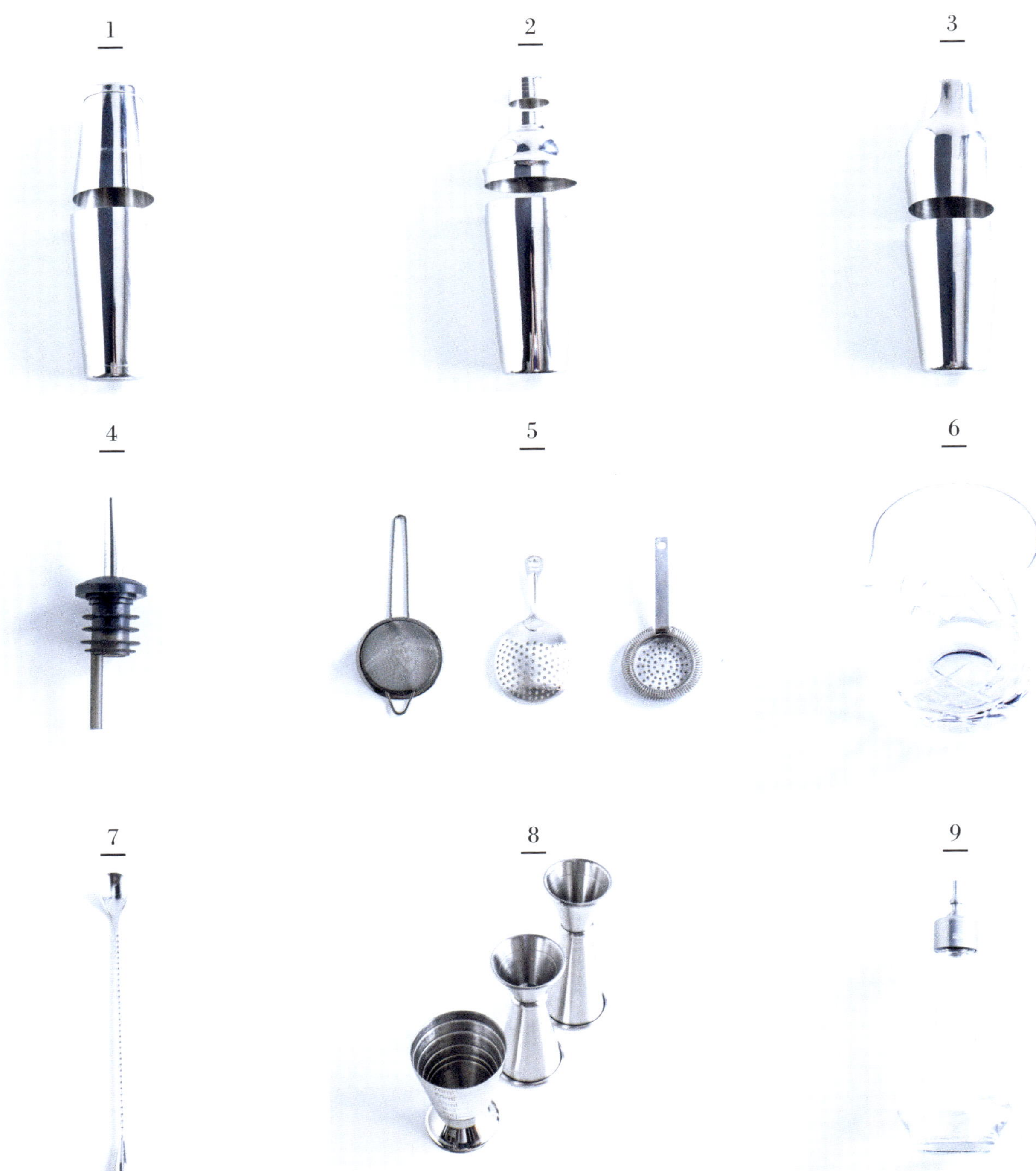

1 BOSTON SHAKER

The most practical and easy to maintain. Choose an all-metal shaker for good thermal conduction.

2 3-PIECE SHAKER

3 PARISIAN SHAKER

4 POURING SPOUT (OR POURER, SPEED POURER)

5 FINE-MESH STRAINER, JULEP STRAINER, SINGLE STRAINER (OR STRAINER)

6 MIXING GLASS

Comes in all shapes and sizes. Opt for ones made of thick glass, as they will provide consistent thermal conduction.

7 BAR SPOON

Comes in all sizes with a great variety of bowls. Choose a spoon with a twisted handle measuring more than 18cm (7in) so it easily reaches the bottom of mixing glasses or shakers.

8 JIGGERS

To accurately measure quantities and pour them. Choose a set of jiggers for the following measures: 10ml (2 tsp), 15ml (½oz), 20ml (⅔oz), 25ml (⅔oz plus 1 tsp), 30ml (1oz), 35ml (1oz plus 1 tsp), 40ml (1⅓oz), 45ml (1½oz), 50ml (1⅔oz). Opt for metal ones to avoid scratches and the transference of tastes or colours. The jiggers must be rinsed each time after use to avoid adding any residual flavour to the next cocktail.

9 BITTERS BOTTLE

Fitted with a measuring spout (or dasher), this will measure more precisely and consistently than commercially available bottles when adding dashes of bitters (aromatic concentrates).

UTENSILS

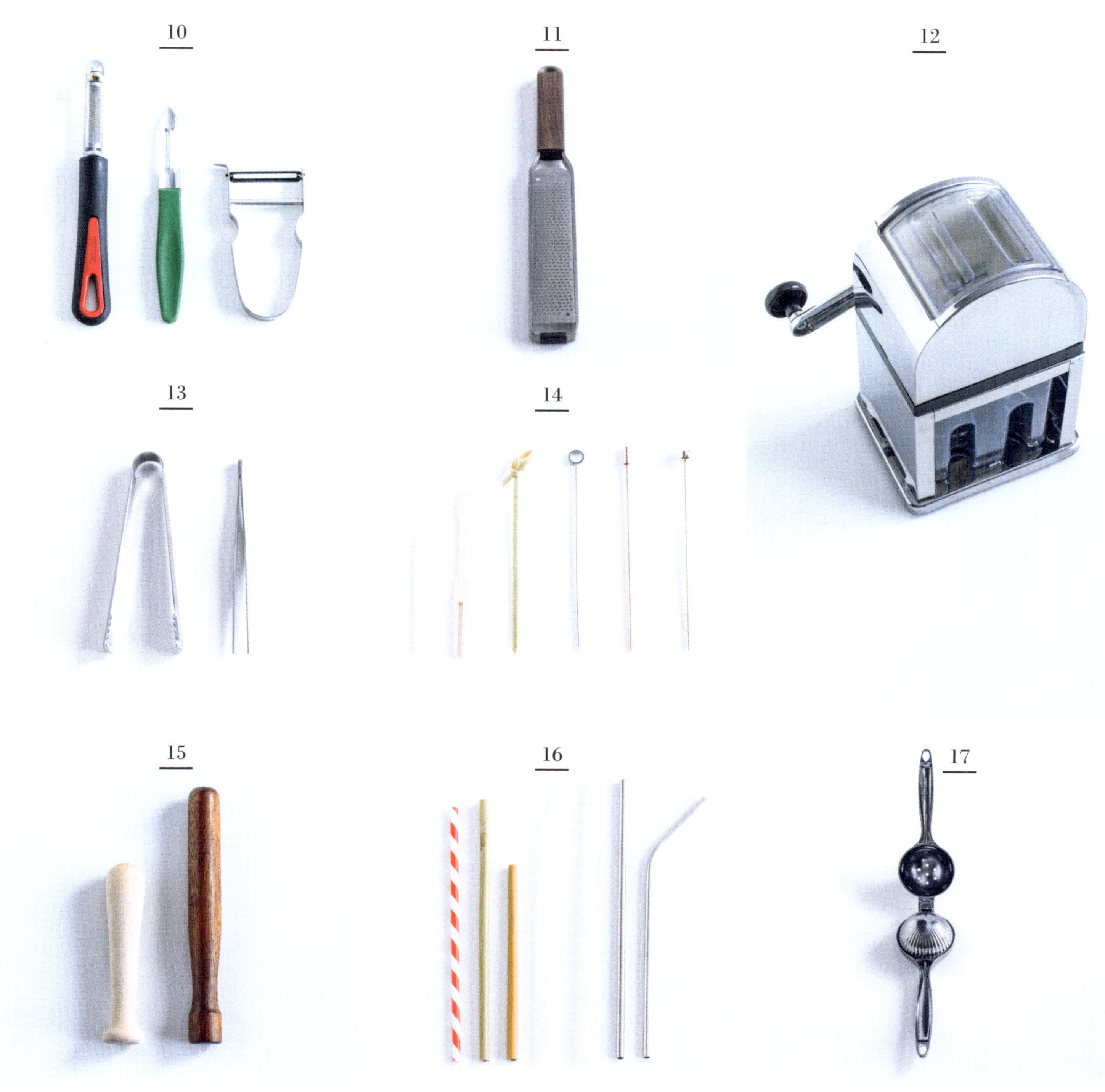

10 TOMATO PEELER, VEGETABLE PEELER, Y (SPEED) PEELER

Essential for removing citrus zest. A tomato peeler with a serrated blade can also be used.

11 FINE GRATER

For grating citrus zest and nutmeg.

12 CRUSHED-ICE MAKER

13 ICE-CUBE TONGS, COCKTAIL TWEEZERS

Ice-cube tongs: these are perfect for avoiding touching ice cubes or blocks of ice with your fingers.

Cocktail tweezers: allow you to pick up decorations and position them accurately. Choose ones long enough (>15cm/6in) so you can get a good grip.

14 COCKTAIL STICKS (PICKS)

15 MUDDLERS (PESTLES)

16 BIODEGRADABLE OR REUSEABLE STRAWS

17 LEMON PRESS (OR MEXICAN ELBOW)

Choose a simple, all-metal model, as it will last longer.

GLASSES

1 Coupe/Coupette

2 Coupette alternatives

3 Flute

4 Single Goblet, Double Goblet

5 Highball

6 Highball Tumblers

7 Irish Coffee

8 Single Old Fashioned

9 Double Old Fashioned

GLASSES

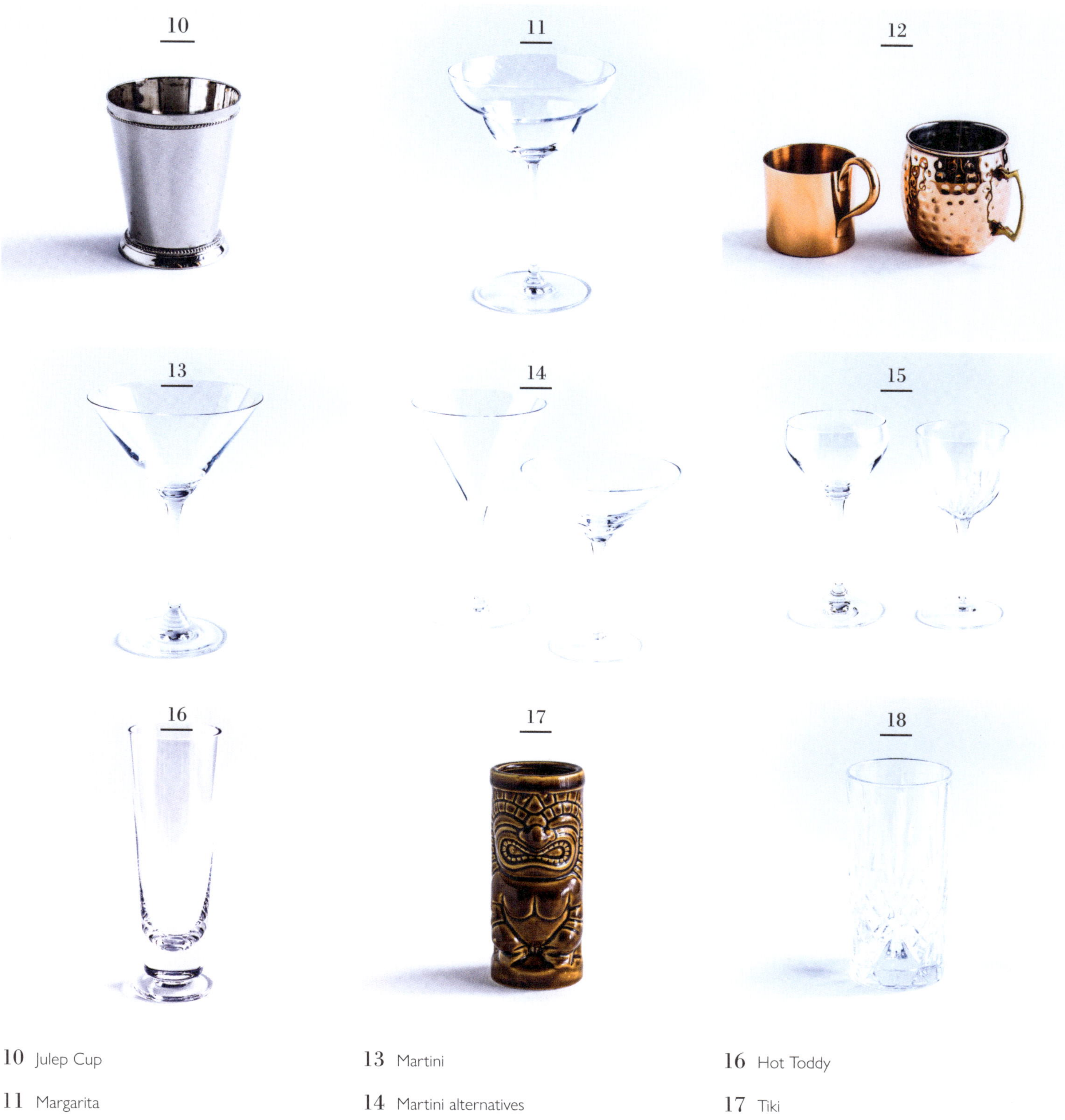

10 Julep Cup
11 Margarita
12 Mule Cups
13 Martini
14 Martini alternatives
15 Nick & Nora styles
16 Hot Toddy
17 Tiki
18 Tumbler

BASIC TERMS/TECHNIQUES

1 CONDITION OF THE ICE

When in the freezer, ice cubes freeze from the outside inwards and air bubbles in the water are trapped on the surface as the water begins to freeze. When taken out of the freezer, a thin opaque veil can be seen over the ice cubes, this cloudiness being caused by the trapped air bubbles. Once this thin layer has melted, water without bubbles is visible and the ice cubes become translucent again. It is at this point that an ice cube is added to a cocktail to continue melting and chill the drink.

2 SHAPING ICE INTO A DOME

Filling a glass with crushed ice and then pressing down on it to make it dome-shaped.

3 DILUTION

When ice is added to a cocktail mixture, it dilutes it a certain amount, depending on the quantity and quality of the ice. To enjoy a cocktail at its best, allow an average of 10–15% dilution in the glass.

4 MUDDLING (CRUSHING)

Crushing an ingredient with a tool to fully release its flavour, so it can infuse the rest of the cocktail.

5 SEALING WITH TEFLON

Wrapping the space between the cap and bottle with Teflon sealing tape to extend the storage life of the bottle's contents.

6 USING A JIGGER

Hold the jigger firmly between your thumb and forefinger or between your forefinger and middle finger. Fill it by pouring over the rim of the jigger so the liquid does not overflow. Jiggers are normally graduated with measures on the side, the largest measure being when the jigger is filled to the brim and not slightly below it. Rinse the jigger after making each individual cocktail to avoid the transference of any lingering flavours. Always check the jigger is perfectly clean by smelling it before starting to make a new cocktail.

BASIC TERMS/TECHNIQUES

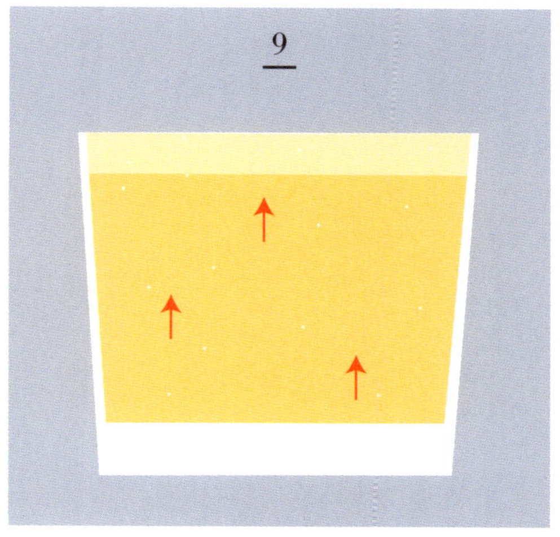

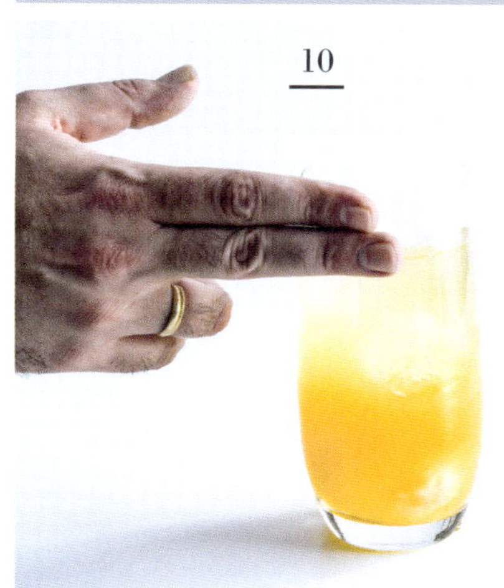

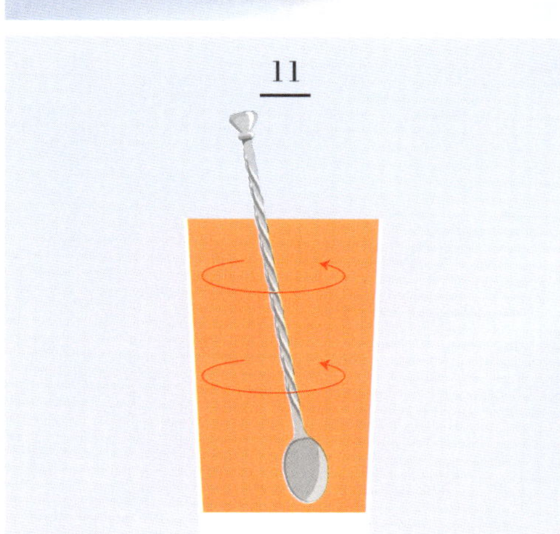

7 BLENDING

Mixing the ingredients together using a blender.

8 EMULSIFYING, INCREASING VOLUME

Incorporating air into a liquid to make it foamy.

9 PRESSING AIR FROM FOAM

A technique that helps take the air out of the foam. Sit the glass on a firm, stable surface, hold it by its base and tap the glass moderately hard four or five times, watching to ensure the number of air bubbles on the surface of the foam decreases each time. Wait for 5–10 seconds before pouring the aerated liquid.

10 WASHLINE

The level to which the liquid in the glass reaches. This should be about two fingers from the rim.

11 MIXING WITH A BAR SPOON

Stirring the liquid in the glass, making small circles with the bar spoon.

12 LOCKING A SHAKER

To lock a shaker, tap the smaller part firmly. Double check by giving a small shake to ensure it is tightly locked and there is no leakage.

13 OPENING A SHAKER

When shaking a cocktail with ice cubes, the cold causes the metal to contract, which tightens the join between the two parts and can make the shaker difficult to open. Hold the shaker with the smaller part on top. Locate one of the crescent-shaped points where the smaller part fits into the larger part and give it a sharp smack with the flat of your hand to open it.

TASTING GUIDE

Basil Smash

REFRESHING COCKTAILS

White Lady

TANGY COCKTAILS

Negroni

SOUR COCKTAILS

TASTING GUIDE

WELL-ROUNDED COCKTAILS

POWERFUL COCKTAILS

SWEET COCKTAILS

INDEX OF CONTENTS

THE BASICS

THE IDEAL BAR: SPIRITS

THE IDEAL BAR: OTHER INGREDIENTS

GLASSWARE

ICE

DECORATIONS

TECHNIQUES FOR MAKING

THE RECIPES

THE ESSENTIALS

MARTINIS

FLIPS

SPIRIT FORWARDS

SOURS

MULES

TIKIS

COLADAS

HIGHBALLS

CHAMPAGNE COCKTAILS

INDEX OF INGREDIENTS

AUTHOR'S ACKNOWLEDGEMENTS

My thanks go to:

Guillaume Guerbois for once again having given me a golden opportunity (in addition to your much valued friendship). Considering all the projects you have allowed me to undertake, I think I owe you a lot more than dinner;

Joseph Biolatto and Britinni Rae for their exceptional ice and for their friendship;

Kevin Rigault, my best 'pupil' who I am so proud of and who long ago surpassed me on so many levels. Thank you for all your invaluable assistance, for giving up your time to help with this book and also for your unwavering friendship;

Kaled Derouiche for helping me move forward in this profession when I felt I was getting nowhere;

Christophe Baudet for showing me that I knew nothing at the time and that this world is much bigger than it seems;

Andréa Solignac Da Silva and her parents for simply being here and I love them;

My father, Michel Tubiana, who let me do what I wanted with my life without passing judgement and to whom I would have loved to dedicate a copy of this book;

Aurélie Legay and Alizée Andrès for taking the plunge into an unknown world and for finishing on time, despite my bad temper;

To Orathay Souksisavanh and Pierre Javelle for the most fun and friendly photoshoot I've ever worked on (and at the same time producing images of the highest quality!);

And, not forgetting, everyone I've met during the course of my career who has enabled me to do what I do today and, of course, the team at Marabout.

ABOUT THE AUTHOR

After graduating from culinary school followed by several years in the restaurant industry, Lucas Tubiana swapped his chef's hat for a cocktail shaker in 2013. He learned his craft in some of Paris's most respected cocktail bars (Le Forvm and Andy Wahloo) and then joined a major Lyon-based group as executive bar manager. Today he consults for numerous businesses, specializing in events and catering.

First published in Great Britain in 2025 by Hamlyn,
an imprint of Octopus Publishing Group Ltd, Carmelite House,
50 Victoria Embankment, London EC4Y 0DZ
www.octopusbooks.co.uk
www.octopusbooksusa.com

An Hachette UK Company
www.hachette.co.uk

The authorized representative in the EEA is Hachette Ireland, 8 Castlecourt Centre, Dublin 15, D15 XTP3, Ireland (email: info@hbgi.ie)

Originally published in France as *Le Grand Manuel des Cocktails* by Marabout in 2022.

Distributed in the US by Hachette Book Group, 1290 Avenue of the Americas, 4th and 5th Floors, New York, NY 10104

Distributed in Canada by Canadian Manda Group, 664 Annette St., Toronto, Ontario, Canada M6S 2C8

ISBN 978-1-784-72980-6
eISBN: 978-1-784-72981-3

A CIP catalogue record for this book is available from the British Library.

Printed and bound in China.

10 9 8 7 6 5 4 3 2 1

Photographs by Pierre Javelle
Illustrations by Yannis Varoutsikos
Additional scientific information by Anne Cazor
Styling by Orathay Souksisavanh

English edition 2025
Commissioning Editor: Jeannie Stanley
Art Director: Jonathan Christie
Senior Editor: Leanne Bryan
Translation from the French: JMS Books LLP, Wendy Sweetser
Designer: Jeremy Tilston
Production Controllers: Lucy Carter and Nic Jones